Learning Salesforce Lightning Application Development

Build and test Lightning Components for Salesforce Lightning
Experience using Salesforce DX

Mohith Shrivastava

BIRMINGHAM - MUMBAI

Learning Salesforce Lightning Application Development

Commissioning Editor: Aaron Lazar
Acquisition Editor: Siddharth Mandal
Content Development Editor: Arun Nadar
Technical Editor: Surabhi Kulkarni
Copy Editor: Safis Editing
Project Coordinator: Sheejal Shah
Proofreader: Safis Editing
Indexer: Pratik Shirodkar
Graphics: Jason Monteiro
Production Coordinator: Shantanu Zagade

First published: July 2018

Production reference: 1300718

Published by Packt Publishing Ltd.
Livery Place
35 Livery Street
Birmingham
B3 2PB, UK.

ISBN 978-1-78712-467-7

www.packtpub.com

`mapt.io`

Mapt is an online digital library that gives you full access to over 5,000 books and videos, as well as industry leading tools to help you plan your personal development and advance your career. For more information, please visit our website.

Why subscribe?

- Spend less time learning and more time coding with practical eBooks and Videos from over 4,000 industry professionals

- Improve your learning with Skill Plans built especially for you

- Get a free eBook or video every month

- Mapt is fully searchable

- Copy and paste, print, and bookmark content

PacktPub.com

Did you know that Packt offers eBook versions of every book published, with PDF and ePub files available? You can upgrade to the eBook version at `www.PacktPub.com` and as a print book customer, you are entitled to a discount on the eBook copy. Get in touch with us at `service@packtpub.com` for more details.

At `www.PacktPub.com`, you can also read a collection of free technical articles, sign up for a range of free newsletters, and receive exclusive discounts and offers on Packt books and eBooks.

Foreword

In the last decade, web technologies have changed beyond anybody's prediction. There was a time when people across industries were talking about moving away from JavaScript. However, it worked the other way around. Frameworks like Angular and React became the backbone of many enterprise applications and emerged as favorite technologies to build an application.

In a nutshell, it is the JavaScript that won and established itself as a winner of this decade. It is not only used for desktop based applications, but also in mobile and server-side programming such as Node.js.

It isn't really about JavaScript, but rather the impact it has created on technology industry and workforce. Salesforce has been awarded as the most innovative company multiple times in the past several years and it wouldn't come as a surprise if we see Salesforce already ahead in the race of adopting cutting-edge technology.

One of many success mantras for Salesforce is to keep developer and admin happy. It offers powerful tools to a developer to create top-notch features and customizations, at the same time it enables Administrators to use, configure, and suggest improvements for those components.

How can we leverage the JavaScript workforce, give developers the tool they want, and how to make administrators superheroes of implementations?

Welcome to the world of *Lightning Experience*! Did you noticed, how many targets this innovative company shot with a single arrow?

Lightning Experience is the future of Salesforce implementations and there is no doubt in saying, Lightning Component is its soul. If you have JavaScript developers, let them work on client controller, if you have Apex developer, let them work on Server controller. Reusable Components built by developers can be used creatively by Salesforce Administrators in Record Page, Home Page, Community, Wave Dashboard and so on.

If you are new to Salesforce development or been a developer for many years working on Visualforce, you would need to skill up in Lightning Component development. Lightning Component is a blend of JavaScript, HTML, CSS, Apex, and Salesforce Platform features, and you need to make sure you got your blend right to build a delicious Lightning recipe.

I believe this book written by Mohith, would give you the right proportion of knowledge about JavaScript and Salesforce platform features to build mind-blowing components and impress your team and clients. This book contains so many tips and pointers which will open up your imagination and would get you excited!

Jitendra Zaa

Salesforce MVP and Sr. Technical Architect at IBM

Contributors

About the author

Mohith Shrivastava has been building and architecting Salesforce applications since 2011, when he graduated from the National Institute of Engineering, Mysore.

He is currently a Salesforce MVP and holds multiple Salesforce certifications. He is an active contributor on Salesforce Stack Exchange Community. Mohith has authored *Learning Salesforce Einstein* and *Salesforce Essentials for Administrators* for Packt publishing. In his leisure time, he loves exploring the latest technologies and spending time with his family.

I would like to thank my parents for nurturing and helping me in all possible ways. I would like thank my wife, Nisha, for her never-ending love and support. The editing team at Packt, as well as my colleagues and the management at Codescience, have been very supportive throughout the journey of this book.
Special thanks to the Salesforce Ohana Community, and to Abhishek Raj and Jitendar Zha for reviewing the content and testing the code.

About the reviewers

Abhishek Raj is a Salesforce consultant working at one of the Big Four consulting firms. He started his career in ISV product development. He has experience with Apex, Visualforce, Lightning, Einstein, predictive analytics, Wave, Java, and the Spring Hibernate frameworks. He has worked on multiple projects in various sectors, such as manufacturing, healthcare, consumer, Insurance, and credit services. He currently holds six certifications from Salesforce. He is a keen and active member of the Bangalore Salesforce Developer group. He is also Meritorious Alumnus of NMIMS University, Mumbai. He has reviewed *Learning Salesforce Einstein* by Packt Publishing.

In his free time, he loves to watch movies and explore the upcoming and the latest trends in technology.

> *I would like to thank my parents, siblings, and my wife for always supporting me and allowing me to give time to this amazing content.*

Jitendra Zaa is a Salesforce MVP and possesses 21 Salesforce certifications. He has worked on the Salesforce platform for more than a decade now. He is also the author of *Apex Design Pattern*, published by Packt Publishing. You can read more about Salesforce-related topics on his blog at JitendraZaa [dot] com.

Packt is searching for authors like you

If you're interested in becoming an author for Packt, please visit authors.packtpub.com and apply today. We have worked with thousands of developers and tech professionals, just like you, to help them share their insight with the global tech community. You can make a general application, apply for a specific hot topic that we are recruiting an author for, or submit your own idea.

Table of Contents

Preface   1

Chapter 1: Introduction to the Lightning Component Framework   9
  Lightning Experience   10
    Lightning Application   11
      Creating a Lightning Application   13
    Creating tabs in Lightning Experience   15
      Lightning Component Tabs   16
      Lightning Page Tabs   16
    Lightning App Builder   18
    Lightning Utility Bar   20
    List views in the Lightning UI   22
    The ability to calendar data in the Date and Datetime fields   24
    Global Actions   25
    Publisher actions   27
  Lightning Component architecture   28
    The concept of web components   29
    Lightning Component Bundle   30
      Lightning Component lifecycle   31
      MVC concepts in the Lightning Component framework   32
  Setting up a Salesforce developer organization to enable the building of Lightning Components   33
    Creating a simple hello world Lightning Component   34
  The Lightning Design system   37
    Creating a simple card component using SLDS   37
  Summary   39

Chapter 2: Exploring Salesforce DX   41
  Enabling the developer hub in your Salesforce organization   42
    Enabling the developer hub   42
  Installing the Salesforce DX CLI   43
  Salesforce DX commands   45
    auth commands   45
    Setting a default Dev Hub for scratch Org creation   46
    Creating a new Salesforce DX project   46
      Configuring a scratch Org definition JSON   47
      Configuring project definition JSON   47
    Creating a scratch Org   48
      Opening the scratch Org   49
      Pulling source from a scratch Org   49
      Push source code to a scratch Org   51

Conflict resolution 53
Ignoring files 53
Lightning commands 53
Creating a Lightning app and components 54
Metadata API commands 55
mdapi:convert and mdapi:retrieve 55
Converting existing managed/unmanaged package code to DX Format 56
Deploy command 57
Data import and export commands in Salesforce DX 57
Data export Salesforce DX command 57
Data import Salesforce DX command 59
Bulk data upsert Salesforce DX command 59
Limitations of bulk upsert commands 60
Installing the Visual Studio extension pack for DX 60
Developer workflow for building a Salesforce application 62
Summary 68

Chapter 3: Lightning Component Building Blocks 69
Component markup and using Lightning base components for layouts 70
Component definition aura:component 70
Access modifier 70
Providing a description to component 71
Implementing interfaces in Lightning Components 71
Lightning base components for layout and layout items 72
Lightning card base component 74
Example layouts using the Lightning layout and card components 75
Horizontal alignment using the Lightning layout base component 78
Vertical alignment using the Lightning layout base component 80
Stretching a LayoutItem using the flexibility attribute 81
Creating multiple rows and controlling the size of the row in Lightning layout 82
Lightning layout to handle multiple devices 83
Nested page layout using Lightning Layouts 86
Understanding attributes 89
Using Expression syntax 90
JavaScript controller and helper 91
Wiring the client-side to the server using Apex controllers 96
Summary 103

Chapter 4: The Lightning JavaScript API 105
Technical requirements 105
Using component get and set methods 106
Using the find function to locate the DOM 106
Introducing Locker Service 108
Strict mode enforcement in Locker Service 108

Understanding the DOM access containment hierarchy in Lightning
Components   110
    The proxy object in Locker Service   111
APIs available in $A top-level functions   112
    Exploring the $A.Util APIs   112
Format date/DateTime using the Aura Localization Service   115
    Find your organization's time zone   115
    Find your organization's local currency   115
    Formatting dates   116
Dynamically creating components using $A.createComponent()   117
    Destroying components using the destory() function   121
**Modifying the DOM in the RENDERER JavaScript file of the
component bundle**   122
    Understanding the rendering life cycle of a component   123
    Understanding re-rendering the life cycle of a component   126
Using custom labels in Lightning Components   128
    Dynamically populating label parameters   129
ES6 support in Lightning Components   129
    An introduction to Promises   130
        Promise support in Lightning Components   131
Summary   132

Chapter 5: Events in the Lightning Component Framework   133
Browser events   133
    Capturing browser events   135
    Event handling in Lightning base components   137
Application events   138
    Creating application events   139
    Registering application events   139
        Firing an application event   139
    Handling application events   140
        Getting event attributes from a handled event   140
    Handling capturing and bubbling events   140
Component events   142
    Creating a component event   142
    Registering a component event   143
        Firing the component event   143
    Handling component events   143
        Alternate syntax to handle events raised by child components   144
        Getting event attributes from handled events   144
Creating a sales LeaderBoard Lightning Application using events   144
Communicating between components   156
    Passing data down the component hierarchy   156
    Using aura:method to call child methods from parent methods   156
        Using the aura method asynchronously   158
    Optimal event architecture design pattern   160

Adding custom events to components dynamically | 164
Summary | 165
Chapter 6: Lightning Data Service and Base Components | 167
Lightning Data Service | 167
Loading Salesforce record context data using force:recordData | 169
Functions available for CRUD records | 171
Saving existing records | 172
Creating a new record | 173
Deleting records | 176
Using SaveRecordResult | 178
Example components using Lightning Data Service | 179
Lightning base components | 183
An introduction to Lightning input field components | 184
Creating an input form using the RecordEdit and Lightning input field components | 184
Introducing events and attributes in Lightning record edit form and input field | 186
Creating a contact edit form using the Lightning input field and RecordEditForm components | 188
Using the Lightning output field component | 189
The list view component | 190
Creating a tree view using the tree and tree grid components | 191
Formatting output data using Lightning base components | 194
Using the datatable component | 197
Using Lightning input components | 199
Using the carousel component | 201
Summary | 202
Chapter 7: Using External JavaScript Libraries in Lightning Components | 203
Third-party JavaScript libraries in Lightning Components | 204
Attributes | 204
Events | 205
Integrating a third-party library into Lightning Components | 205
Integrating the Select2 JavaScript library into Lightning Components | 207
Integrating the MomentJs library into Lightning Components | 211
Creating a Locker Service-compliant JavaScript bundle using webpack | 213
Introduction to webpack | 214
Entry | 214
Output | 215
Loaders | 215
Plugins | 216
Integrating choices.js into Lightning Components | 217
Structuring a JS-heavy project in Salesforce DX | 219
Creating a Locker Service-compatible bundle with webpack | 219
ChartJs in Lightning Components | 225
Making client-side calls to external sites using JavaScript | 227
Communication between the Lightning main frame and iframe | 232

Communication from the Visualforce page to the Lightning Component   232
Communication from the Lightning Component to the Visualforce page   234
Rendering a React application in a Lightning Component using
Lightning:container   235
   Rendering reactApp using the LCC npm module in a Lightning Component   236
   Limitations of Lightning:container   243
Summary   243

Chapter 8: Debugging Lightning Components   245
   Enabling Debug Mode   245
   Salesforce Lightning Inspector   246
     Lightning Salesforce Inspector tabs   250
      Component Tree   250
       $auraTemp   251
      Transactions tab   252
      Performance tab   252
      Event Log tab   254
      Actions tab   255
      Storage tab   255
   Salesforce community page optimizer   256
   Using the Chrome developer Console   258
     Setting breakpoints in the Chrome developer Console   259
     Pause on caught exceptions   261
   Apex debugging   261
     Using the Salesforce CLI to stream logs   263
     Advanced debugging with the Replay Debugger   264
   Summary   268

Chapter 9: Performance Tuning Your Lightning Component   269
   Storable actions   270
     When to use storable actions?   270
   Avoiding nested aura:if in aura:iteration   271
     $A.createComponent() for lazy loading   275
     Using plain old JavaScript to gain maximum performance   275
   Events strategy for performance and ease of code maintenance   277
     Event anti-patters that can cause a performance bottleneck   277
      <aura:iteration> – multiple items set   277
   Optimizing JavaScript in Lightning Components   279
   Unbound expression bindings   279
   Using the Lightning data service   281
   Leveraging Lightning base components   281
     Creating a record form, using Lightning:recordForm   282
   Optimizing Apex code   282
     Limiting data rows for lists   282
     Reducing server response time, using the platform cache   283
     Avoiding sending responses from Apex as wrapper objects   284

Disabling Debug Mode for production   286
Summary   286
Chapter 10: Taking Lightning Components out of Salesforce Using Lightning Out   287
Lightning Out in Visualforce   287
  Creating a Lightning dependency application   288
  Adding Lightning Components for the Visualforce JavaScript library   289
  Adding JavaScript to create a component on a Visualforce page   289
Lightning Out in a Node.js application   291
  Creating a connected application   291
  Setting up a Node.js application   293
    Creating a Lightning Out application   295
    Deploying Node.js application on Heroku   298
Lightning Out for unauthenticated users   299
Lightning Out limitations and considerations   303
Summary   303
Chapter 11: Lightning Flows   305
Introducing Flows   305
  Creating the Lead Finder app using the Flow builder   307
  Running Flows in Lightning Experience   316
  Debugging Flows   318
Adding custom components in Flow builder   318
  Using asynchronous XHR calls in customized Lightning Components   322
  Using Lightning Components as local Flow actions   329
  Embedding Flows into a Lightning Component   333
Summary   336
Chapter 12: Making Components Available for Salesforce Mobile and Communities   337
Using Lightning Components in a Salesforce mobile application   338
  Setting up the Chrome browser to simulate the Salesforce mobile app experience   339
  Adding a Lightning Component to the Salesforce mobile navigation   340
  Adding Lightning Components as global and object-specific actions   345
Lightning Components in Community Cloud   348
  Creating communities in Salesforce   348
  Creating a theme layout   352
  Creating custom content layouts   359
  Overriding search, profile menu, and navigation in communities using customized Lightning Components   363
    Overriding a standard search interface   363
    Overriding a profile menu   363
    Adding custom navigation   364
Summary   366

Chapter 13: Lightning Navigation and Lightning Console APIs 367
  Adding navigation support using Lightning :navigation 368
  Introducing the Lightning Console 374
    Utility Bar component 375
      Page context in the Utility Bar API 379
    Workspace API 380
    Standard Lightning tab events in the console 385
  Summary 386

Chapter 14: Unit Testing Lightning Components 387
  Introduction to Jasmine 388
    Jasmine syntax and terminology 388
      Suite 388
      Spec 389
      Setup and teardown 390
      Spies 391
    Quickstart example 392
  LTS 395
    Writing tests for a YouTubeSearchApp 396
      Installing LTS 397
      Creating a Lightning Component test via CLI 398
        Testing for search terms rendered via two-way binding 399
        Verifying the response by mocking the server response using Jasmine spy 401
      Testing application events 404
  Summary 405

Chapter 15: Publishing Lightning Components on AppExchange 407
  Namespacing Salesforce developer instances for managed package generation 408
  The impact of namespacing Salesforce instances on the component bundle 409
  Creating scratch Orgs with namespaces 415
  Creating a managed package 417
  Documenting your components using the auradoc file 421
  Using the design file to allow admins to configure attributes 424
  Publishing components on AppExchange 427
  Summary 429

Other Books You May Enjoy 431

Index 435

Preface

The Salesforce Lightning platform is widely used today in a number of Fortune 500 companies for building applications that are used in sales, services, marketing, collaboration, and various other business areas. Salesforce provides the most popular Customer Relationship Management (CRM) system, and the demand for Salesforce developers and consultants is increasing every year. Applications built on top of the Lighting platform are cloud based, secure, and require no on-premises software installation.

Salesforce Lightning Experience is a redesigned user interface that allows users to be more productive and innovative. Lightning Experience comprises pages and layouts that can be customized using Lightning Application Builder (a drag-and-drop interface that allows administrators to build pages by dropping various components) and Lightning Components. Salesforce provides out-of-the-box Lightning components that administrators can leverage for most business needs. However, not all user interface challenges can be solved with these out-of-box components. The Lightning Components Framework allows Salesforce developers to build custom Lightning components. A Lightning component is made up of HTML (markup) and JavaScript (secured using Salesforce Locker Service) and forms a component bundle that can be placed in Salesforce Lightning Experience, Salesforce Communities, Salesforce Mobile App, Salesforce for Outlook, Chatter Publisher, and other Salesforce interfaces.

Salesforce DX allows developers to adopt source-driven development techniques. Salesforce DX simplifies developer workflows on the platform and helps to build and iterate Salesforce applications faster. Salesforce DX provides a command line interface (CLI) tool that simplifies setting up the developer environment for development, debugging, unit testing, and deploying Salesforce applications.

This book will teach you how to build custom Lightning components by using the Lightning Components Framework and leveraging Salesforce DX CLI commands. In this book, we cover the fundamentals and capabilities of the framework. The end goal of this book is to provide Salesforce developers with enough information so that they can start designing and building components on their own to meet their custom component needs.

Who this book is for

The target audience for this book includes beginner, intermediate, and advanced Salesforce developers and architects who want to fully understand the capabilities of the Lightning Components Framework and learn about application development on the Salesforce platform.

This book can also be used by JavaScript frontend developers who are familiar with JavaScript and want to understand the capabilities and boundaries of the Lightning Components Framework. The book also covers the integration capabilities of the framework with other open source JavaScript libraries and how to take Lightning components built on the platform to outside world.

What this book covers

Chapter 1, *Introduction to the Lightning Component Framework*, introduces you to the basics of the Lightning Components architecture and tells you why you should learn about the Lightning Components Framework. The chapter also covers Lightning Experience UI capabilities and where in the Lightning Experience you can leverage custom Lightning components to customize.

Chapter 2, *Exploring Salesforce DX*, covers basics of the Salesforce DX CLI capabilities and commands. The chapter focuses on how to leverage Salesforce DX to create a source-driven development workflow on the platform. You will learn how to use Salesforce DX to create Salesforce applications.

Chapter 3, *Lightning Component Building Blocks*, teaches you how to build a custom Lightning component. This chapter covers how to write component markup, JavaScript client-side controllers and helper functions, server-side Apex code that client-side helper functions can talk to, and Lightning Base components to create layouts.

Chapter 4, *The Lightning JavaScript API*, covers the native APIs that are provided by the framework and the Locker Service security model for the components. This chapter also talks about differences between the native JavaScript APIs and the APIs available under Locker Service.

Chapter 5, *Events in the Lightning Component Framework*, teaches you the syntax for creating and firing application and component events. The chapter also covers various intercommunication patterns available in the framework for passing data between components.

Chapter 6, *Lightning Data Service and Base Components*, covers the syntax and capabilities of Lightning Data Service and how it simplifies fetching context data, as well as how it enables you to create, read, edit, and delete records when it comes to contextual data. You will also explore how the Lightning Data Service can make custom components react to data changes in the UI. This chapter also teaches you how to work with Salesforce-provided base components.

Chapter 7, *Using External JavaScript Libraries in Lightning Components*, covers how you can integrate third-party libraries, such as Chart.js, Moment.js, and ReactJS with the Lightning Components Framework. You will also learn about the debugging procedure in the case of a library not working under Locker Service, and you'll discover how to use open source JavaScript bundlers, such as webpack, to make them Locker Service compatible.

Chapter 8, *Debugging Lightning Components*, teaches you about the debugging techniques for client-side JavaScript controllers and helpers using Chrome Developer Tools, and debugging techniques for Apex using the new Apex Replay Debugger.

Chapter 9, *Performance Tuning Your Lightning Components*, covers how you can improve the performance of your Lightning components with techniques such as using storable actions, platform caching, and paginating data rows that are returned from the server. You will learn about the Chrome extensions and plugins available for figuring performance bottlenecks.

Chapter 10, *Taking Lightning Components out of Salesforce Using Lightning Out*, teaches you how to work with the Lightning Out technology. You will learn about the steps and processes required to take your Lightning components outside the Salesforce platform.

Chapter 11, *Lightning Flows*, teaches you how to use Lightning components with the Salesforce Flow builder. You will learn about how components can pass data to flows and how you can embed flows inside Lightning components.

Chapter 12, *Making Components Available for Salesforce Mobile and Communities*, teaches how to use Lightning components in Salesforce mobile applications (Salesforce1), and Salesforce Community Builder. We will learn how to customize communities using custom theme layouts and custom navigation. You will also learn how to override profile menus and create your own templates.

Chapter 13, *Lightning Navigation and Lightning Console APIs*, covers how to work with the Navigation API, the Workspace API, and the Messaging API for the Utility Bar component. The chapter also teaches you about the options available for customizing components in Salesforce Console.

Chapter 14, *Unit Testing Lightning Components*, teaches you how to write unit tests for Lightning components using the Lightning Testing Service. You will learn about Jasmine and how to leverage Jasmine with the Lightning Testing Service to write unit tests for the custom Lightning components.

Chapter 15, *Publishing Lightning Components on AppExchange*, teaches you how to publish components on Salesforce AppExchange so that components can be installed in multiple Salesforce instances.

To get the most out of this book

The book assumes that the reader has had some exposure to programming. The book also assumes that you are familiar with the Salesforce Apex programming language, JavaScript fundamentals (especially the concepts of variables, callbacks, and promises), HTML, and CSS. The book expects that you are familiar with Salesforce administration capabilities, such as creating objects and fields, and navigating through Salesforce.

To get most out of the book, sign up for a promotional Salesforce Org with Salesforce DX enabled at https://developer.Salesforce.com/promotions/Orgs/dx-signup, and a developer Org at https://developer.Salesforce.com/signup, and try all the code snippets discussed in the book by creating scratch Orgs for every chapter. Instructions for creating scratch Orgs, with the accompanying code, can be found in the following GitHub repository: https://github.com/PacktPublishing/Learning-Salesforce-Lightning-Application-Development.

The book uses the following software, all of which is freely available:

- Salesforce DX CLI (https://developer.Salesforce.com/tools/sfdxcli)
- Visual Studio Code editor (https://code.visualstudio.com/)
- Salesforce DX plugin for Visual Studio from the Visual Studio marketplace (https://marketplace.visualstudio.com/items?itemName=Salesforce.Salesforcedx-vscode)

Download the example code files

You can download the example code files for this book from your account at www.packtpub.com. If you purchased this book elsewhere, you can visit www.packtpub.com/support and register to have the files emailed directly to you.

You can download the code files by following these steps:

1. Log in or register at `www.packtpub.com`.
2. Select the **SUPPORT** tab.
3. Click on **Code Downloads & Errata**.
4. Enter the name of the book in the **Search** box and follow the onscreen instructions.

Once the file is downloaded, please make sure that you unzip or extract the folder using the latest version of:

- WinRAR/7-Zip for Windows
- Zipeg/iZip/UnRarX for Mac
- 7-Zip/PeaZip for Linux

The code bundle for the book is also hosted on GitHub at `https://github.com/PacktPublishing/Learning-Salesforce-Lightning-Application-Development`. In case there's an update to the code, it will be updated on the existing GitHub repository.

We also have other code bundles from our rich catalog of books and videos available at `https://github.com/PacktPublishing/`. Check them out!

Download the color images

We also provide a PDF file that has color images of the screenshots/diagrams used in this book. You can download it here: `https://www.packtpub.com/sites/default/files/downloads/LearningSalesforceLightningApplicationDevelopment_ColorImages.pdf`.

Conventions used

There are a number of text conventions used throughout this book.

`CodeInText`: Indicates code words in the text, database table names, folder names, filenames, file extensions, pathnames, dummy URLs, user input, and Twitter handles. Here is an example: "To override New, Edit, or View, the Lightning component must implement the `Lightning:actionOverride` interface."

A block of code is set as follows:

```
function StringUtils() {};

StringUtils.prototype.concatenate = function(str1,str2) {
  return str1.concat(str2);
};

StringUtils.prototype.camelcase = function(string) {
  string = string.toLowerCase().replace(/(?:(^.)|([-_\s]+.))/g,
function(match) {
      return match.charAt(match.length-1).toUpperCase();
  });
  return string.charAt(0).toLowerCase() + string.substring(1);
};
```

When we wish to draw your attention to a particular part of a code block, the relevant lines or items are set in bold:

```
describe("when string operations are performed", function(){
    //Spec for Concatenation operation
    it("should be able to concatenate hello and world", function() {
expect(stringUtil.concatenate('Hello','World')).toEqual('HelloWorld');
    });

    //Spec for camelcase operation
    it("should be able to camelcase", function() {
        expect(stringUtil.camelcase('hello-
world')).toEqual('helloWorld');
    });

    //Spec for capitalizeFirstLetter
    it("should be able to capitalize First Letter", function() {
expect(stringUtil.capitalizeFirstLetter('world')).toEqual('World');
    });
});
```

Any command-line input or output is written as follows:

```
sfdx force:lightning:test:run
```

Bold: Indicates a new term, an important word, or words that you see onscreen. For example, words in menus or dialog boxes appear in the text like this. Here is an example: "Once in the **Setup** menu, find **App Manager** from the search box. A new Lightning app can be created using the **New Lightning App** button."

Warnings or important notes appear like this.

 Tips and tricks appear like this.

Get in touch

Feedback from our readers is always welcome.

General feedback: Email feedback@packtpub.com and mention the book title in the subject of your message. If you have questions about any aspect of this book, please email us at questions@packtpub.com.

Errata: Although we have taken every care to ensure the accuracy of our content, mistakes do happen. If you have found a mistake in this book, we would be grateful if you would report this to us. Please visit www.packtpub.com/submit-errata, selecting your book, clicking on the Errata Submission Form link, and entering the details.

Piracy: If you come across any illegal copies of our works in any form on the Internet, we would be grateful if you would provide us with the location address or website name. Please contact us at copyright@packtpub.com with a link to the material.

If you are interested in becoming an author: If there is a topic that you have expertise in and you are interested in either writing or contributing to a book, please visit authors.packtpub.com.

Reviews

Please leave a review. Once you have read and used this book, why not leave a review on the site that you purchased it from? Potential readers can then see and use your unbiased opinion to make purchase decisions, we at Packt can understand what you think about our products, and our authors can see your feedback on their book. Thank you!

For more information about Packt, please visit packtpub.com.

1

Introduction to the Lightning Component Framework

Salesforce Classic, also known as **Aloha**, has been around for a few years. Reimagining the user experience was essential to making the Salesforce application modern, efficient, and more user-friendly. Lightning Experience provides Salesforce users with a much better user experience than Aloha. It's more flexible and easy to customize the UI and the entire UI has been re-imagined to make sales and support representatives more efficient and productive.

At the heart of Lightning Experience are unified design systems across various Salesforce offerings. The Lightning Design System used by Salesforce for all its product offerings is an open source CSS framework and a set of design patterns. The Lightning Component framework is a Salesforce UI framework that is based on the concept of web components and glues the client and server together. The framework is built on the open source Aura framework. The Lightning Component framework uses HTML, CSS, and JavaScript on the frontend and connects to Salesforce objects and business logic on the server via a strongly typed object-oriented language (similar to Java) known as Apex. Lightning Components are the building blocks that power the Lightning Experience application. A **Lightning Application** page consists of one or more Lightning Components, which are arranged by Salesforce system administrators to provide end users with a 360-degree view of their Salesforce application data and enable them to be more efficient by providing easy mechanisms to take necessary actions on data.

If you have a background in either the old-school Salesforce way of building applications (using Visualforce for the frontend and Apex for the backend) or you are new to development on the platform, this book aims to cover both the depth and breadth of the Lightning Component framework. The end goal is to make you a fearless Salesforce Lightning developer.

The aim of this chapter is to answer why and how important it is to be familiar with the Lightning Component framework and start learning how to build Lightning Components and Lightning Applications.

In this chapter, we will be covering the following topics:

- Lightning Experience
- Lightning Component framework architecture
- Setting up a Salesforce developer organization to enable the building of Lightning Components
- The Lightning Design system

Lightning Experience

Lightning Experience is new Salesforce user interface. As a developer, to explore Lightning Experience, all you need is a free Salesforce developer instance. You can sign up for a developer instance at `https://developer.Salesforce.com/signup`.

If you already have one of these instances, you can switch to Lightning Experience. To see how to switch to Lightning Experience from Classic, please check out the following screenshot:

This shows how one can switch to Lightning Experience From Classic Salesforce

In some instances, one would need to enable Lightning Experience. Once Lightning Experience is enabled, you will notice the **Switch To Lightning Experience** link.

Lightning Experience, like Salesforce Classic, consists of applications (**Apps**), **Tabs**, **List views**, and **Detail Record View pages**. Additionally, beyond all these, the Lightning UI provides the following additions:

- App Builder for Salesforce administrators to drag and drop Lightning Components
- Lightning Utility Bar (located at the footer)
- The ability to create Kanban views
- The ability to calendar custom objects

Let's examine each of these views with some screenshots and further explore the various ways a Salesforce administrator can customize them with Lightning Components.

Custom Lightning Components can also be installed by administrators from the Salesforce application store, known as *AppExchange*. To explore the components available on Salesforce *AppExchange*, visit `https://appexchange.Salesforce.com/components`.

Lightning Application

The App Launcher allows you to switch between different Salesforce applications.

The following screenshot shows the App Launcher. All of the applications are represented by cards:

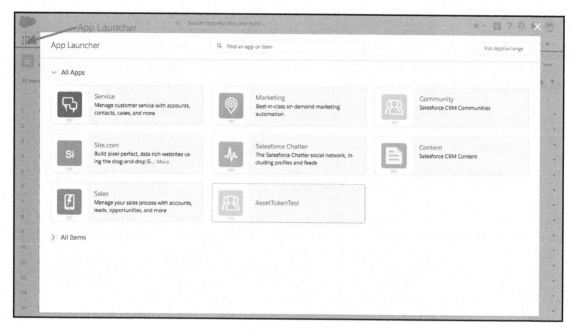

App Launcher helps to switch between apps

The setup link for Lightning Experience takes you to the standard **Setup** page for Salesforce administrators to execute admin-related tasks. The following screenshot shows the **Setup** menu:

This shows how one can navigate to Setup Screen from the Setup Menu

Once in the **Setup** menu, find **App Manager** from the search box. A new Lightning app can be created using the **New Lightning App** button, and if the application is Classic, you can upgrade it to a Lightning Application.

Creating a Lightning Application

To create a Lightning Application, follow the steps from the **App Launcher**:

1. Click on the **New Lightning App** button.
2. Follow the prompt and enter the name of the application (note that the developer name gets auto-populated once you click on the **Developer Name** field), description, and configure **App Branding**:

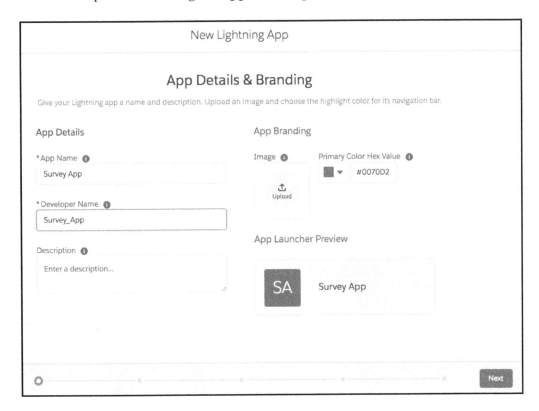

New Lightning App

App Details & Branding

Give your Lightning app a name and description. Upload an image and choose the highlight color for its navigation bar.

App Details

*App Name
Survey App

*Developer Name
Survey_App

Description
Enter a description...

App Branding

Image   Primary Color Hex Value
             #0070D2
Upload

App Launcher Preview

SA   Survey App

Next

3. Choose between a console app and a standard app.

4. Optionally, select **Utility Bar** items. Utility bars are used to carry quick functionalities that need to be accessed quickly, such as taking notes during sales calls, or quickly finding contact details when a service representative is on a call with a customer.

5. Select the **Navigation** tab:

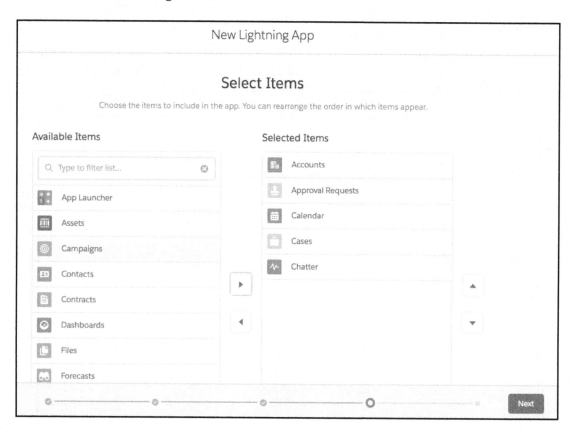

6. Select the profiles that the application will have access to:

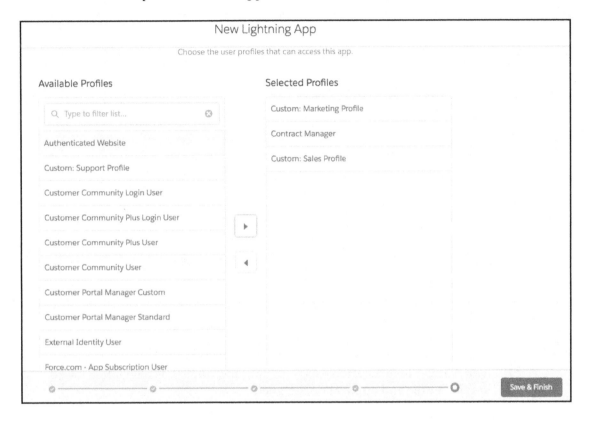

 The process of upgrading a classic application to Lightning involves the same steps as highlighted in this section. Classic apps in Salesforce do not appear in Lightning Experience unless you upgrade them.

Creating tabs in Lightning Experience

The creation of a Lightning tab can be achieved by searching for **Tabs** in the **Setup** menu. The navigation path for the creation of a tab is **Setup** | **User Interface** | **Tabs**.

The following screenshot shows the tab creation screen:

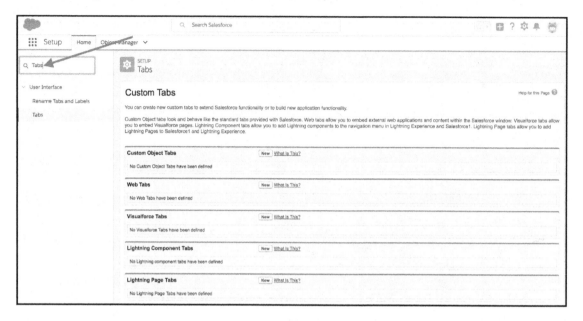

Screenshot shows Custom Tab Creation Screen In Setup Menu

 The creation of **Custom Object Tabs**, **Web Tabs**, and **Visualforce Tabs** is very similar to in Salesforce Classic, and they appear as navigation based on the profile and application assigned.

Lightning Component Tabs

A custom Lightning Component can be assigned as a **Lightning Component** tab. The component must implement a `force:appHostable` interface for it to appear as a **Lightning Component** tab.

Lightning Page Tabs

Lightning page tabs are created from a Lightning page using the App Builder.

From the **Setup** menu, navigate to **User Interface | Lightning App Builder**. The screenshot that follows shortly shows the navigation path for finding the **Lightning App Builder**.

There are three different types of Lightning pages, explained in the following table:

Lightning Page Type	Description
App Page	Used to create an app's navigation for Lightning Experience and Salesforce 1
Home Page	Used to customize the **Home Page** of Lightning Experience
Record Page	Used to customize the **Record Page** of Lightning Experience

The following screenshot shows the selection options when choosing the type of Lightning page:

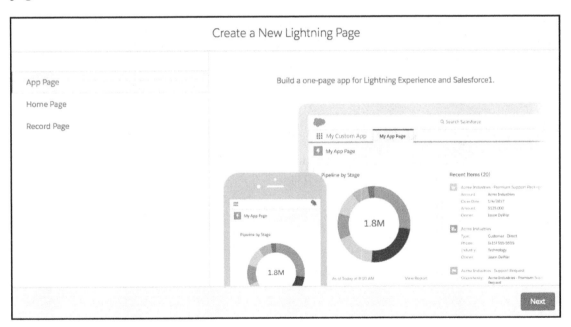

A Lightning page comprises multiple Lightning Components. You can use a combination of standard Lightning Components, custom-built **Lightning Components**, and components installed from Salesforce AppExchange.

There are also multiple options to choose the type of layout for a Lightning page. The following screenshot shows the various options:

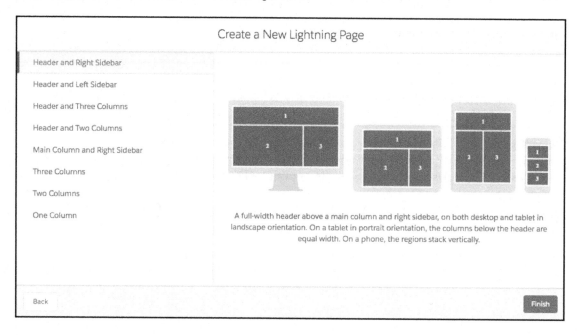

Lightning App Builder

Lightning App Builder allows administrators to drag and drop various standard and custom components to create a Lightning page.

The following screenshot shows the Lightning App Builder screen that administrators use to create a Lightning page:

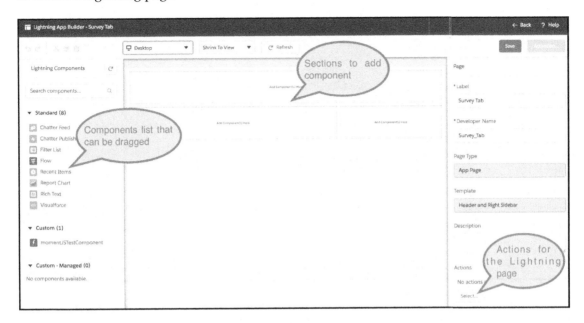

Screenshot shows the Lightning App Builder Screen

Once a Lightning page is saved, the activation screen provides options to configure the profile for the page.

On the **Record Page**, the assignment configuration can be understood with the help of the following screenshot:

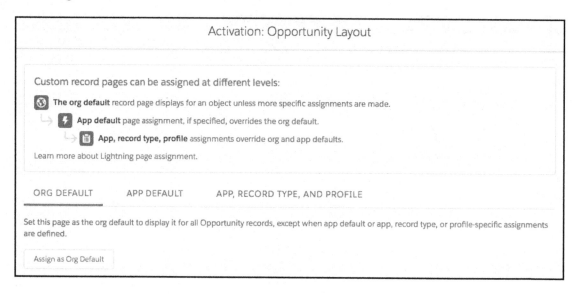

Clearly, one overrides the other. **ORG DEFAULT** is the top level, followed by **APP DEFAULT**, and then by **APP, RECORD TYPE, AND PROFILE**.

Lightning Utility Bar

In a Lightning Application, you can add Lightning Components to the horizontal footer. This can be very useful for adding productive tools such as a simple calculator, reports, recent items, a **Computer Telephony Interface** (CTI) softphone, and any other quick access tools that your sales or support representatives might find useful.

To make a Lightning Components available as a utility, the component must implement the `flexipage:availableForAllPageTypes` interface.

> We will explore all of the interfaces later, as we learn how to build Lightning Components.

The following screenshot shows how you can edit a Lightning Application from the **App Manager** and add a **Utility Bar** to a **Lightning Application**:

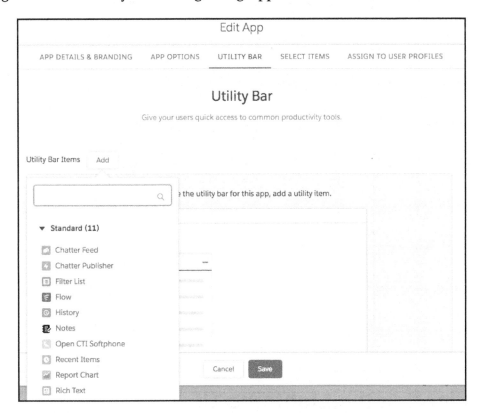

The horizontal footer is where Components added to the Utility Bars are displayed. You can control the height and width of utility components, and their ability to load in the background.

The following screenshot shows a utility Component added to a sales application:

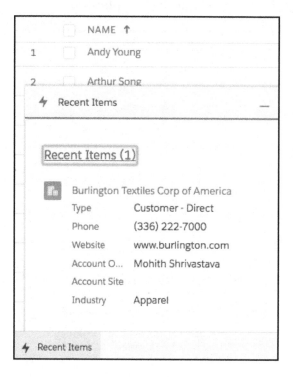

List views in the Lightning UI

List views in Lightning Components are similar to those in Salesforce Classic, but with some additional capabilities, such as creating a Kanban view, using quick charts to display data in graph format, inline editing, adding filters, sorting, and the ability to take mass actions.

In List views, currently, there is no way to overwrite an object List view with a custom Lightning Components.

The following screenshot shows functionalities present on the List view that can help end users to visualize data and perform actions on it:

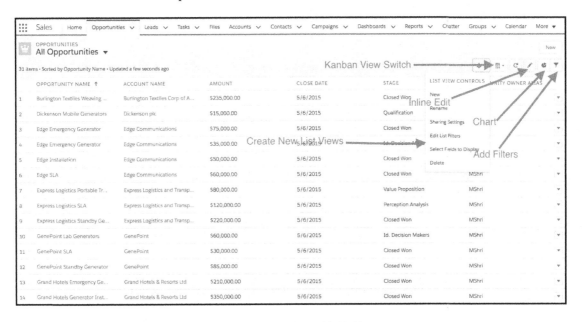

Screenshot shows the All Opportunities List View

Note that the **New Edit** and **View** buttons can also be overridden with a custom Lightning Component. To override these standard buttons and views, the navigation path is **Setup** | **Object Manager** | <select object> | **Button, Links, and Actions**. The following screenshot shows how you can override the **New button** (a similar screen appears for other overrides):

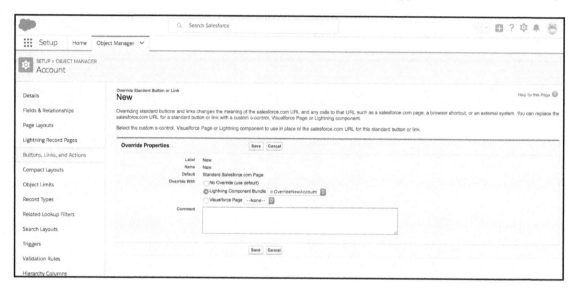

Screenshot shows how you can override New button on Account with a Custom Lightning Component

 To override **New, Edit**, or **View**, the Lightning Component must implement the `Lightning:actionOverride` interface.

The ability to calendar data in the Date and Datetime fields

Lightning Experience provides end users with the ability to calendar any object. The following screenshot shows how you can use the **Calendar** tab to calendar data across objects. The user can follow the prompts and select **Field for Start** and **Field Name to Display** to create a calendar:

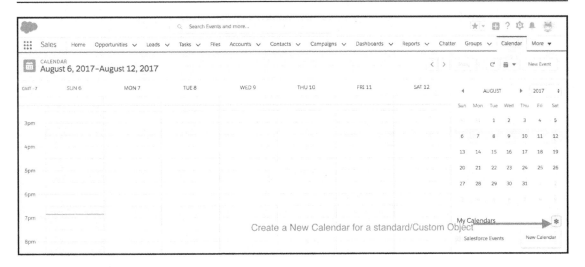

Global Actions

Global Actions are available on all pages. The following screenshot shows **Global Actions**:

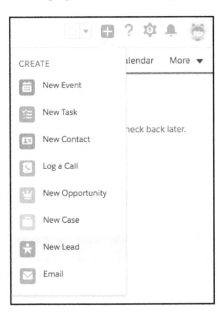

You can also create a new custom global action by using a custom Lightning Component. The navigation path from set up manager page is **Setup** | **Global Actions**.

The following screenshot shows how you can add a custom **Global Action** using a Lightning Component:

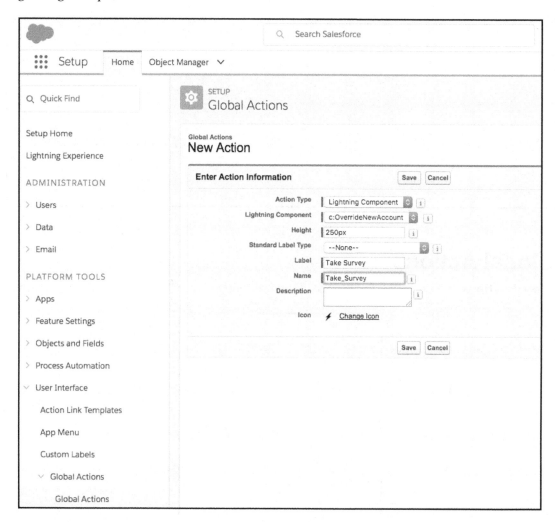

 For custom **Global Actions** to appear, the Salesforce administrator needs to add the action to **Publisher Layouts**. The navigation path for **Publisher Layouts** is **Setup** | **Global Actions** | **Publisher Layouts**.

Publisher actions

Publisher actions are available in Salesforce 1 and Lightning Experience, and these are object-specific and available on the Object Detail Lightning page.

To create a publisher action, you can use the **Object Manager** tab from the **Setup** menu. The navigation path is **Setup** | **Object Manager** | <select object> | **Buttons, Links, and Actions**.

The following screenshot shows how you can create a publisher action for an **Account** object using a custom Lightning Component:

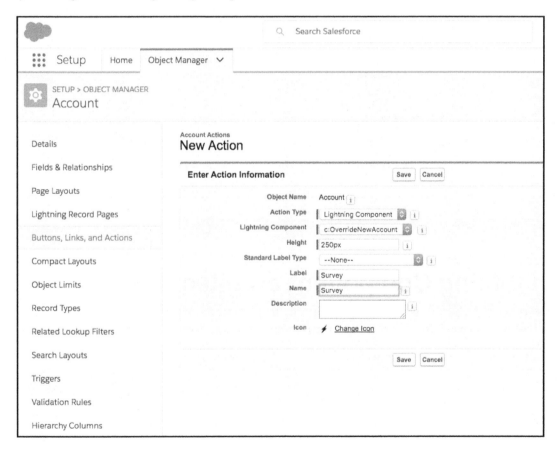

The Publisher Action also needs to be configured based on the page layout. This can be achieved via **Object Manager**. The following screenshot shows how you can configure a custom publisher action:

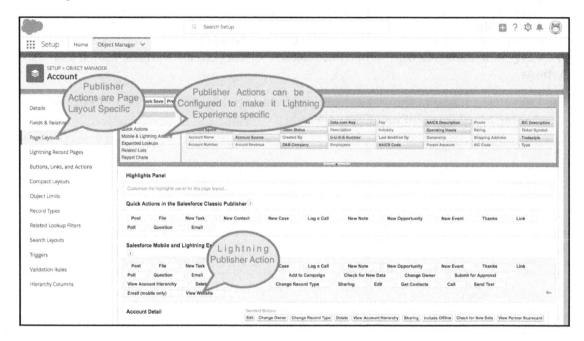

The Screenshot shows Page Layout Editor In Lightning Experience

Lightning Component architecture

Before we start building Lightning Components, let's understand the architectural differences between how Lightning Components and Salesforce Classic Visualforce work.

In a traditional Classic Salesforce UI, every time a user clicks a link, an HTML page is loaded from the server. Even for small interactions, the whole web page or tab needs to be reloaded.

Lightning Experience is based on the concept of a **Single-Page Application** (SPA). In SPAs, once the page is loaded, for any other subsequent request of data from the server, an Ajax callout is made and the page is re-rendered with new data. The aim is to avoid the whole page refreshing.

The following diagram helps to visualize the difference between a single-page architecture and a traditional web page rendering mechanism:

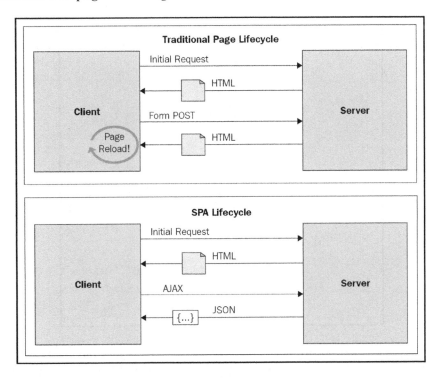

The concept of web components

With web components, you can do almost anything that can be done with HTML, CSS, and JavaScript, and they can be a portable component that can be re-used easily.

Lightning Components are based on this idea, where each individual component consists of one or multiple components that use Apex, JavaScript, HTML, and CSS on top of Salesforce metadata to build a completely functional unit that can work on multiple Salesforce instances and multiple pages.

To understand how web components work, let's consider the following image. This shows how a page can have multiple components. It's also important to note that, since each of the components can consist of data from a third party, and if components from different namespaces can scrap data, it can diminish data security. Hence, Salesforce has a security mechanism known as **Locker service** to prevent data from being accessed.

It locks the DOM of the component and, hence, the JavaScript code from the component cannot access data from other components:

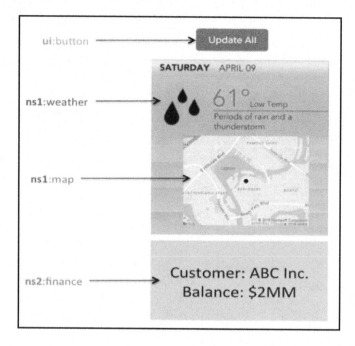

A Lightning page can have multiple components. They can be as small as a button component or can consist of components from different namespaces and different vendors. A component is a reusable unit and can be reused in Lightning Experience and Salesforce 1. To make these components interact with each other, the framework provides events. We will explore Lightning events in later chapters.

Lightning Component Bundle

A Lightning Component bundle consists of four primary sections (there are also Renderer, Design, and SVG sections apart from these four, which we will cover in upcoming chapters):

- **Lightning Component Markup file** (.cmp) file: This is an XML component definition and consists of HTML markup.
- **CSS** file (.css): This consists of CSS for the component.

- **JavaScript** `helper` **and controller** (`.js`): This consists of JavaScript code. The `helper` file is used to keep all the reusable code for the component.
- **Apex controller** (`.cls`): This is not a part of the bundle, but every component that uses Salesforce data uses a server-side controller to fetch and post data to the Salesforce servers.

In the last section of this chapter, we will create a Lightning Component using the Salesforce **Developer Console**. In `Chapter 3`, *Working with Lightning Component Building Blocks*, we will dig deeper into each of these files and explore how to build a functional component for Lightning Experience.

Lightning Component lifecycle

A basic understanding of the sequence of steps that takes place when a Lightning Component communicates with a client and a server will help a great deal before we dive deep into how to build a Lightning Component.

The following diagram shows how a Lightning Component works between the client and server:

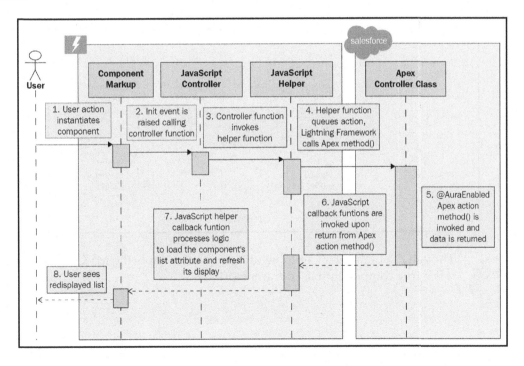

The key things to note from the previous diagram are as follows:

- A user action instantiates the component and an init event is raised
- The JavaScript controller function calls the `helper` function to perform any server-side action
- The Apex controller method is invoked from the `helper` function, the data is returned, and JavaScript `callback` functions are invoked
- The JavaScript client-side logic can be written to manipulate the DOM, set attributes, and refresh the view

MVC concepts in the Lightning Component framework

The Lightning Components framework follows the **Model, View, Controller (MVC)** paradigm. The component file provides the view layer, the JS controller and `helper` files provide the controller part, and the controller interacts with the Salesforce server via Apex. Apex connects to the Salesforce database, which acts as the Model.

The following diagram illustrates how the Lightning Component framework is based on the MVC paradigm:

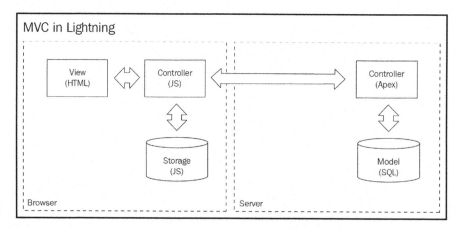

 Though the Lightning Component framework adopts the MVC paradigm, it is a true component-based framework first.

Setting up a Salesforce developer organization to enable the building of Lightning Components

Before we start building Lightning Components, there are some things that need to be done to your developer organization.

If you have not signed up for a Developer organization yet, you can get one for free at `https://developer.Salesforce.com/signup`

1. Enabling **My domain** is a necessary step, and if you have not enabled it, then it's not possible to test your Lightning Component. To enable **My domain**, the navigation path is **Setup** | **Company Settings** | **My Domain**. Register for a domain name, walk through the wizard, and make sure you deploy the new domain to all users. The following screenshot shows the navigation path and also the end result once **My Domain** is enabled:

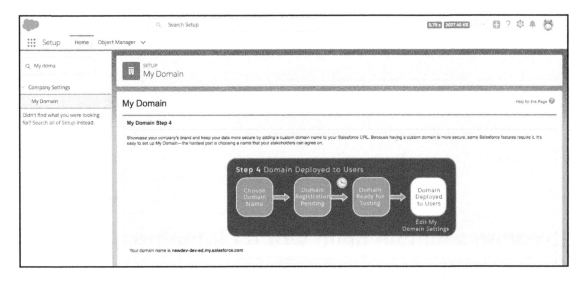

The preceding screen is for deploying My Domain to users

2. Disabling caching for development purposes is very important. Lightning Experience performs caching to improve performance, and this may interfere with the testing of Lightning Components because your code changes might not immediately reflect upon page reload.

3. The navigation path to disable caching is **Setup| Security | Session Settings**. The following screenshot shows the checkbox that needs to be unchecked:

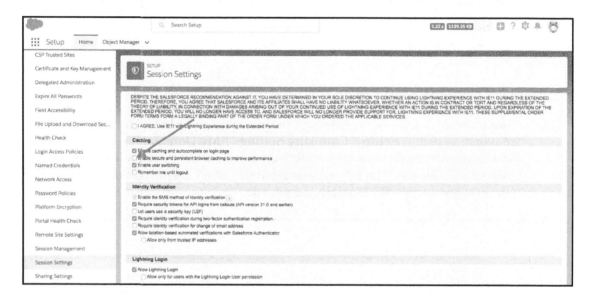

This is how you can disable persistent cache in salesforce environment for Lightning Component development Purpose

For production, these settings need to be enabled to improve performance.

Creating a simple hello world Lightning Component

The aim of the section is to demonstrate how to build a simple Lightning Component via the Salesforce **Developer Console**. We will also explore how to create a simple application to test our component.

The simplest way to create a Lightning Component is to use the Salesforce **Developer Console**. In later chapters, we will get familiar with source-driven development and the use of an **Integrated Development Editor** (IDE). For now, let's use the Salesforce **Developer Console**:

1. Open the Salesforce **Developer Console**:

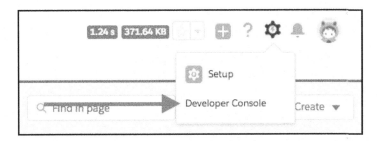

2. Use the **File** menu to create a new **Lightning Component**:

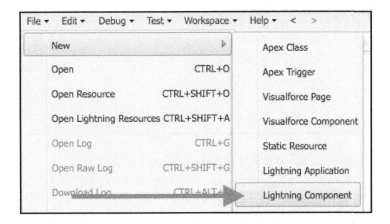

3. Name the component. Let's name it HelloWorld for now.
4. Enter the following code in the component markup and save it (command + *S*):

```
<aura:component >
    HelloWorld
</aura:component>
```

5. Let's test this on the browser. To test this, we will need to create a **Lightning Application**. Go to the **File** menu, as we did in *step 2*, to create a **Lightning Application**. Let's name the application `HelloWorldApp`, enter the following code, and save it (command + *S*). Notice we have used the `HelloWorld` component in the `aura:application` tag to reference the component.

```
<aura:application >
    <c:HelloWorld/>
</aura:application>
```

6. Click on **Preview** in the application and make sure the browser renders **HelloWorld**. The following screenshot shows the preview and the application:

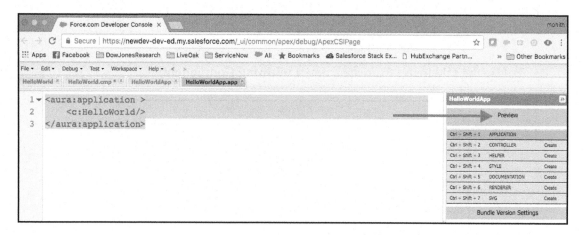

7. You will see that there was a unique URL generated as `Salesforce_domain/c/HelloWorldApp.app`. Notice that `c` is the default namespace. For a managed package application, your organization may have a namespace and then the namespace is used in the URL generated instead of `c`. Also, note that `Salesforce_domain` is the domain name of your Salesforce instance. The following screenshot shows how the component markup is rendered on the browser:

The Lightning Design system

A real-world application involves UI widgets such as lists, tables, cards, modal, and many more. For its Lightning Experience UI, Salesforce uses a common design pattern, which is an open source project known as the Lightning Design System. You can read more about the Lightning Design System, and the patterns and components provided from the official documentation located at `https://www.Lightningdesignsystem.com`.

Lightning Components can use the styles provided by the Lightning Design System. Let's modify our `HelloWorld` component to display `HelloWorld` in a card format, using the card components provided by the **Salesforce Lightning Design System (SLDS)**.

Creating a simple card component using SLDS

Let's open the `Helloworld` application we have built so far again and modify it to include the SLDS:

1. To open the existing Lightning Component, in **Developer Console**, use **File | Open Lightning Resource**, search for the `HelloWorld` component, and select **Open Selected**.
2. Copy the code that is in the SLDS card component from SLDS (`https://www.Lightningdesignsystem.com/components/cards/`).
3. Paste the markup as it is on the `HelloWorld` component file. You will get an error, as shown in the following screenshot:

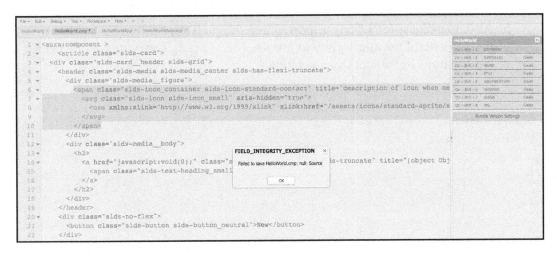

Error when you try using SVG tags in component markup

4. The error is because of the SVG tag (we will see how to use SVG tags in later chapters). Let's remove the highlighted portion for now to allow the save operation. The complete code for the component is as follows:

```
<aura:component >
  <article class="slds-card">
  <div class="slds-card__header slds-grid">
    <header class="slds-media slds-media_center slds-has-flexi-
truncate">
      <div class="slds-media__figure">
      </div>
      <div class="slds-media__body">
        <h2>
          <a href="JavaScript:void(0);" class="slds-card__header-
link slds-truncate" title="[object Object]">
            <span class="slds-text-heading_small">Card
Header</span>
          </a>
        </h2>
      </div>
    </header>
    <div class="slds-no-flex">
      <button class="slds-button slds-button_neutral">New</button>
    </div>
  </div>
  <div class="slds-card__body slds-card__body_inner">Card Body
(custom goes in here)</div>
  <footer class="slds-card__footer">Card Footer</footer>
</article>
</aura:component>
```

5. Also, to make sure SLDS is imported into the shell application for testing, we will need to extend the application to use the force:slds base component. Let's modify our HelloworldApp as follows:

```
<aura:application extends="force:slds">
    <c:HelloWorld />
</aura:application>
```

6. Let's preview the application and see the SLDS card in the browser. The following screenshot shows the results rendered on the browser:

 If you drag these components into the Lightning App Builder, the SLDS will be automatically imported by Salesforce, but for the application created using `<aura:application>` use `extends="force:slds"`.

The preceding is a simple demonstration of how to use the Salesforce SLDS in Lightning Component Framework. The Lightning Component framework is pretty powerful and provides many components and patterns. As a designer, you can build a complete application using the component set provided. Through this book, as we move ahead, we will use the SLDS extensively to build the UI for our components.

Summary

Now that we are familiar with Lightning Experience, the Lightning Component framework architecture, and the Lightning Design System, we are ready to dive deep and explore the Lightning Component framework further.

Let's also address the question of why we should invest time in learning this framework. The primary reason for learning this framework is that to customize Lightning Experience or Lightning pages, we will need to build custom Lightning Components. Also, as we will see later, the Lightning Component framework can be used to build Salesforce communities. It can also be used to build chatter extensions, Salesforce extensions for Outlook, and extensions in other Salesforce products.

In the next chapter, we will explore how to use Salesforce DX and an IDE to set up our development workflow for source-driven development.

Exploring Salesforce DX

2

Salesforce DX is a modern tool for building Salesforce applications. It allows Salesforce developers to carry out source-driven development. In a source-driven development workflow, the source code can be kept in a version control system such as GitHub, **Team Foundation Server (TFS)**, **Subversion (SVN)**, or any other equivalent source control system. A developer can deploy the source code into a Salesforce instance, referred to as scratch Orgs, using commands provided by the Salesforce DX CLI. The CLI also provides commands to push the source code from your machine (referred to as local) to a Salesforce instance, create a Lightning Component Bundle, test Lightning Components, and many others. Source-driven development makes it easier for developers to work in a team and to adopt **Continuous Integration (CI)**. CI automates the verification of builds (compiling code and making it ready for a production environment) and helps to detect regression bugs early. Throughout this book, we will be using the Salesforce DX CLI to push code to scratch Orgs and using GitHub as our version control system to manage our source code. This chapter covers the installation of the Salesforce DX CLI and various commands, and walks through a simple example of how to use Salesforce DX to build and test Lightning Components.

In this chapter, we will cover the following:

- Enabling the developer hub in your Salesforce organization
- Installing the Salesforce DX CLI
- Salesforce DX commands
- Force Lightning namespace commands
- Force metadata API commands
- Installing the Visual Studio extension pack for DX
- Creating a Lightning Component using the Visual Studio extension pack for SFDX

Enabling the developer hub in your Salesforce organization

Salesforce DX allows you to create scratch Orgs, where developers can enhance the source code of their applications and test them.

Scratch Org creation is possible only once your business organization (if you are a Salesforce **Independent Software Vendor** (ISV), Salesforce assigns a business organization) or your production application (if you are a Salesforce customer) has the **Dev Hub** enabled.

The **Dev Hub** allows you to do two critical tasks:

- Manage the scratch Orgs created by your developers. With scratch Orgs, each developer can build an application separately in their own scratch Org without stepping on each other's code.
- If you are an ISV vendor (that is, you build and distribute Salesforce applications on the Salesforce platform), you can register for your application namespace on the **Dev Hub**. A Salesforce managed package application requires a namespace when packaging and the **Dev Hub** provides a way to register a namespace.
- A managed package Salesforce application is one where, once installed in a subscriber Org, the IP of the source code is protected and there is no way to access it in the Salesforce organization that installed the application.
- Scratch Orgs can have the same namespace as your managed package application.

Enabling the developer hub

You will need to perform the steps that follow in your business or in your production organization to enable the developer hub.

Salesforce also provides a trial edition of the **Dev Hub** for developers to experiment with. To start using the trial edition of the developer hub, create a Salesforce instance using the URL https://developer.Salesforce.com/promotions/Orgs/dx-signup. Note that your trial edition is valid only for 30 days, but that should be sufficient time for you to play with and explore Salesforce DX.

Carry out the following steps:

1. Log in to your production Org (if you're a customer), your business Org (if you're an ISV), or your trial Org as the system administrator

2. From Setup, enter `Dev Hub` in the **Quick Find** box and select **Dev Hub**

3. Click Non-GA Service Agreement to read the service agreement

4. To enable the **Dev Hub**, click **Enable**

5. After you have enabled the **Dev Hub**, you can't disable it. If you're using a trial Org, **Dev Hub** is already enabled

6. The following screenshot shows the tabs that are visible in the developer hub. The **Namespace Registry** allows you to find the namespaces you have used for your managed package applications:

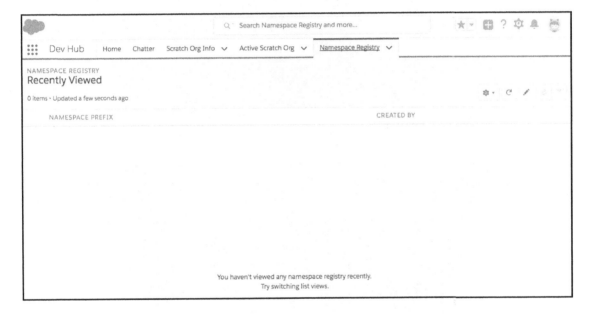

Installing the Salesforce DX CLI

The Salesforce CLI enables you to do the following major tasks from the command line:

- Create and manage Scratch Orgs
- Push and pull code and configuration from source control to Salesforce scratch Orgs

- Load sample datasets into scratch Orgs
- Assign Permission sets
- Install and uninstall managed package applications from the command line

To install the CLI, visit the Salesforce CLI website at `https://developer.Salesforce.com/tools/sfdxcli`.

Depending on your operating system, you can download the executable. The following screenshot shows the selection screen for the installation:

Once your installation is done, make sure to type the sfdx command in your terminal to ensure that the Salesforce DX CLI is installed. The following screenshot shows a successful installation on a Mac Terminal:

```
Mohiths-MacBook-Air:Desktop mohith$ sfdx
Usage: sfdx COMMAND [command-specific-options]

Help topics, type "sfdx help TOPIC" for more details:

  sfdx force    # tools for the salesforce developer
  sfdx plugins  # manage plugins
  sfdx update   # update sfdx-cli

Mohiths-MacBook-Air:Desktop mohith$
```

In the next few sections, we will explore some basic commands to familiarize ourselves with the CLI commands. Specifically, we will explore how to connect to the developer hub, how to create scratch Orgs using the CLI, how to scaffold Lightning bundles, and how to push code changes to a Salesforce Org. We won't be covering the full list of commands provided by DX, but it's recommended to refer to the official documentation at `https://developer.Salesforce.com/docs/atlas.en-us.sfdx_cli_reference.meta/sfdx_cli_reference/`.

You will need your **Dev Hub** username for the upcoming section. If you have not signed up for the trial edition, you can sign up for it here: `https://developer.Salesforce.com/promotions/Orgs/dx-signup`.

Salesforce DX commands

In this section, we will cover some basic commands to authorize Salesforce, set a default **Dev Hub** username, and scaffold a Salesforce DX application.

auth commands

The first thing you will need to do is to connect the CLI to Salesforce. The CLI provides commands to connect using web-based OAuth flow, JWT token-based flow, and an sfdx auth URL.

Use JWT-based flow for CI. If you are using Salesforce DX with Travis, Circle, or Jenkins, then it's always recommended to use JWT-based flow.

To connect the **Dev Hub** to the CLI, run the following command:

```
sfdx force:auth:web:login -r https://login.Salesforce.com
```

For Sandbox Orgs, use test.Salesforce.com instead.

The following screenshot shows the Terminal once the CLI has been authorized to connect to Salesforce:

```
Mohiths-MacBook-Air:DXProject mohith$ sfdx force:auth:web:login -r https://login.salesforce.com
Successfully authorized mohith+devhub@codescience.com with org id 00D1I000000nmA2UAI
You may now close the browser
Mohiths-MacBook-Air:DXProject mohith$
```

Setting a default Dev Hub for scratch Org creation

To configure the default Dev Hub globally, execute the following command:

```
sfdx force:config:set defaultdevhubusername=mohith@dx.com -g  //use your
developer hub username instead of mohith@dx.com
```

Here, -g denotes global and hence, by default, for all the DX projects, the same **Dev Hub** username will be used to create a scratch Org for other DX projects.

If you want to set a different **Dev Hub**, then omit -g and execute the same command in your project directory. The following screenshot shows that the default **Dev Hub** username has been set:

Creating a new Salesforce DX project

To create a new DX project, run the following command in the directory that you want the new project to reside in:

```
sfdx force:project:create -n SampleDXProject
```

Here, SampleDXProject is the name of the project. Once you have the project created, you will see the folder structure, as shown in the following screenshot:

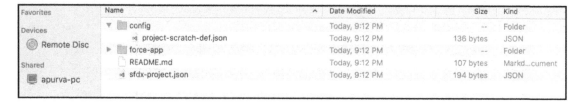

Configuring a scratch Org definition JSON

The configuration in the `project-scratch-def.json` file defines the structure of the scratch Org. Let's look at the following sample `project-scratch-def.json` file:

```
{
  "OrgName": "Acme",
  "country": "US",
  "edition": "Enterprise",
  "features": "MultiCurrency;AuthorApex",
  "OrgPreferences": {
    "enabled": ["S1DesktopEnabled", "ChatterEnabled"],
    "disabled": ["SelfSetPasswordInApi"]
  }
}
```

In the preceding file, we define editions and features we want to enable. It also shows that the scratch Org that we create here will be of `Enterprise` edition with Salesforce features such as `MultiCurrency` and `AuthorApex` enabled. Also, the Salesforce scratch organization will be created, which will have chatter and Salesforce1 enabled, but `SelfSetPasswordInAPI` will not be enabled.

Look at the supported features and Org preferences list in the official docs at `https://developer.Salesforce.com/docs/atlas.en-us.sfdx_dev.meta/sfdx_dev/sfdx_dev_scratch_Orgs_def_file_config_values.htm`.

Configuring project definition JSON

The `sfdx-project.json` file enables the configuration parameter to set `sourceAPIVersion` and namespace if you are building a managed package application.

A sample `sfdx-project.json` file is as follows:

```
{
  "packageDirectories": [{
    "path": "force-app",
    "default": true
  }],
  "namespace": "",
  "sfdcLoginUrl": "https://login.Salesforce.com",
  "sourceApiVersion": "40.0"
}
```

packageDirectories is the location of the directory to which the source from the scratch Org (managed package, unmanaged package, or unpacked code) will be pulled and pushed. We can specify multiple paths, but only one path can be the default. The following code shows an example of how to specify multiple paths:

```
{
"packageDirectories" : [
    { "path": "force-app", "default": true},
    { "path" : "unpackaged" },
    { "path" : "utils" }
  ],
"namespace": "",
"sfdcLoginUrl" : "https://login.Salesforce.com",
"sourceApiVersion": "40.0"
}
```

You can specify the directory name when pulling and pushing source code to scratch Orgs.

Creating a scratch Org

A scratch Org is the Org where developers will build source code and configure an application. To create a scratch Org from the command line, you can execute the following command (cd into the project before running this command):

```
sfdx force:org:create -f project-scratch-def.json -a LighntningScratchOrg
```

Note that, here, LightningScratchOrg is the alias of the Org. Also, note that we have to be in the path of the config file. The following screenshot depicts what is shown following the successful creation of a scratch Org:

```
Mohiths-MacBook-Air:DXProject mohith$ cd /Users/mohith/Desktop/ForceProjects/DXProject/SampleDX
Project
Mohiths-MacBook-Air:SampleDXProject mohith$ cd /Users/mohith/Desktop/ForceProjects/DXProject/Sa
mpleDXProject/config
Mohiths-MacBook-Air:config mohith$ sfdx force:org:create -f project-scratch-def.json
Successfully created scratch org: 00D0m0000000ZnpEAE, username: test-fuovl3z2shti@mohith_compan
y.net
Mohiths-MacBook-Air:config mohith$
```

Notice from the screenshot that a `username` is automatically assigned and an `OrgId` is also generated.

Opening the scratch Org

Before opening the scratch Org, you can set the default scratch Org for source push and pull using the following command:

```
sfdx force:config:set defaultusername=<username>
```

To open a scratch Org, use the command shown here:

```
sfdx force:org:open -u <username/alias>
```

The following is a screenshot of the command line when the Org is opened:

```
Mohiths-MacBook-Air:config mohith$ sfdx force:org:open -u test-fuovl3z2shti@mohith_company.net
Access org 00D0m0000000ZnpEAE as user test-fuovl3z2shti@mohith_company.net with the following U
RL: https://page-power-9638-dev-ed.cs65.my.salesforce.com/secur/frontdoor.jsp?sid=00D0m0000000Z
np!ARIAQBIPTuQhTXnzVYvAs6NUsTCbeztMNa_rXxnLGGkV2A1Vv0rzm418cjvOV5DLCEXJd3yQntyy3DnZs8dABh039n0Y
AX.7
```

Pulling source from a scratch Org

To pull source code components from a scratch Org, use the following command:

```
sfdx force:source:pull
```

Let's create a simple component bundle named `HelloWorld` in the scratch Org and retrieve into the local folder using the preceding command.

To open the Org from the command line, use the following command:

```
sfdx force:org:open -u <username>
```

Once you are in the Org, use the **Developer Console** to create a `HelloWorld` component, as shown in the following screenshot:

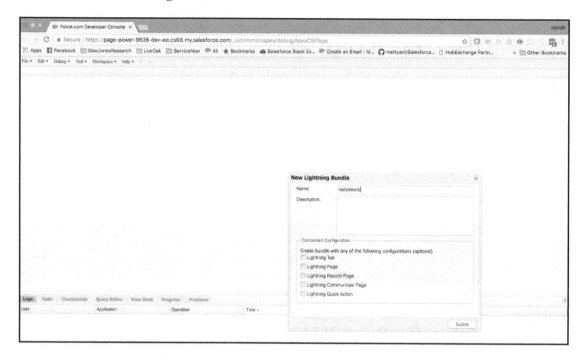

The preceding shows how to use **Developer Console** to create a Lightning Component Bundle

The code for the component can be very simple, as shown here:

```
<aura:component >
  <div> Test Component </div>
</aura:component>
```

The following screenshot shows the command-line screen once a source pull has been performed:

```
Mohiths-MacBook-Air:config mohith$ sfdx force:source:pull
STATE    FULL NAME    TYPE                 PROJECT PATH
─────    ─────────    ────                 ────────────

Add      HelloWorld   AuraDefinitionBundle /Users/mohith/Desktop/ForceProjects/DXProject/SampleDX
Project/force-app/main/default/aura/HelloWorld
```

You should also see the file in your local folder.

If you use Visual Studio Code, then you can open the folder to see the file structure, as shown in the following screenshot:

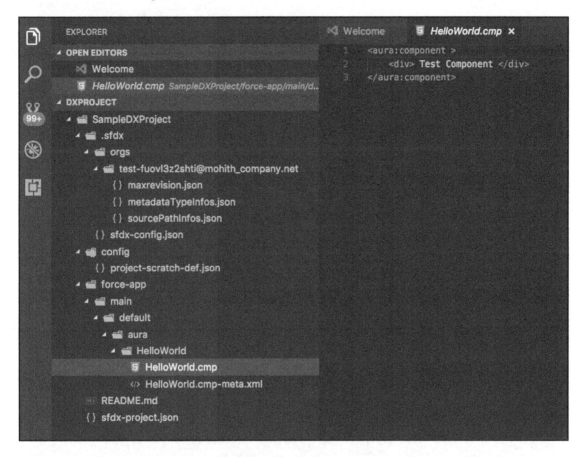

If you want to download and install Visual Studio Code, follow this link: `https://code.visualstudio.com/download`.

Push source code to a scratch Org

To push source to scratch Org, run the following command:

```
sfdx force:source:push
```

For our use case, we can change the `HelloWorld.cmp` file code, as shown in the following screenshot:

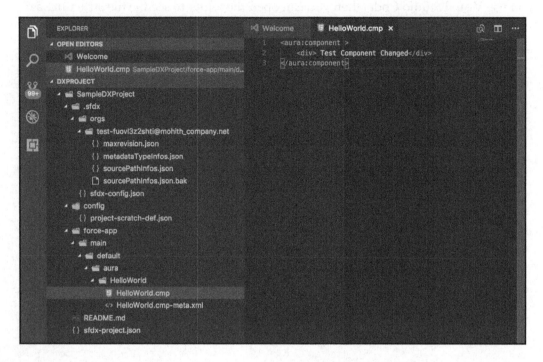

Once you run:

sfdx force:push

the code is deployed to the scratch Org. The screenshot shows the command-line interface once the code has been deployed successfully:

```
Mohiths-MacBook-Air:config mohith$ sfdx force:source:status
STATE            FULL NAME                TYPE                    PROJECT PATH

Local Changed   HelloWorld/HelloWorld.cmp    AuraDefinitionBundle    force-app/main/default/aura/Hel
loWorld/HelloWorld.cmp-meta.xml
Local Changed   HelloWorld/HelloWorld.cmp    AuraDefinitionBundle    force-app/main/default/aura/Hel
loWorld/HelloWorld.cmp
Mohiths-MacBook-Air:config mohith$ sfdx force:source:push
STATE       FULL NAME    TYPE            PROJECT PATH

Changed     HelloWorld   AuraDefinitionBundle    force-app/main/default/aura/HelloWorld
```

Also, note that you can always find the status change between your local folder and scratch Org using the following command:

```
sfdx force:source:status
```

Conflict resolution

If there is a conflict between a server and your local machine, when you do a force push the conflict will be shown. You can overwrite the file onto the local system remotely using the following command:

```
sfdx force:source:push --forceoverwrite
```

To overwrite local files from the server use the command:

```
sfdx force:source:pull --forceoverwrite
```

Ignoring files

You might want to untrack certain files and folders when pushing code from the local system to the scratch Org. To do this, you have to create a file named forceignore. The sample format for forceignore is as follows:

```
# Specify a relative path to a directory from the project root
helloWorld/main/default/classes

# Specify a wildcard directory - any directory named "classes" is excluded
**classes

# Specify file extensions
**.cls
**.pdf

# Specify a specific file
helloWorld/main/default/HelloWorld.cls
```

Lightning commands

In this section, we will explore commands provided by DX to create a Lightning bundle via the command line.

Creating a Lightning app and components

Note that you will need to be in the aura directory to create a Lightning Application or component. If you do not have one, create a directory named `aura` in the <app dir> I `main` I `default`.

Hence, let's cd into the aura directory using the command-line utility:

```
Mohiths-MacBook-Air:config mohith$ cd /Users/mohith/Desktop/ForceProjects/DXProject/SampleDXPro
ject/force-app/main/default/aura
Mohiths-MacBook-Air:aura mohith$ 
```

To create a simple Lightning app named `TestApp`, execute the following command:

```
sfdx force:Lightning:app:create -n TestApp
```

The following screenshot shows the files that were automatically added to the local folder once the preceding commands had been executed:

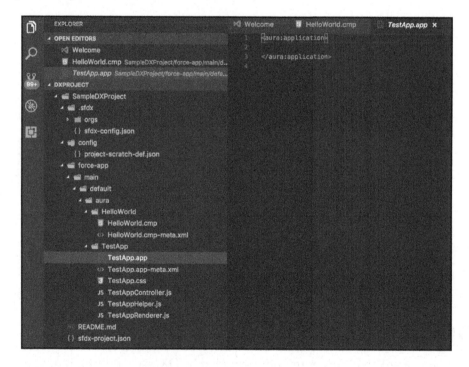

Along similar lines, to create a component bundle named `Testcomponent`, execute the following command in the aura directory:

```
sfdx force:Lightning:component:create -n Testcomponent
```

The following table summarizes the commands available to create Lightning Components, Lightning Application, events, and interfaces:

Command	Description
`Lightning:app:create`	Creates a Lightning app bundle in the specified directory or the current working directory. The bundle consists of multiple files in a folder with the designated name.
`Lightning:component:create`	Creates a Lightning Component Bundle in the specified directory or the current working directory. The bundle consists of multiple files in a folder with the designated name.
`Lightning:event:create`	Creates a Lightning event bundle in the specified directory or the current working directory. The bundle consists of multiple files in a folder with the designated name.
`Lightning:interface:create`	Creates a Lightning interface bundle in the specified directory or the current working directory. The bundle consists of multiple files in a folder with the designated name.

Metadata API commands

If you have been working with the Salesforce platform, you will already be aware that the Metadata API format is used for the deployment of code and configuration from one Salesforce instance to another.

Salesforce DX has a different folder format than the Metadata API format. The Salesforce DX force Metadata API commands allow you to convert the Metadata API file format into the Salesforce DX format for development, and also provides a command to deploy file representations into your production Orgs or package Orgs for ISV applications.

mdapi:convert and mdapi:retrieve

Metadata API commands allow you to convert the retrieved source code from the Metadata API to the Salesforce DX project format. To retrieve the source code from your Org, you can use `mdapi:retrieve`.

If you already have an unmanaged package, managed package, or existing source code in your Orgs, you can use mdapi:retrieve to retrieve them to a ZIP format and then use mdapi:convert to convert them to DX format.

Converting existing managed/unmanaged package code to DX Format

To convert existing source code from an unmanaged package, you can take the following steps:

1. Authenticate with your Developer Edition Org. Type the following command, then authenticate with your developer edition Org credentials, and accept to provide access to Salesforce DX. Type the command. Note that targetOrg is an alias that is assigned to the target Org. Alias is a shorthand string, so you don't have to type the username:

   ```
   sfdx force:auth:web:login -a targetOrg
   ```

2. Export the unmanaged package into a temp directory using the retrieve command and you will notice that, once the following commands have been executed, you will see a ZIP file in the temp folder:

   ```
   mkdir temp
   sfdx force:mdapi:retrieve -s -r./temp -u targetOrg -packagename
   ```

   Here, packagename is the name of your unmanaged package.

3. Unzip the file using the ZIP file utility.
4. Execute the following command to convert the source code to the Salesforce DX project structure:

   ```
   sfdx force:mdapi:convert -r./temp
   ```

5. The preceding code assumes that you have created a DX project using the following commands:

   ```
   sfdx force:project:create -n myproject
   cd myproject
   ```

Deploy command

Use the deploy command to deploy files to production or your packaging Org:

```
sfdx force:mdapi:deploy
```

To convert the source back to the Metadata API format so that you can deploy it, using execute the following command:

```
sfdx force:source:convert
```

The Salesforce SFDX CLI is a great utility and provides a lot of functions to create Apex, Visualforce, and Lightning Components, as well as to create a dataset, to install packages, and to deploy applications. It's out of the scope of this book to discuss each and every command. You can explore every command provided by Salesforce DX in the official document at: https://developer.Salesforce.com/docs/atlas.en-us.sfdx_cli_reference.meta/sfdx_cli_reference/cli_reference.htm.

Throughout the book, we will use Salesforce DX to build and test Lightning Components. Wherever applicable, if we introduce new commands that are not covered, we will highlight them.

Data import and export commands in Salesforce DX

The Salesforce DX CLI also provides ways to create, export, and import data into scratch Orgs. This can be very helpful to get a sample dataset in scratch Orgs.

Let's explore the ones that we will be using regularly.

Data export Salesforce DX command

The data export command allows exporting a dataset from a scratch Org into JSON files.

Let's try to export the dataset to the data folder in your local project from one of the Dev Orgs. Note that you will need to connect your CLI with the Org you are trying to export data into using the auth commands we discussed in the previous section.

Let's try and run the following command:

```
sfdx force:data:tree:export -p -q "SELECT Id, Name, (SELECT Id, LastName,
FirstName FROM Contacts) FROM Account" -u MyTPO --outputdir./data
```

Note that, here, -u is followed by the Org alias. It can be a username as well of the Org. In this case, I have an Org with the alias MyTPO.

-p indicates that multiple subject files should be generated, followed by the automatic generation of plan file definitions.

The preceding command exports the data using the **Salesforce Object Query Language (SOQL)** into an output directory data in the root folder. Remember to run this command from the root of your project.

The preceding command creates a folder named data with the following file structure:

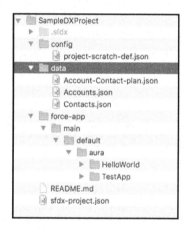

Observe the structure of all the files that were generated here.

A couple of things you can infer from the JSON files are as follows:

- A referenceId is self-generated for both contact and account files.
- The plan file maps which objects should have the saved Refs and which ones should be resolved. The sample plan file would look like the following for the Account and Contact objects in Salesforce:

```
[{
    "sobject": "Account",
    "saveRefs": true,
    "resolveRefs": false,
    "files": [
```

```
      "Accounts.json"
    ]
  },
  {
    "sobject": "Contact",
    "saveRefs": false,
    "resolveRefs": true,
    "files": [
      "Contacts.json"
    ]
  }
]
```

Data import Salesforce DX command

Once you have the data files, you can import data into scratch Orgs or any other Orgs using the following commands:

```
sfdx force:data:tree:import --plan./data/Account-Contact-plan.json -u MyTPO
```

That `--plan` is used to provide the path of the plan JSON file.
Here, `MyTPO` is, again, the alias of the Org we want to import the dataset to.

Once you import the data, the command prompt will have the results and the IDs of the dataset.

Bulk data upsert Salesforce DX command

If you need large volumes of data to be imported to the Org, the CLI also provides bulk API commands, which allow you to upsert data from the CSV file into the Org.

The following is a sample command to upsert data using the CSV file:

```
$ sfdx force:data:bulk:upsert -s Account -f./path/to/file.csv -i
ExternalId__c -w 2
```

The preceding command will upsert Account data from the file with the name `file.csv`, which is in the `/path/to/` path, using the `ExternalId` field `ExternalId__c`, and will wait for two minutes before refreshing the command-line display.

You can also track the status of the job and the batch using a job or a combination of job and batch IDs. The following command shows the sample command set for this:

```
sfdx force:data:bulk:status -i 750xx000000005sAAA -b 751xx000000005nAAA
```

Limitations of bulk upsert commands

As you might notice, bulk upsert can take only one sobject at a time, so, to insert or upsert multiple objects, you would have to maintain the CSV files and manage their own CSV files.

There are a lot of other commands related to data that we will not cover as they are beyond the scope of this book. To gain an understanding of them, refer to the official documentation here:

```
https://developer.Salesforce.com/docs/atlas.en-us.sfdx_cli_reference.meta/sfdx_
cli_reference/cli_reference_force_data.htm.
```

Installing the Visual Studio extension pack for DX

Visual Studio Code from Microsoft is a lightweight editor. Salesforce has an extension pack for it, which provides an IDE-like experience. The DX commands we looked into are all baked into it. In this section, we will explore that extension by installing it and taking a quick walk through it.

Throughout the book, we will use Visual Studio Code as our IDE, but you are free to use any IDE or the Salesforce **Developer Console** to explore the Lightning Components covered in this book.

If you have not downloaded Visual Studio Code, download it from `https://code.visualstudio.com/download`.

Once you are inside Visual Studio Code, you can look for extensions and search for the Visual Studio Code extensions for DX.

The following screenshot shows how to find and install it:

Once installed, make sure to open your DX project folder that has sfdx-project.json as root.

Once you type `sfdx` in the command palette, you will notice that most of the DX commands can be executed from Visual Studio Code.

The following screenshot shows where you should type the `sfdx` command. Also note that the editor has an integrated terminal, where you can execute commands:

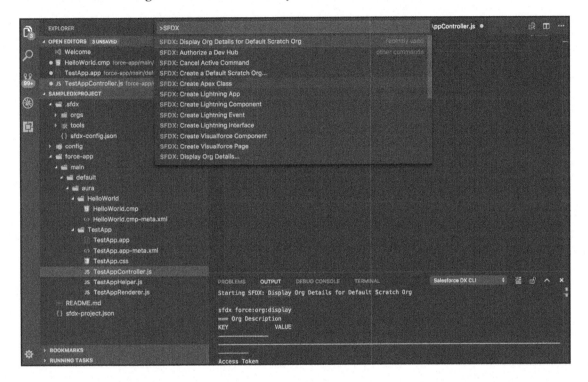

As you can see, some of the commands that we executed via the **Dev Hub** are also available in the extension, and this allows us to use a combination of the CLI, Visual Studio Code, and the Visual Studio Code extension pack for Salesforce to set up an efficient workflow.

Developer workflow for building a Salesforce application

This section covers a simple developer workflow, which we will be adapting to build Apex and Lightning Components using the Salesforce DX CLI, Visual Studio Code, and the Visual Studio Code extension pack for the Salesforce plugin.

The following is a rough diagram of one of the developer workflows that we will be following for all of the components and code in subsequent chapters:

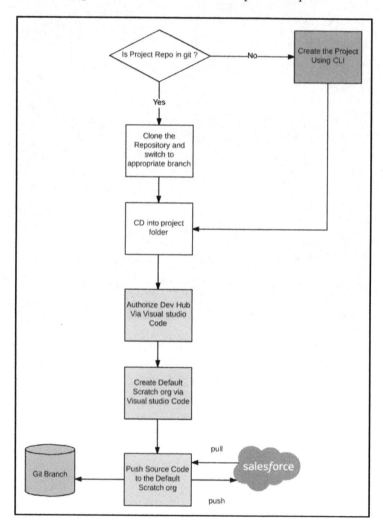

Let's follow the preceding workflow step by step using Salesforce DX commands.

Create a Salesforce DX project in the directory you would like the project folder to be in. The following command shows a sample command:

```
sfdx force:project:create -n HelloWorldProject
```

The following screenshot shows the command-line Terminal:

```
Mohiths-MacBook-Air:ForceProjects mohith$ sfdx force:project:create -n HelloWorldProject
target dir = /Users/mohith/Desktop/ForceProjects
   create HelloWorldProject/sfdx-project.json
   create HelloWorldProject/README.md
   create HelloWorldProject/config/project-scratch-def.json
```

Note that `HelloWorldProject` is the name of the project directory. Once you create the project, you will see the following file structure:

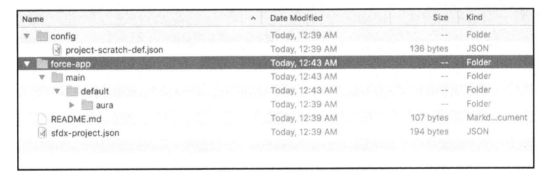

Name	^	Date Modified	Size	Kind
▼ config		Today, 12:39 AM	--	Folder
project-scratch-def.json		Today, 12:39 AM	136 bytes	JSON
▼ force-app		Today, 12:43 AM	--	Folder
▼ main		Today, 12:43 AM	--	Folder
▼ default		Today, 12:43 AM	--	Folder
▶ aura		Today, 12:39 AM	--	Folder
README.md		Today, 12:39 AM	107 bytes	Markd...cument
sfdx-project.json		Today, 12:39 AM	194 bytes	JSON

Then, follow these steps:

1. Open the project folder in Visual Studio Code.

2. Authorize the **Dev Hub** using Visual Studio Code. On the command palette, type SFDX:Authorize a **Dev Hub**. This is shown in the following screenshot. Once the command executes, enter the credentials for your Org, and once logged in, close the window:

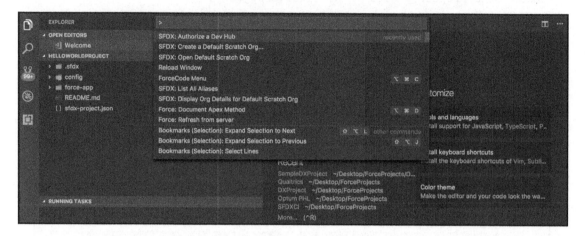

3. Create a default scratch Org for your project. Again, this can be done from the Visual Studio Code View menu and using the command palette. On the command palette, type **SFDX: Create a Default Scratch Org...**.

4. You will be prompted to use scratch def JSON and an alias. Note that the alias is optional. The following screenshot shows the default scratch Org creation command:

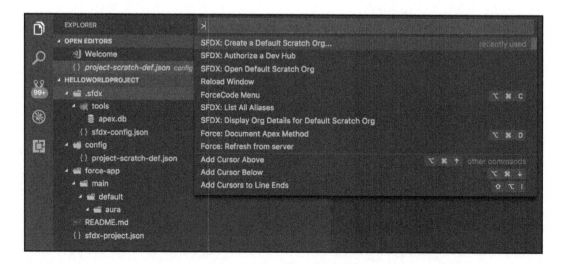

5. The next step is to create a Lightning Components and code components locally. Again, use the **View** option and the **Command Palette** to create a Lightning component bundle. Use the **SFDX:Create Lightning Components**:

6. Push to the scratch Org. Again, use the View option and the command palette to push code to the scratch Org. To do this, use SFDX:Pushsource to default scratch Org. Open the scratch Org using SFDX:Open Default Scratch Org.

7. You can work locally and push code to the server or work in the scratch Org directly and then you can pull back the source using SFDX:Pull source from scratch Org. Note that you can create objects, workflows, and other components directly, and force:pull will retrieve everything from the scratch Org into the local folder.

8. To experiment with this, let's open the scratch Org and use the **Developer Console** to edit the components:

9. Use `SFDX:Pull` source from default scratch Org to get the changes to the local folder.

10. The following are some of the utilities listed in the table provided by the DX plugin for VS Code to compare local and changes on the server:

Command	Usage
`SFDX:View` local changes	This shows all the changes in the Terminal that are in the local folder compared to source on the Salesforce server
`SFDX:View` changes in default scratch Org	This shows all the changes in the Terminal in the scratch Org compared to the local folder
`SFDX:View` all changes	Combined changes in server and local
`SFDX:Pull` source from default scratch Org and override conflicts	Allows you to override all of the source code from a Salesforce scratch Org to a local folder
`SFDX:Push` source and override conflicts	Overrides the source in the scratch Org to exactly the same as that of the local folder

11. The final step is to always make sure you synchronize the code to the Git repository. VS Code has GitHub integration built in, so it's easier to set up a repository and push source code. Note that, for this, you will need to install Git the instructions for this are documented here: `https://git-scm.com/book/en/v2/Getting-Started-Installing-Git`.

12. To get started with creating your own Git repository at github.com and note the repository URL, execute the following commands in the project folder:

1. Initialize the Git repository:

```
git init
```

2. Create a .gitignore file in the root of the project with the following contents. Feel free to add more files that you do not want to commit:

```
.DS_Store
.sfdx
.project
.Salesforce
.settings
node_modules
.idea
```

3. Add all of the local files and commit them to the repository using the following command:

```
git add.

git commit -m "commit message"
```

4. Set up a stream for pushing to remote Git:

```
git remote add origin <reposiortyURL>
```

5. If you run into conflicts and need to overwrite, use the following command:

```
git pull origin master --allow-unrelated-
histories
git merge origin origin/master
//Fix any conflicts if found
git add.
git commit -m "merge conflicts"
git push origin master
```

6. You will notice that VS Code has built-in support for committing changes to the Git repository. This is indicated in the following screenshot:

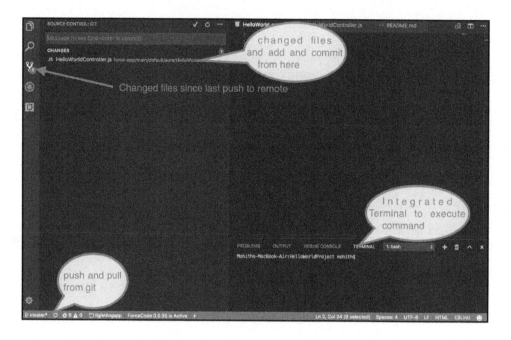

Summary

In this chapter, we explored the developer workflow and the toolsets required to start building Lightning Components. It's always recommended to use an IDE to accelerate the building of Lightning Components. We covered the Salesforce extension pack for Salesforce DX for Visual Studio Code. There are lot more IDE options, such as Eclipse with the Force.com plugin (https://developer.Salesforce.com/tools/forceide2), Illuminated Cloud (http://www.illuminatedcloud.com/), the Welkin Suite (https://welkinsuite.com/), or one of the many other alternatives, and you can use the one that best suits your needs. The general developer workflow that we covered in this chapter will remain the same irrespective of your choice of IDE.

Now that we have equipped ourselves with the appropriate tools, in the next chapter, we will explore how to build a complete functional Lightning Components. We will build a component that can search for YouTube videos based on a keyword input by a user.

Lightning Component Building Blocks

3

In the last chapter, we equipped ourselves with tools and a developer workflow using Salesforce DX. In this chapter, we will build our first working Lightning Component. As we build the application, we will explore the basic building blocks of the Lightning Component framework, which includes Component Markup, the JavaScript controller, and `helper`. We will also learn how to wire a server-side Apex controller to client-side JavaScript. By the end of the chapter, we will have a Lightning Component that allows users to input a search string and search YouTube content.

This chapter assumes that you are familiar with Salesforce server-side Apex programming. If you are not familiar with Salesforce Apex programming, you can explore it on Trailhead (`https://trailhead.Salesforce.com/en/modules/Apex_database/units/Apex_database_intro`).

In this chapter, we will be covering the following topics:

- Component markup and using Lightning base components for layouts
- Lightning Component attributes and Expressions
- Writing a JavaScript controller and `helper`
- Wiring client-side JavaScript to Apex controllers

Component markup and using Lightning base components for layouts

Component markup resides in the `.cmp` file. Markup consists of HTML elements, aura components (`aura:component` provides default rendering implementation), and other custom child components. Custom components start with the default namespace c. Apart from the c namespace, Salesforce provides out-of-the-box components with a UI and the Lightning namespace (components with the Lightning namespace are referred to as base components).

 It is recommended to use a new Lightning namespace when using out-of-the-box components because Lightning namespace components automatically apply the **Salesforce Lightning Design System** (**SLDS**), CSS, and also provide in-built JavaScript functions such as validations, currency formatting, and localization.

The syntax for the component is as follows:

```
<aura:component>
<!-- Optional coponent attributes here -->
<!-- Optional HTML markup -->
</aura:component>
```

Component definition aura:component

`aura:component` defines the root of the hierarchy. There are optional attributes and, in this section, we will cover an explanation of a few attributes.

Access modifier

An access attribute defines whether a component is available globally or is just public. Global components can be accessed outside the namespace. If an AppExchange vendor allows subscriber organizations to use components, they will be marked as `global`.

 By default, components are public. This means they cannot be accessed outside of the current namespace.

The syntax with the `access` attribute should be as follows:

```
<aura:component access="global">
<!-- Optional coponent attributes here -->
<!-- Optional HTML markup -->
</aura:component>
```

Providing a description to component

Provide a component description. Use this attribute to some description. The syntax with the `description` attribute is shown as follows. This is extremely when your component is previewed in the document previewer:

```
<aura:component access="global" description="Youtube Search Component">
<!-- Optional coponent attributes here -->
<!-- Optional HTML markup -->
</aura:component>
```

Implementing interfaces in Lightning Components

A comma-separated list of interfaces that the component implements. An interface defines where Lightning Components are available. The following some of the available interfaces and their importance:

Interface	Description
`force:appHostable`	Creates a component for use as a navigation element in Lightning Experience or Salesforce mobile apps.
`forceCommunity:availableForAllPageTypes`	Creates a component that's available for drag and drop in the **Community Builder**.
`flexipage:availableForAllPageTypes`	Creates a component for use in Lightning pages or the **Lightning App Builder**.
`flexipage:availableForRecordHome`	Creates a component for use on a record **Homepage** in Lightning Experience.
`force:LightningQuickAction`	Creates a component that can be used with a Lightning quick action.
`Lightning:actionOverride`	Overrides a standard action in **Lightning Experience**.

The syntax with multiple interfaces for the component is as follows:

```
<aura:component access="global" description="Youtube Search Component"
implements="flexipage:availableForAllPageTypes,flexipage:availableForRecord
Home,force:appHostable">
<!-- Optional coponent attributes here -->
<!-- Optional HTML markup -->
</aura:component>
```

You can also define your own interface using `aura:interface`. To know more refer the docs here `https://developer.salesforce.com/docs/atlas.en-us.lightning.meta/lightning/oo_interfaces.htm`.

In `Chapter 1`, *Introduction to the Lightning Component Framework*, we briefly touched upon the *Lightning Design System*. The Lightning Design System provides pre-defined patterns to build a UI without having to reinvent or code much. However, the Lightning Design System alone is not sufficient to attain a working application. That requires the developer to use JavaScript code to add client-side interactivity. Salesforce has simplified this by providing some out-of-the-box components with the Lightning namespace. Your goal, as a developer, should be to use these components as much as possible. They simplify the application build by having to code lots of JavaScript. However, note that, if you need functionality, that's not provided by out-of-the-box components; you could always custom code the entire markup.

To explore the Lightning Component documentation in your Salesforce environment, visit `https://<myDomain>.Lightning.force.com/`, component reference/`suite.app?page=home`. Note that, here, `myDomain` is your Salesforce custom domain. The document is also available on the Salesforce developer website at `https://developer.Salesforce.com/docs/component-library/`.

Lightning base components for layout and layout items

The `Lightning:layout` and `Lightning:layoutItem` components allow you to create the layout inside `aura:component`. The attributes for the `Lightning:layout` and `Lightning:layoutitem` components are shown in the following table:

- Lightning:layout:

Name	Type	Description
class	string	A CSS class for the outer element, in addition to the component's base classes.
title	string	Displays tooltip text when the mouse moves over the element.
horizontalAlign	string	Determines how to spread the layout items horizontally. The alignment options are center, space, spread, and end.
verticalAlign	string	Determines how to spread the layout items vertically. The alignment options are start, center, end, and stretch.
multipleRows	Boolean	Determines whether to wrap the child items when they exceed the layout width. If true, the items wrap to the following line. This value defaults to false.
pullToBoundary	string	Pulls layout items to the layout boundaries and corresponds to the padding size on the layout item. Possible values are small, medium, or large.

- Lightning:layoutitem:

Name	Type	Description
class	string	A CSS class for the outer element, in addition to the component's base classes.
title	string	Displays tooltip text when the mouse moves over the element.
size	integer	If the viewport is divided into 12 parts, size indicates the relative space the container occupies. Size is expressed as an integer from 1 through 12. This applies for all device-types.
smallDeviceSize	integer	If the viewport is divided into 12 parts, this attribute indicates the relative space the container occupies on device-types larger than a mobile. It is expressed as an integer from 1 through 12.
mediumDeviceSize	integer	If the viewport is divided into 12 parts, this attribute indicates the relative space the container occupies on device-types larger than a tablet. It is expressed as an integer from 1 through 12.
largeDeviceSize	integer	If the viewport is divided into 12 parts, this attribute indicates the relative space the container occupies on device-types larger than a desktop. It is expressed as an integer from 1 through 12.

flexibility	object	Make the item fluid so that it absorbs any extra space in its container or shrinks when there is less space. Allowed values are: `auto` (columns grow or shrink equally as space allows), `shrink` (columns shrink equally as space decreases), `no-shrink` (columns don't shrink as space reduces), `grow` (columns grow equally as space increases), `no-grow` (columns don't grow as space increases), `no-flex` (columns don't grow or shrink as space changes). Use comma-separated values for multiple options, such as `auto, no-shrink`.
padding	string	Sets padding to either the right or left sides of a container, or all sides of a container. Allowed values are `horizontal-small`, `horizontal-medium`, `horizontal-large`, `around-small`, `around-medium`, and `around-large`.

Lightning card base component

The Lightning card component displays a simple card. You can set the title, the footer, and the body. You can also add action buttons.

The code for the Lightning card component is as follow:

```
<aura:component>
    <Lightning:card footer="Card Footer" title="Hello">
        <aura:set attribute="actions">
            <Lightning:button label="Search"/>
        </aura:set>
        <p class="slds-p-horizontal_small">
            Card Body (custom component)
        </p>
    </Lightning:card>
</aura:component>
```

The following table contains more detailed descriptions of the attributes:

NAME	TYPE	ACCESS	REQUIRED	DEFAULT	DESCRIPTION
body	component[]	GLOBAL	No		Inherited from `aura:component`. The body of the component. In markup, this is everything in the body tag.

NAME	TYPE	ACCESS	REQUIRED	DEFAULT	DESCRIPTION
title	object	GLOBAL	Yes		The title can include text or another component and is displayed in the `header`.
iconName	string	GLOBAL	No		The Lightning design system name of the icon. Names are written in the format `utility:down` where `utility` is the category, and down is the specific icon to be displayed. The icon is displayed in the `header` to the left of the `title`.
actions	component[]	GLOBAL	No		Actions are components such as button or `buttonIcon`. Actions are displayed in the `header`.
variant	string	GLOBAL	No	base	The variant changes the appearance of the card. Accepted variants include base or narrow. This value defaults to base.
class	string	GLOBAL	No		A CSS class for the outer element, in addition to the component's base classes.
footer	object	GLOBAL	No		The footer can include text or another component.

Example layouts using the Lightning layout and card components

In this section, we will explore some examples of how to create the layout using `Lightning:layout`, `Lightning:layoutItem`, and `Lightning:card`.

> You can use Salesforce DX format for all of the code shared in this chapter. Clone the repository using the `git clone https://github.com/PacktPublishing/Learning-Salesforce-Lightning-Application-Development` command. Once you have the project, `cd` into `chapter3` and follow the instructions to create a scratch org and push the source code.

Take the following steps to observe the output of the examples covered in this section:

1. Start by creating a Lightning Application via the **Developer Console**, as follows:

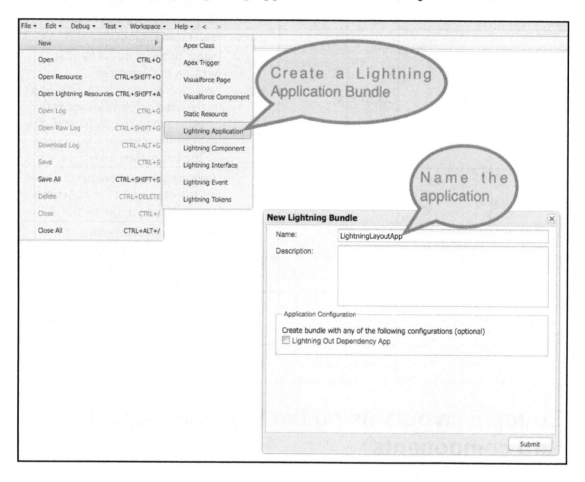

2. Copy the markup code provided in the following examples for each section into the application file of the bundle created in *step 1*, as follows:

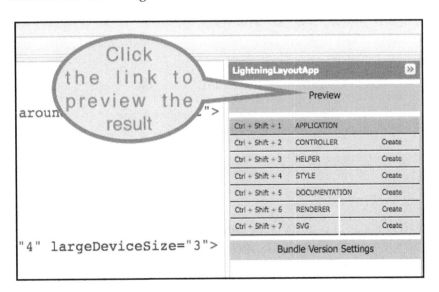

```
1 ▼ <aura:application extends="force:slds">
2 ▼     <lightning:layout verticalAlign="start" multipleRows="true">
3 ▼         <lightning:layoutItem flexibility="auto" smallDeviceSi...          eviceSize="3" padding="around-small" size="12">
4 ▼             <lightning:card title="1">
5 ▼                 <p class="slds-p-horizontal_small">
6                     Card 1
7                 </p>
8             </lightning:card>
9         </lightning:layoutItem>
10 ▼         <lightning:layoutItem flexibility="auto" size="12" padding="around-small" smallDeviceSize="6" mediumDeviceSize="4" largeDeviceSize="3">
11 ▼             <lightning:card title="2">
12 ▼                 <p class="slds-p-horizontal_small">
13                     Card 2
14                 </p>
15             </lightning:card>
16         </lightning:layoutItem>
17 ▼         <lightning:layoutItem flexibility="auto" size="12" padding="around-small" smallDeviceSize="6" mediumDeviceSize="4" largeDeviceSize="3">
18 ▼             <lightning:card title="3">
19 ▼                 <p class="slds-p-horizontal_small">
20                     Card 3
21                 </p>
22             </lightning:card>
23         </lightning:layoutItem>
24 ▼         <lightning:layoutItem flexibility="auto" size="12" padding="around-small" smallDeviceSize="6" mediumDeviceSize="4" largeDeviceSize="3">
25 ▼             <lightning:card title="4">
26 ▼                 <p class="slds-p-horizontal_small">
27                     Card 4
28                 </p>
29             </lightning:card>
30         </lightning:layoutItem>
```

Screenshot shows how one can use developer console to create a test application

3. Preview the application using the **Preview** link provided in the **Developer Console**. The following screenshot shows the **Preview** link:

Horizontal alignment using the Lightning layout base component

In this section, we will create an application that demonstrates how to use
`Lightning:layout` base components and achieve horizontal and vertical alignments.

Create a simple Lightning Application via the **Developer Console** and let's name the
application `LightningLayoutApp`. Now copy the following code:

```
<aura:application extends="force:slds">
    <Lightning:layout horizontalAlign="space">
        <Lightning:layoutItem padding="around-small">
            <Lightning:card title="1">
                <p class="slds-p-horizontal_small">
                    Card 1
                </p>
        </Lightning:card>
        </Lightning:layoutItem>
        <Lightning:layoutItem padding="around-small">
            <Lightning:card title="2">
                <p class="slds-p-horizontal_small">
                    Card 2
                </p>
        </Lightning:card>
        </Lightning:layoutItem>
        <Lightning:layoutItem padding="around-small">
            <Lightning:card title="3">
                <p class="slds-p-horizontal_small">
                    Card 3
                </p>
        </Lightning:card>
        </Lightning:layoutItem>
        <Lightning:layoutItem padding="around-small">
            <Lightning:card title="4">
                <p class="slds-p-horizontal_small">
                    Card 4
                </p>
        </Lightning:card>
        </Lightning:layoutItem>
    </Lightning:layout>
</aura:application>
```

When we **Preview** the application via the **Developer Console**, we get the following layout.
Notice that there is a space across the border equivalent to the card size:

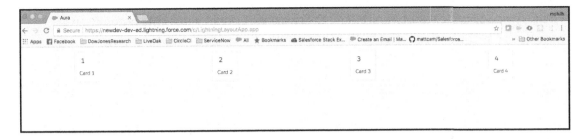

Now lets change `horizontalAlign` to stretch and observe the output. The updated code should be as follows:

```
<aura:application extends="force:slds">
    <Lightning:layout horizontalAlign="spread">
            <Lightning:layoutItem padding="around-small">
                <Lightning:card title="1">
                    <p class="slds-p-horizontal_small">
                        Card 1
                    </p>
            </Lightning:card>
            </Lightning:layoutItem>
            <Lightning:layoutItem padding="around-small">
                <Lightning:card title="2">
                    <p class="slds-p-horizontal_small">
                        Card 2
                    </p>
            </Lightning:card>
            </Lightning:layoutItem>
            <Lightning:layoutItem padding="around-small">
                <Lightning:card title="3">
                    <p class="slds-p-horizontal_small">
                        Card 3
                    </p>
            </Lightning:card>
            </Lightning:layoutItem>
            <Lightning:layoutItem padding="around-small">
                <Lightning:card title="4">
                    <p class="slds-p-horizontal_small">
                        Card 4
                    </p>
            </Lightning:card>
            </Lightning:layoutItem>
        </Lightning:layout>
</aura:application>
```

When we preview the result, notice how the cards are spread across the border now:

Vertical alignment using the Lightning layout base component

With vertical-align, you can align the layout vertically. Let's use the following code to observe how the cards are aligned:

```
<aura:application extends="force:slds">
    <Lightning:layout verticalAlign="start">
        <Lightning:layoutItem padding="around-small">
            <Lightning:card title="1">
                <p class="slds-p-horizontal_small">
                    Card 1
                </p>
            </Lightning:card>
        </Lightning:layoutItem>
        <Lightning:layoutItem padding="around-small">
            <Lightning:card title="2">
                <p class="slds-p-horizontal_small">
                    Card 2
                </p>
            </Lightning:card>
        </Lightning:layoutItem>
        <Lightning:layoutItem padding="around-small">
            <Lightning:card title="3">
                <p class="slds-p-horizontal_small">
                    Card 3
                </p>
            </Lightning:card>
        </Lightning:layoutItem>
        <Lightning:layoutItem padding="around-small">
            <Lightning:card title="4">
                <p class="slds-p-horizontal_small">
                    Card 4
                </p>
            </Lightning:card>
```

```
            </Lightning:layoutItem>
          </Lightning:layout>
      </aura:application>
```

The following screenshot shows the cards that are vertically aligned:

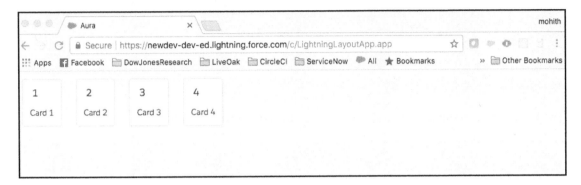

Stretching a LayoutItem using the flexibility attribute

Let's stretch the cards by setting the flexible attribute of the component to auto:

```
<aura:application extends="force:slds">
    <Lightning:layout verticalAlign="start">
          <Lightning:layoutItem flexibility="auto" padding="around-
small">
              <Lightning:card title="1">
                  <p class="slds-p-horizontal_small">
                      Card 1
                  </p>
        </Lightning:card>
          </Lightning:layoutItem>
          <Lightning:layoutItem flexibility="auto" padding="around-
small">
                <Lightning:card title="2">
                    <p class="slds-p-horizontal_small">
                        Card 2
                    </p>
        </Lightning:card>
          </Lightning:layoutItem>
          <Lightning:layoutItem flexibility="auto" padding="around-
small">
                <Lightning:card title="3">
                    <p class="slds-p-horizontal_small">
                        Card 3
                    </p>
```

```
        </Lightning:card>
          </Lightning:layoutItem>
          <Lightning:layoutItem flexibility="auto" padding="around-
small">
                <Lightning:card title="4">
                    <p class="slds-p-horizontal_small">
                        Card 4
                    </p>
                </Lightning:card>
            </Lightning:layoutItem>
        </Lightning:layout>
</aura:application>
```

The following screenshot shows the application with cards stretched:

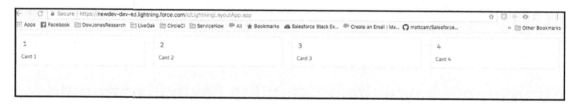

Creating multiple rows and controlling the size of the row in Lightning layout

The `size` attribute on the `Lightning:layoutItem` allows you to control the size of the item and, with multiple rows, the cards can span across various rows.

Let's use the following code in a Lightning Application created via the **Developer Console**:

```
<aura:application extends="force:slds">
    <Lightning:layout verticalAlign="start" multipleRows="true">
            <Lightning:layoutItem flexibility="auto" padding="around-small"
size="6">
                <Lightning:card title="1">
                    <p class="slds-p-horizontal_small">
                        Card 1
                    </p>
                </Lightning:card>
            </Lightning:layoutItem>
            <Lightning:layoutItem flexibility="auto" size="6"
padding="around-small">
                <Lightning:card title="2">
                    <p class="slds-p-horizontal_small">
                        Card 2
```

```
                </p>
            </Lightning:card>
          </Lightning:layoutItem>
          <Lightning:layoutItem flexibility="auto" size="2"
padding="around-small">
              <Lightning:card title="3">
                  <p class="slds-p-horizontal_small">
                      Card 3
                  </p>
            </Lightning:card>
          </Lightning:layoutItem>
          <Lightning:layoutItem flexibility="auto" size="2"
padding="around-small">
              <Lightning:card title="4">
                  <p class="slds-p-horizontal_small">
                      Card 4
                  </p>
            </Lightning:card>
          </Lightning:layoutItem>
        </Lightning:layout>
</aura:application>
```

The output should look like the following screenshot:

1	2
Card 1	Card 2
3	4
Card 3	Card 4

Lightning layout to handle multiple devices

The layoutItem has attributes to specify the size of different device types. To further understand this, consider the following markup code. Use the **Developer Console** to create a Lightning Component, copy the markup, and preview the application to observe the output. For this, shrink your browser window to observe the output.

The code is as follows:

```
<aura:application extends="force:slds">
    <Lightning:layout verticalAlign="start" multipleRows="true">
        <Lightning:layoutItem flexibility="auto" smallDeviceSize="6"
mediumDeviceSize="4" largeDeviceSize="3" padding="around-small" size="12">
            <Lightning:card title="1">
                <p class="slds-p-horizontal_small">
```

```
                         Card 1
                 </p>
         </Lightning:card>
           </Lightning:layoutItem>
           <Lightning:layoutItem flexibility="auto" size="12"
padding="around-small" smallDeviceSize="6" mediumDeviceSize="4"
largeDeviceSize="3">
                 <Lightning:card title="2">
                     <p class="slds-p-horizontal_small">
                         Card 2
                     </p>
         </Lightning:card>
           </Lightning:layoutItem>
           <Lightning:layoutItem flexibility="auto" size="12"
padding="around-small" smallDeviceSize="6" mediumDeviceSize="4"
largeDeviceSize="3">
                 <Lightning:card title="3">
                     <p class="slds-p-horizontal_small">
                         Card 3
                     </p>
         </Lightning:card>
           </Lightning:layoutItem>
           <Lightning:layoutItem flexibility="auto" size="12"
padding="around-small" smallDeviceSize="6" mediumDeviceSize="4"
largeDeviceSize="3">
                 <Lightning:card title="4">
                     <p class="slds-p-horizontal_small">
                         Card 4
                     </p>
         </Lightning:card>
           </Lightning:layoutItem>
         </Lightning:layout>
</aura:application>
```

The output for various device sizes are as follows. The following is the output for a large device:

The following is the output for a medium device:

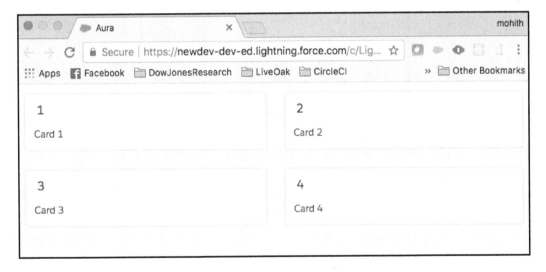

The following is the output for smaller devices:

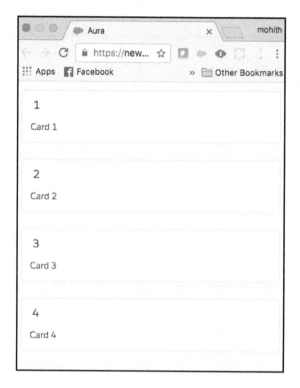

Nested page layout using Lightning Layouts

The following example shows how one can nest Lightning:layoutItem and Lightning layout to create various layouts. The following example shows how you can add custom CSS to the application using the Style file of the component bundle. The markup code is as follows:

```
<aura:application extends="force:slds">
    <div class="c-container">
        <Lightning:layout multipleRows="true">
            <Lightning:layoutItem padding="around-small" size="12">
                <div class="page-section page-header">
                    <h2>Header</h2>
                </div>
            </Lightning:layoutItem>
            <Lightning:layoutItem padding="around-small" size="12">
                <Lightning:layout>
                    <Lightning:layoutItem padding="around-small" size="3">
```

```
                    <div class="page-section page-right">
                        <h2>Left Sidebar</h2>
                        <p>
                                Test SideBar Content
                        </p>
                    </div>
                </Lightning:layoutItem>
                <Lightning:layoutItem padding="around-small" size="6">
                    <div class="page-section page-main">
                        <h2>Main</h2>
                        <p>
                            Main Page Content
                        </p>
                    </div>
                </Lightning:layoutItem>
                <Lightning:layoutItem padding="around-small" size="3">
                    <div class="page-section page-right">
                        <h2>Right Sidebar</h2>
                        <ul>
                            <li><a href="#">Archive 1</a>
                            </li>
                            <li><a href="#">Archive 2</a>
                            </li>
                            <li><a href="#">Archive 3</a>
                            </li>
                            <li><a href="#">Archive 4</a>
                            </li>
                            <li><a href="#">Archive 5</a>
                            </li>
                        </ul>
                    </div>
                </Lightning:layoutItem>
            </Lightning:layout>
        </Lightning:layoutItem>
        <Lightning:layoutItem flexibility="auto" padding="around-small"
size="12">
            <div class="page-footer page-section">
                <h2>Footer</h2>
            </div>
        </Lightning:layoutItem>
    </Lightning:layout>
  </div>
</aura:application>
```

The CSS code should be placed in the `Style` file of the component bundle. The CSS code is as follows:

```css
.THIS.c-container {
    border: 1px solid #d8dde6;
    margin: 10px 0 20px 0;
}
.THIS.page-section {
    border: solid 1px #ccc;
    padding: 1rem;
}
.THIS.page-header,
.THIS.page-footer {
    height: 50px;
}
.THIS.page-main {
    background: #f8f8f8;
}
.THIS.page-left,
.THIS.page-right {
    background: #f0efef;
}
```

The output will as follows:

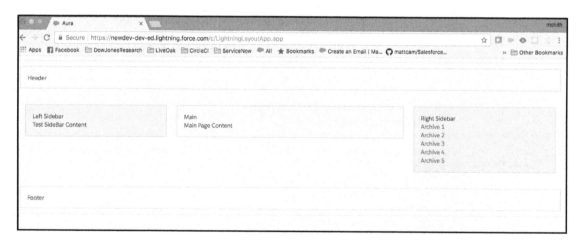

Understanding attributes

Let's understand value providers in Lightning Components, before diving deeper into attributes. Value providers hold data and provide a way to access that data. Lightning Components have two types of value providers out of the box. They are listed in the following table:

Value provider	Description
v (view)	This allows access to the value of the attribute in the Component Markup.
c (controller)	This allows you to wire events and actions .

An attribute is a placeholder to hold data. You can treat attributes like Java variables. The following is the syntax to define attributes:

```
<aura:component>
    <aura:attribute name="searchString" type="String" default="lighnting
components"/>
</aura:component>
```

Name and data type are mandatory when defining attributes. An attribute can be one of the following types: primitive (string, integer, decimal, Boolean, double, date, dateTime), arrays (sets, list, maps), objects, custom Apex, functions, or Salesforce `sobject`. To explore more, head to the standard documentation at `https://developer.Salesforce.com/docs/atlas.en-us.Lightning.meta/Lightning/ref_aura_attribute.htm`.

Use the Expression syntax to display a value from an attribute. The Expression syntax format is shown here:

```
<aura:component>
    <aura:attribute name="searchString" type="String" default="lighnting
components"/>
    <p>{!v.searchString}</p>
</aura:component>
```

For objects, use the " . " notation to traverse properties. For arrays, use `aura:iteration` to loop over results.

Using Expression syntax

The syntax for the Expression is `{!expression}`. The Expression syntax can be used inside the Component Markup. Let's take a look at the following table to see the syntax for Expressions in different scenarios:

Expression Example	Syntax	Example Code

Expression to reference a value from an attribute	`{!v.attributeName}`	<pre><aura:component>
		    <aura:attribute name="searchString"
		type="String" default="lighnting
		components"/>
		    <p>{!v.searchString}</p>
		</aura:component></pre>

Expression for calling client-side controller actions	`{!c.handleClick}`	<pre><Lightning:button label="Framework Button"
		onclick="{!c.handleClick}"/>
		
		The client-side JavaScript controller will
		be as following
		
		({
		    handleClick : function(component, event)
		{
		    }
		})</pre>

Expression operator	The operators supported are listed in the standard docs. Please refer to: `https://developer.Salesforce.com/docs/atlas.en-us.Lightning.meta/Lightning/expr_operators.htm`	<pre><aura:component>
		    <aura:attribute name="searchString"
		type="String" default="lighnting
		components"/>
		    <p>{!'Hello' + v.searchString}</p>
		</aura:component></pre>

Expression function	The supported functions are listed here: `https://developer.Salesforce.com/docs/atlas.en-us.Lightning.meta/Lightning/expr_functions.htm`	<pre><aura:component>
		    <aura:attribute name="searchString"
		type="String" default="lighnting
		components"/>
		    <p>{!concat('Hello',v.searchString)}
		</p>
		</aura:component></pre>

To become familiar with all the operators and functions, refer to the Lightning Component Developer guide documentation at: `https://developer.Salesforce.com/docs/atlas.en-us.Lightning.meta/Lightning/expr_overview.htm`

JavaScript controller and helper

Lightning Components are not just static markup; they interact with Salesforce data to send data back and forth between a browser and Salesforce servers.

JavaScript is used in web applications to add interactivity to web pages. It allows you to manipulate DOM elements (by applying new styles, removing styles, changing HTML markup), communicate with the server to send data back and forth, or pass data to the server, add animations, add visual effects, add audio effects, and many other things.

A Lightning Component bundle comprises JavaScript controllers and `helpers` that allow you to write client-side JavaScript to add interactivity and retrieve and push data to Salesforce servers.

When you create a Lightning bundle, let's assume that the name of the component is YouTube **Search** component, a JavaScript controller file is created with the name `youtubeSearchController.js`, and a JavaScript `helper` file is created with the name `youtubeSearchHelper.js`.

Controller files consist of methods and are invoked from the Component Markup via actions or event handlers. Component methods usually call `helper` functions. Component `helper` files consist of all the reusable code, that can be called from a JavaScript controller method, or a `helper` method can call other methods in the `helper` file using the `this` keyword. Later, we will see that even a `Renderer` method can reuse methods from a `helper` file.

Let's look at a short example that demonstrates how we wire up a JavaScript controller, `helper`, and Component Markup. Let's assume we have a small amount of text input and a **Search** button. Once the user inputs the search keyword, we display the entered text.

A rough wireframe for the preceding requirement is as follows:

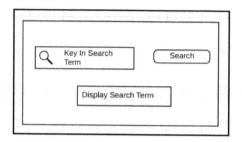

Let's create the component bundle and use the component reference document. In your Salesforce org, you can use `https://<myDomain>.Lightning.force.com/componentReference/suite.app?page=home` to refer to the docs. Note that `<myDomain>` should be replaced with the domain name of your Salesforce instance.

The documentation is also available on the developer site at: `https://developer.Salesforce.com/docs/component-library/`.

The Component markup code for the preceding example is as follows. Observe that we are using `lighnting:layout` and `Lightning: layoutItem`, which we learned about in the previous section, to create the layout. Let's name the component bundle `youtubeSearch`. The `youtubeSearch.cmp` file will be as follows:

```
<!-- youtubesearch.cmp-->
<aura:component
implements="force:appHostable,flexipage:availableForAllPageTypes"
access="global" >
    <div class="c-container">
        <Lightning:layout multipleRows="true" horizontalAlign="center"
verticalAlign="center">
            <Lightning:layoutItem flexibility="auto" size="6">
              <div class="slds-form-element">
                <label class="slds-form-element__label" for="text-input-
id-1">Enter search term</label>
                   <div class="slds-form-element__control">
                     <input type="search" id="text-input-id-1" class="slds-
input" placeholder="Enter Search Term" aura:id="searchBox"/>
                   </div>
              </div>
            </Lightning:layoutItem>
            <Lightning:layoutItem flexibility="auto" size="4"
padding="horizontal-small">
```

```
                    <Lightning:button variant="brand" label="Search" title=""
onclick="{! c.handleClick }" class="c-btn"/>
            </Lightning:layoutItem>
            <Lightning:layoutItem flexibility="auto" padding="around-large"
size="6">
                <p> You searched for </p>
            </Lightning:layoutItem>
        </Lightning:layout>
    </div>
</aura:component>
```

Add the following to the CSS file of the bundle to adjust the margin of the button. The file that's modified is `youtubeSearch.css`:

```
.THIS.c-container {
    padding-top :50px;
}

.THIS.c-btn{
    margin-top :15px;
}
```

To view the result, create a shell Lightning Application called `youtubeSearchApp`. This will look as follows:

```
<!-- youtubeSearchApp.app -->

<aura:application extends="force:slds">
    <c:youtubeSearch />
</aura:application>
```

The application with static markup should look like the following:

Let's add a functionality that, once a user clicks on the **Search** button, changes the text at the bottom depending on the search term.

To add this interactivity, we will need the following:

1. An attribute to hold the search term and the Expression syntax to refer to the attribute in the markup.
2. A click action on the **Search** button that calls a JavaScript controller action.
3. A simple `helper` file that sets the attribute value equal to the search term entered in the input text box.
4. Let's update the Component markup to add the attribute and the Expression in the markup to refer the attribute. Also notice that we have added `aura:id` to the input element. Observe the code lines that are highlighted in bold:

```
<!-- youtubesearch.cmp-->

<aura:component
implements="force:appHostable,flexipage:availableForAllPageTypes"
access="global" >
  <aura:attribute name="searchTerm" type="String" />
  <div class="c-container">
  <Lightning:layout multipleRows="true" horizontalAlign="center"
verticalAlign="center">
  <Lightning:layoutItem flexibility="auto" size="6">
  <div class="slds-form-element">
  <label class="slds-form-element__label" for="text-input-id-1">
  Enter search term
  </label>
  <div class="slds-form-element__control">
  <input type="search" id="text-input-id-1" class="slds-input"
placeholder="Enter Search Term" aura:id="searchBox"/>
  </div>
  </div>
  </Lightning:layoutItem>
  <Lightning:layoutItem flexibility="auto" size="4"
padding="horizontal-small">
  <Lightning:button variant="brand" label="Search" title=""
onclick="{! c.handleClick }" class="c-btn"/>
  </Lightning:layoutItem>
  <Lightning:layoutItem flexibility="auto" padding="around-large"
size="6">
  <p> You searched for {!v.searchTerm} </p>
  </Lightning:layoutItem>
  </Lightning:layout>
  </div>
</aura:component>
```

5. The `youtubesearchController.js` file is shown as follows. Notice how we do not write a lot of logic in the controller file. It's usually kept light and invokes `helper` functions present in the `youtubesearchHelper.js` file.

```
//youtubesearchController.js
({
  handleClick : function(component, event, helper) {
    helper.setSearchTerm(component, event);
  }
})
```

6. The `helper` function is as follows:

```
//youtubesearchHelper.js
({
  setSearchTerm : function(component, event) {
      var searchTerm =
component.find('searchBox').getElement().value;
      console.log(searchTerm);
    component.set("v.searchTerm", searchTerm);
  }
})
```

7. As expected, the output is the following:

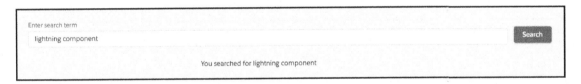

There are a couple of things you might have noticed that might be new to you in JavaScript `helper` code:

1. To locate a DOM element by ID, we used the `component.find()` function, and then we can use DOM functions
2. To set the attribute, the syntax is as follows:

```
component.set(<v.attributename>,<attributevalue>)
```

`attributevalue` is the value you want to set

3. Note that, to get the value of the attribute, the syntax is:

```
component.get("v.attributename");
```

To find the different supported methods of the component, you can reference the auraDocs from your org. The auraDocs can be found at: `https://<myDomain>/auradocs/reference.app#reference?topic=api:Component`, where `<myDomain>` is your custom Salesforce domain.

Wiring the client-side to the server using Apex controllers

So far, we have learned how to write client-side JavaScript controllers and `helpers`. In this section, we will learn how to wire client-side calls to the server-side Apex. Apex is an object-oriented programming language similar to Java. Apex allows you to write database logic and queries such as stored procedures. This section assumes that the reader is familiar with Salesforce Apex programming.

In your Salesforce org, whitelist Google APIs via **Remote Site Settings** for the following application so that your org can reach out to the YouTube API. The navigation path is **Setup | Security | Remote Site Settings**.

The following screenshot shows the **Remote Site Settings**:

The code to search YouTube results from the YouTube REST API follows here. The instructions for registering the API key can be obtained here: `https://developers.google.com/youtube/v3/getting-started`.

Use Visual Studio IDE and create an Apex class. The class consists of `http callout` to search YouTube based on the search string provided. The code for this is as follows:

```
public with sharing class Youtubesearch {
```

```
    public static final string key = '<your API key>';//Replace with your
API key here

    public static final string youtubesearchURL =
'https://www.googleapis.com/youtube/v3/search?key='+key+'&part=snippet';

    @AuraEnabled
    public Static String search(String searchstr){
        // Instantiate a new http object
        Http h = new Http();
         // Instantiate a new HTTP request, specify the method (GET) as well
as the endpoint
        HttpRequest req = new HttpRequest();
        String url = youtubesearchURL+'&q=' +
EncodingUtil.urlencode(searchstr,'UTF-8');
        //String url = youtubesearchURL;
        req.setEndpoint(url);
        req.setMethod('GET');
        // Send the request, and return a response
        HttpResponse res = h.send(req);
//system.debug('RESULTS..>>>'+YoutubeDataParser.parse(res.getBody()));
        //return YoutubeDataParser.parse(res.getBody());
        return res.getBody();
    }


}
```

Notice that we have annotated variables and methods with the @auraEnabled annotation.
While working with Lightning Components, it's important to note that to call server-side
methods from the client-side JavaScript, the method should be annotated with
the @auraEnabled annotation, and also notice that any property of the Apex class that
needs to be exposed to the Lightning Component framework needs to have this annotation.

To wire, the server-side code to the client-side JavaScript, let's use the JavaScript controller
and helper we built in the prior section.

The code to enqueue the server-side action is as follows:

1. Add the Apex controller that your helper will be calling to the Component
    Markup using the controller attribute. The code for this as follows:

    ```
    <aura:component
    implements="force:appHostable,flexipage:availableForAllPageTypes"
    access="global" controller="YoutubeSearch">
    ```

2. To hold the results obtained from the server, we require an attribute at the frontend. This is defined as follows, shown in bold:

```
<aura:component
implements="force:appHostable,flexipage:availableForAllPageTypes"
access="global" controller="YoutubeSearch">
    <aura:attribute name="searchTerm" type="String" />
    <aura:attribute name="data" type="Map"/>
```

3. The JavaScript controller invokes the `helper` on the **Search** button click is as follows:

```
({
  handleClick : function(component, event, helper) {
    helper.setSearchTerm(component, event);
  }
})
```

4. The `helper` that invokes the server-side search method is shown as follows. Notice how we take the response from the server and assign it to the attribute (using `component.set()`):

```
({
  setSearchTerm : function(component, event) {
        var searchTerm =
component.find('searchBox').getElement().value;
        console.log(searchTerm);
         component.set("v.searchTerm",searchTerm);
        // create a one-time use instance of the search action
        // in the server-side controller
        var action = component.get("c.search");
        action.setParams({ searchstr : searchTerm});
        action.setCallback(this, function(response) {
            var state = response.getState();
            if (state === "SUCCESS") {
                var youtube_res =
JSON.parse(response.getReturnValue());
                console.log(response.getReturnValue());
                console.log(youtube_res);
                component.set("v.data",youtube_res);
            }
            else if (state === "INCOMPLETE") {
                // do something
            }
            else if (state === "ERROR") {
                var errors = response.getError();
                if (errors) {
```

```
                        if (errors[0] && errors[0].message) {
                            console.log("Error message: " +
                                    errors[0].message);
                        }
                    } else {
                        console.log("Unknown error");
                    }
                }
            });
            $A.enqueueAction(action);
        }
    })
```

5. The code in the `callback` function is shown as follows. It sets the `data` attribute to hold a `response` object from a server. Notice that we also parse the JSON string into the JavaScript object using `JSON.parse()`:

```
action.setCallback(this, function(response) {
        var state = response.getState();
        if (state === "SUCCESS") {
            var youtube_res =
JSON.parse(response.getReturnValue());
            console.log(response.getReturnValue());
            console.log(youtube_res);
            component.set("v.data",youtube_res);
        }
    });
```

If you are not familiar with the `callback` function, I recommend reading the following article: `https://developer.mozilla.org/en-US/docs/Glossary/Callback_function` .

6. Finally, let's enhance the frontend markup code to iterate and show the results. The following is the final code for the markup. Notice that the newly added code is highlighted. The code for the `youtubesearch.cmp` file is as follows:

```
<aura:component
implements="force:appHostable,flexipage:availableForAllPageTypes"
access="global" controller="YoutubeSearch">
    <aura:attribute name="searchTerm" type="String" />
    <!--ATTRIBUTES DECLARATION -->
    <aura:attribute name="data" type="Map"/>
    <div class="c-container">
        <Lightning:layout multipleRows="true"
horizontalAlign="center" verticalAlign="center">
            <Lightning:layoutItem flexibility="auto" size="6">
```

```
                    <div class="slds-form-element">
                        <label class="slds-form-element__label" for="text-
input-id-1">Enter search term</label>
                        <div class="slds-form-element__control">
                            <input type="search" id="text-input-id-1"
class="slds-input" placeholder="Enter Search Term"
aura:id="searchBox"/>
                        </div>
                    </div>
                </Lightning:layoutItem>
                <Lightning:layoutItem flexibility="auto" size="4"
padding="horizontal-small">
                    <Lightning:button variant="brand" label="Search"
title="" onclick="{! c.handleClick }" class="c-btn"/>
                </Lightning:layoutItem>
                <Lightning:layoutItem flexibility="auto" padding="around-
large" size="6">
                    <p> You searched for {!v.searchTerm} </p>
                </Lightning:layoutItem>
                <Lightning:layoutItem flexibility="auto"
padding="horizontal-small" size="8">
                    <aura:iteration items="{!v.data.items}" var="cardItem">
                        <Lightning:card title="{!cardItem.snippet.title}">
                            <p class="slds-p-horizontal_small">
                                {!cardItem.snippet.description}
                            </p>
                            <div class="slds-media__figure">
                                <a
href="{!'https://www.youtube.com/watch?v='+cardItem.id.videoId}"
target="_blank">
                                    <img
src="{!cardItem.snippet.thumbnails.high.url}" style="height:100px;"
alt="Placeholder" />
                                </a>
                            </div>
                        </Lightning:card>
                    </aura:iteration>
                </Lightning:layoutItem>
            </Lightning:layout>
        </div>
</aura:component>
```

7. If you have an end-to-end working application, the output screen will be as follows. To preview, use the test application URL. The URL will be `https://<myDomain>/c/youtubeSearchApp.app`. This assumes that you have created a **Lightning App Bundle** from the **Developer Console** named `youtubeSearchApp`, as discussed earlier:

8. Let's look at the following diagram, which summarizes the chain of actions and events from the user interaction on the client-side code to the server-side call:

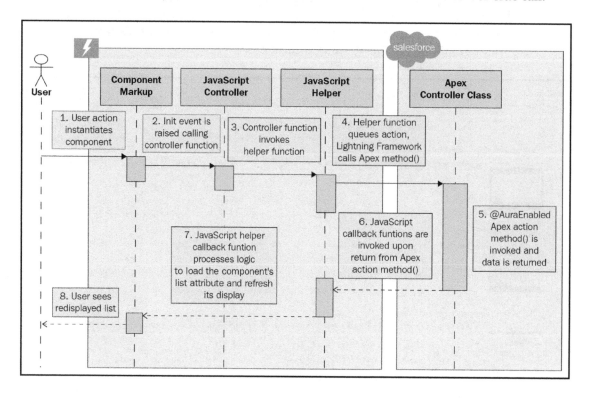

The diagram shows the chain of events and actions that takes place from the browser to the server when a Lightning Component loads or an action is performed. The diagram mentions an `init` event. The `init` event is the event that is raised by the component when the component loads (you can treat this as being similar to an `onload` event). The syntax for the `init` event is as follows:

```
<aura:handler name="init" value="{!this}" action="{!c.doInit}"/>
```

Notice that, via the action, we can invoke the controller function just as we invoked the search function on the button click.

The `value="{!this}"` setting marks *this* as a value event. You should always use this setting for an `init` event.

Summary

In this chapter, we covered how to create Lightning layouts in depth. Using an example of a Lightning Component, we learned how to write JavaScript controllers, `helpers`, and how to wire client-side JavaScript controllers to backend Apex programs to send data to the server and handle responses. In the next chapter, we will dig further into various methods, functions, and APIs that come out of the box with the Lightning Component framework.

The Lightning JavaScript API 4

In this chapter, we will dig deeper into the Lightning component rendering life cycle and its JavaScript API. The Lightning Component framework typically uses the ES5 version of JavaScript. However, some ES6 support is built in, including the use of `Promises` and, array functions. The Lightning component framework does not support all of the APIs in JavaScript ES5 specifications, due to security. Only APIs that are considered safe from a web security perspective are supported by the framework. Salesforce runs the custom JavaScript that we write in the `helper`, controller, or `RENDERER` files, through a service known as a locker service, which ensures that your JavaScript code is safe and compliant with security.

This chapter will start with the various system-specific JavaScript functions and APIs provided by the Lightning framework, and we will then dig deeper into its rendering cycle, followed by a section on Locker Services.

In this chapter, we will cover the following topics:

- Setting attributes
- Finding DOM elements using the `find` function
- The Locker Service security model of Lightning Components
- The Aura Localization Service
- `$A.util` functions
- Dynamically creating components using $A.createComponent()

Technical requirements

This chapter assumes that you are familiar with JavaScript programming. If you are new to JavaScript programming, refer to the Mozilla developer documentation at `https://developer.mozilla.Org/en-US/docs/Web/JavaScript` before diving into this chapter.

Using component get and set methods

Attributes are declared in a component's markup. You can treat attributes as similar to Java variables or JavaScript variables. To extract the values from them, we use `component.get()`, and to set the values, we use `component.set()`.

Let's suppose that you have defined an attribute for a component using `aura:attribute`, as follows:

```
<aura:component access="global">
  <aura:attribute name="searchTerm" type="String" />
</aura:component>
```

You can get the value of the attribute by using the following:

```
component.get("v.searchTerm")
```

To set the value of the attribute, the syntax is as follows:

```
component.set("v.searchTerm", 'Lightning')
```

 Here, `Lightning` is the value of the attribute that we are setting.

Using the find function to locate the DOM

To locate the DOM, you need to assign an `aura:id` to the DOM element. If there are multiple elements with same ID, an array is returned.

Let's look at an example component to observe the console output for the following component bundle. Let's name the component bundle `DemoCmp`:

```
<aura:component >
  <div aura:id="div1" class="div1" id="div1">
        <span class="span1"> 1</span>
        <span class="span2"> 2</span>
        <span class="span3"> 3</span>
    </div>
    <Lightning:button variant="brand" label="Submit" onclick="{!
c.handleClick }" />
</aura:component>
```

The `DemoCmpController.js` file for the preceding component is as follows:

```
({
   handleClick : function(component, event, helper) {
         console.log("cmp.getElement(): ",
component.find("div1").getElement());
         var div = component.find("div1").getElement();
         //[].forEach.call(div.childNodes, v => console.log(v.className));
         for(var i=0 ; i<div.childNodes.length ;i++){
               console.log(div.childNodes[i].outerHTML);
               console.log(div.childNodes[i].className);
            }
      }
})
```

To test this, create a simple application bundle with the following code, and click on **Preview** to view the component:

```
<aura:application extends="force:slds">
    <c:DemoCmp />
</aura:application>
```

The console output will look like the following screenshot (after you click on the **Submit** button). Use the browser console to view the output:

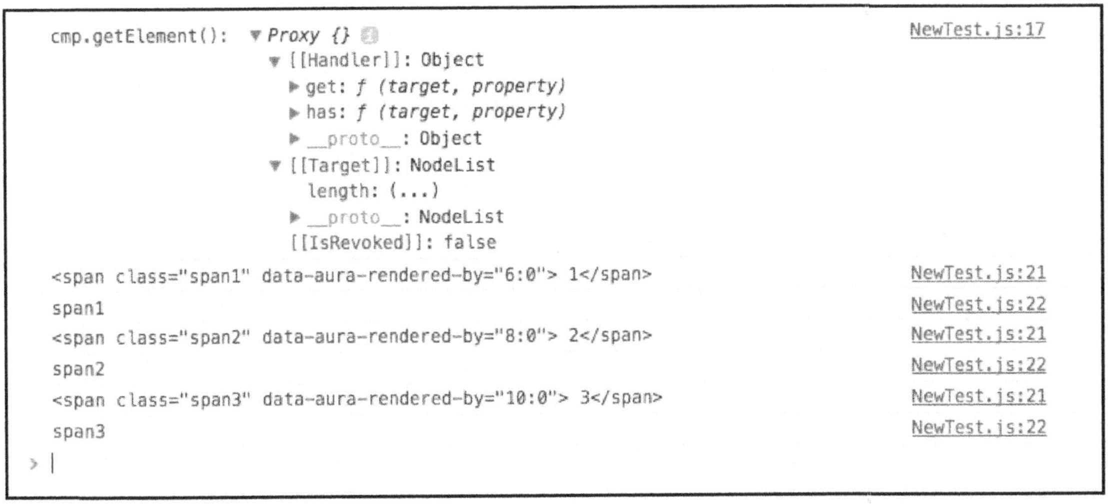

```
cmp.getElement():    ▼ Proxy {} ⓘ                                              NewTest.js:17
                       ▼ [[Handler]]: Object
                          ▶ get: ƒ (target, property)
                          ▶ has: ƒ (target, property)
                          ▶ __proto__: Object
                       ▼ [[Target]]: NodeList
                           length: (...)
                          ▶ __proto__: NodeList
                           [[IsRevoked]]: false
<span class="span1" data-aura-rendered-by="6:0"> 1</span>                     NewTest.js:21
span1                                                                         NewTest.js:22
<span class="span2" data-aura-rendered-by="8:0"> 2</span>                     NewTest.js:21
span2                                                                         NewTest.js:22
<span class="span3" data-aura-rendered-by="10:0"> 3</span>                    NewTest.js:21
span3                                                                         NewTest.js:22
> |
```

Interestingly, when we used `component.find("div1").getElement()`, we expected an HTML element as the output. However, if you observe carefully, you will notice that the console output a proxy object instead. That behavior is due to the Salesforce Locker Service, which we will discuss in the next section.

You might be wondering how a developer can find out what APIs are supported for a component. In your Salesforce instance,
visit `https://<myDomain>.Lightning.force.com/auradocs/reference.app#reference?topic=api:Component`, where `myDomain` is the custom domain of your Salesforce instance.

Introducing Locker Service

The Lightning Locker Service enforces security in single-page applications built using Lightning Components. Locker uses a browser **content security policy (CSP)** to protect a web page against **cross-site scripting (XSS), clickjacking,** and other **code injection** attacks that result from the execution of malicious content in a trusted web page context.

Locker Services serve the following purposes:

- Protection against web security vulnerabilities.
- Adding namespaces to your components, preventing component code from accessing data from other components.
- A component code only has access to the DOM that was created by your component.

The preceding factors allow for the coexistence of components from multiple vendors on the same web page. Salesforce ISVs can build components and publish on AppExchange (`https://appexchange.Salesforce.com/`) if the components adhere to locker security principles.

Strict mode enforcement in Locker Service

Locker Service automatically enforces ES5 strict mode for the JavaScript. If you write JavaScript that is not valid in strict mode, you will see unexpected errors. Let's take a look at some of the best practices that one must follow for the JavaScript code in controllers and helper files:

- Using a variable without declaring it is not allowed. Suppose that you declare a variable as follows:

  ```
  a = component.set("v.name",'Test');
  ```

  This is invalid; instead, use the `var` keyword. The correct syntax is as follows:

  ```
  var a = component.set("v.name",'Test');
  ```

- Using an object without declaring it is also not allowed:

```
x = {x:4, y:20};        // This will cause an error
```

  The fix for the preceding is as follows:

```
var x = {x:4, y:20};        // This will cause an error
```

- Deleting a variable (or an object) is not allowed. The following is not allowed:

```
var x = 5;
delete x;
```

- Deleting a function (or an object) is also not allowed:

```
function x(p1, p2) {};
delete x;
```

- Duplicating a parameter name is not allowed:

```
function x(p1, p1) {};
```

- Writing to a read-only property is not allowed:

```
var obj = {};
Object.defineProperty(obj, "x", {value:0, writable:false});
obj.x = 3;
```

- Writing to a get-only property is not allowed:

```
var obj = {get x() {return 0} };
obj.x = 3;
```

- Writing to a get-only property is not allowed:

```
var obj = {get x() {return 0} };
obj.x = 3;
```

The following future reserved keywords are not allowed in strict mode:

- `implements`
- `interface`
- `let`
- `package`
- `private`

- protected
- public
- static
- Yield

 The `eval()` function evaluates JavaScript code that is represented as a string. Recently, Salesforce decided to support this inside of Locker Service, in global mode.

Understanding the DOM access containment hierarchy in Lightning Components

Locker Services restrict component code from reaching out to other components DOMs that are in a different namespace. For example, a custom component cannot reach out to the DOM of the component in the Lightning namespace (a base component).

Let's look at the following code, in order to understand DOM access containment:

```
<aura:component >
  <div aura:id="div1" class="div1" id="div1">
        <span class="span1"> 1</span>
        <span class="span2"> 2</span>
        <span class="span3"> 3</span>
    </div>
    <Lightning:button variant="brand" label="Submit" aura:id="btn"
onclick="{! c.handleClick }" />
</aura:component>
```

The controller code is as follows:

```
({
  handleClick : function(component, event, helper) {
        console.log("cmp.getElement(): ",
component.find("btn").getElement());//This will not work and a ugly error
is thrown
})
```

Upon a button click, you will see an error, as follows:

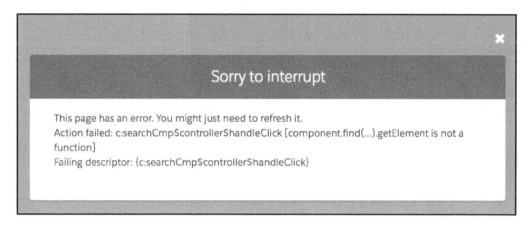

Locker Service doesn't allow components to access the DOM for `<Lightning:button>`, because the button is in the Lightning namespace, and our component is in the c namespace.

A component can only traverse the DOM and access elements created by a component in the same namespace. This behavior prevents the anti-pattern of reaching into DOM elements owned by components in other namespaces.

The proxy object in Locker Service

Locker Service relies on the proxy object for its underlying implementation. The `proxy` function in JavaScript allows for adding custom behaviors to the JavaScript objects.

For intrinsic JavaScript objects, such as arrays, Boolean, string, dates, JSON, objects, and more, Locker Service returns raw JavaScript objects.

For non-intrinsic JavaScript objects, Locker Service filters and returns the proxy objects.

Locker Service provides documentation for modified, non-intrinsic JavaScript objects. The Locker API viewer documentation can be accessed at `http://documentation.auraframework.Org/lockerApiTest/index.app?aura.mode=DEV`. Observe the objects highlighted in orange; it shows that they have different implementations than the actual browser API.

The following table shows some of the objects that Locker Service filters and returns as proxy objects:

JavaScript Object	Locker Service Filtered Object
HTML collection	Proxy object
Window object	Secure window
Document object	Secure document object
HTML element object	Secure HTML element object

Locker Service is supported by Chrome, Firefox, Safari, and Microsoft Edge. Note that Locker Service is not supported in IE11.

APIs available in $A top-level functions

The Aura object is the top-level object in the JavaScript framework code. In this section, we will explore some of the utility functions that the Lightning component framework supports. To explore all of the supported JavaScript functions and APIs of the Lightning component framework, refer to the documentation in your Salesforce instance at `https://<myDomain>.Lightning.force.com/auradocs/reference.app#referen ce`, where `myDomain` is the custom domain set for the application.

Exploring the $A.Util APIs

The following table shows supported Util functions:

Util Class	Description	Example Code
addClass (Object elementString newClass)	Adds a CSS class to a component.	```var myCmp = component.find("myCmp"); $A.util.addClass(myCmp, "myClass");```
getBooleanValue (object val): Boolean	Coerces truthy and falsy values into native Booleans.	

hasClass (Object elementString className): Boolean	Checks whether the component has the specified CSS class.	```//find a component with aura:id="myCmp" in markup var myCmp = component.find("myCmp"); $A.util.hasClass(myCmp, "myClass");```
isArray (Object obj): Boolean	Checks whether the specified object is an array.	
isEmpty (Object obj): Boolean	Checks whether the object is empty. An empty object's value is undefined, null, an empty array, or an empty string. An object with no native properties is not considered empty.	
isObject (Object obj): Boolean	Checks whether the specified object is a valid object. A valid object is not a DOM element; a native browser class (XMLHttpRequest) is not falsely; and it is not an array, error, function string, or number.	
isUndefined (Object obj): Boolean	Checks whether the object is undefined.	
toggleClass (Object: elementString className)	Checks whether the object is undefined or null.	
isUndefinedOrNull (Object obj): Boolean	Removes a CSS class from a component.	

removeClass (Object: elementString newClass)	Toggles (adds or removes) a CSS class from a component.	`//find a component with aura:id="toggleMe" in markup var toggleText = component.find("toggleMe"); $A.util.toggleClass(toggleText, "toggle");`

The following is a simple application to create a toggle. Create a simple application and copy the following code, then click on the **Toggle** button to understand how a CSS class is added and removed.

The `HideAndShowUpApp.app` code is as follows:

```
<aura:application extends="force:slds">
    <div class="spinner" aura:id="spinner">
     <Lightning:spinner alternativeText="Loading" />
    </div>
    <Lightning:button label="Toggle" variant="brand" onclick="{!
c.handleClick }" class="btn"/>
</aura:application>
```

The CSS-style code is as follows (for `HideAndShowUpApp.css`):

```
.THIS.spinner {
    position: absolute;
    display: inline-block;
    width: 80px;
    height: 80px;
    margin :50px
}

.THIS.btn {
    margin-top :150px;
    margin-left :50px;
}

/*toggleCss.css*/
.THIS.toggle {
    display: none;
}
```

The controller code is in the `HideAndShowUpAppController.js` file, as follows:

```
({
  handleClick : function(component, event, helper) {
        var spinnerComponent = component.find("spinner");
        console.log(spinnerComponent);
      $A.util.toggleClass(spinnerComponent, "toggle");
  }
})
```

Notice that the CSS class toggle has the `display:none` attribute, for CSS.

Format date/DateTime using the Aura Localization Service

The localization service of the Aura components takes care of providing localization support to the client-side JavaScript input and output. In this section, we will cover a few of the functions provided by the localization service. For a comprehensive list of the functions supported, refer to the official documentation at `https://<myDomain>/auradocs/reference.app#reference?topic=api:AuraLoc alizationService`. Here, `myDomain` is the custom domain name of your organization.

Find your organization's time zone

To find the local time zone of the running user, copy the following snippet of code into your component JavaScript:

```
var OrgtimeZone = $A.get("$Locale.timezone");
```

Find your organization's local currency

To find the local currency, copy the following snippet of code in your component's JavaScript:

```
var Orgcurrency = $A.get("$Locale.currency");
```

Formatting dates

To understand how to format dates, let's copy the following code files into a new Lightning app (create a Lightning app bundle by using the **Developer Console**, and name it DateFormatterApp):

- DateformatterApp.app

```
<aura:application extends="force:slds">
  <aura:attribute name="DateTimeInput" type="DateTime" />
  <aura:attribute name="output" type="DateTime" />
      <Lightning:input type="datetime-local" label="Input Date"
name="date" value="{!v.DateTimeInput}"/>
      <Lightning:select aura:id="select" name="select"
label="Select a pie" onchange="{! c.onChange }">
        <option value="">choose one...</option>
        <option value="YYYY MM DD">YYYY MM DD format</option>
        <option value="MMMM DD YYYY, hh:mm:ss a">MMMM DD YYYY,
hh:mm:ss a format</option>
        <option value="yyyy-MM-dd HH:mm:ss.SSS">yyyy-MM-dd
HH:mm:ss.SSS format</option>
    </Lightning:select>
      <p>outputDate {!v.output}</p>
</aura:application>
```

- The controller code is as follows:

```
({
  onChange : function(component, event, helper) {
    console.log(component.get("v.DateTimeInput"));
        var dateInput = component.get("v.DateTimeInput")
        var selectedformat =
component.find('select').get('v.value') ;
        var output =
$A.localizationService.formatDate(dateInput,selectedformat);
        component.set("v.output",output);
  }
})
```

The output component's preview will look as follows:

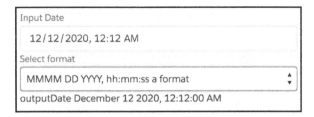

Notice that we used the formatDate function of localizationService to format the date and time. Also, notice that we used lighting:select to create a picklist selector and its onChange event and finds function to get the values.

Dynamically creating components using $A.createComponent()

Components can be dynamically injected by using the $A.createComponent() function. The syntax for this function is as follows:

```
$A.createComponent(String type, Object attributes, function callback)
```

The parameters used in the $A.createComponents function are described as follows:

- type: The type of component to create; for example, ui:button.
- attributes: A map of attributes for the component, including the local ID (aura:id).
- callback(cmp, status, errorMessage): The callback to invoke after the component is created. The callback has three parameters:
- cmp: The component that was created. This enables you to do something with the new component, such as add it to the body of the component that creates it. If there's an error, cmp is null.
- status: The status of the call. The possible values are SUCCESS, INCOMPLETE, or ERROR. Always check that the status is SUCCESS before you try to use the component.
- errorMessage: The error message, if the status is ERROR.

A simple example snippet to create a text component would look as follows:

```
$A.createComponent("aura:text",{value:'Hello World'},
function(auraTextComponent, status, statusMessagesList){
    // auraTextComponent is an instance of aura:text containing the value
Hello World
});
```

If you want to add multiple components, you can use the $A.createComponents() function. The syntax is as follows:

```
createComponents (Array components, function callback)
```

An example sample code would look as follows:

```
$A.createComponents([
    ["aura:text",{value:'Hello'}],
    ["Lightning:button",{label:'Button'}],
    ["aura:text",{value:'World'}]
], function(components,status,statusMessagesList){
    // Components is an array of 3 components
    // 0 - Text Component containing Hello
    // 1 - Button Component with label Button
    // 2 - Text component containing World
});
```

Let's create a simple application to dynamically create a form, using lightning:input.

The code for the application markup (let's name it DynamicForm.app) is as follows:

```
<aura:application extends="force:slds">
  <aura:attribute name="dynamicForm" type="Aura.Component[]"/>
  <aura:handler name="init" value="{!this}" action="{!c.onInit}"/>
    {!v.dynamicForm}
    <br/>
    <Lightning:button variant="brand" label="Submit" onclick="{!
c.handleClick }" />
</aura:application>
```

The dynamicForm attribute is a special type of Aura.Component array. It's a framework-specific markup that can hold an array of the component.

The controller code is as follows:

```
({
  onInit : function(component, event, helper) {
    helper.doInit(component, event, helper);
  },
```

```
        handleClick : function(component, event, helper) {
            var components = component.find("dynamicFormId");//Extract all the
components
            components.forEach(function(cmp) {
                console.log(cmp.get("v.value"));//Display the value and the
type
                console.log(cmp.get("v.type"));
                if (cmp.get("v.type") === 'checkbox'){
                    console.log(cmp.get("v.checked"));
                }
            });
        }
    })
```

The `helper` function that creates the dynamic markup is shown as follows. We leverage `$A.createComponents` to create multiple components. Note that `A.createComponents` accepts an array of objects as parameter, where each object defines an input tag with a data type and `label` attribute.

```
({
  doInit : function(component,helper,event) {
    var dynamicFormInput = [
    ["Lightning:input",{
        "label" : "Text Field",
        "name" : "TextField",
        "aura:id" : "dynamicFormId"
    }],
    ["Lightning:input",{
        "type" : "search",
        "label" : "search",
        "name" : "search",
        "aura:id" : "dynamicFormId"
    }],
        ["Lightning:input", {
          "type" : "checkbox",
        "label" : "Red",
        "name" : "red",
        "aura:id" : "dynamicFormId"
        }],
    ];
    $A.createComponents(dynamicFormInput,
    function(components, status, errorMessage){
        if (status === "SUCCESS") {
            var formBody = component.get("v.dynamicForm");
            components.forEach(function(element) {
            formBody.push(element);
            console.log(element);
```

```
        });
            component.set("v.dynamicForm", formBody);
        }
        else if (status === "INCOMPLETE") {
            console.log("Error In Creating Component")
            // Show offline error
        }
        else if (status === "ERROR") {
            console.log("Error: " + errorMessage);
            // Show error message
        }
    }
  );
 }
})
```

The output preview of the component will look as follows:

There are some key things to observe in the preceding code:

- We have looped over each of the newly created components and added the `dynamicForm` attribute, appended to the body.
- The `handleClick` function can be used with the same `aura:id` to loop over multiple elements, to extract the values of the input from the dynamic markup.

Destroying components using the destory() function

One can destroy components manually by using the `component.destory()` function. The following code shows an example of destroying a component with a specified ID:

```
var componentToDestory = component.find("newCmp");//newCmp is the aura:id
of the component to destroy
componentToDestory.destroy();
```

After a component that is declared in the markup is no longer in use, the framework automatically destroys it and frees up its memory. If you create a component dynamically in JavaScript and that component isn't added to a facet (`v.body`, or another attribute of the type `Aura.Component[]`), you have to destroy it manually by using `destroy()`, to avoid memory leaks.

Modifying the DOM in the RENDERER JavaScript file of the component bundle

The Lightning component framework takes care of rendering and re-rendering the DOM element when the values change. However, if you want to modify the DOM or take control of the DOM modification, you can do so in the render file. The following screenshot illustrates how you can find the RENDERER file for the component or the Lightning application:

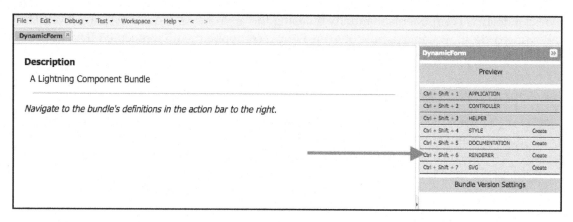

To customize, modify, and interact with DOM elements, you must follow the following template in the RENDERER JavaScript file:

```
({
  // Your RENDERER method overrides go here
  render : function(component, helper) {
      var ret = this.superRender();
      // do custom rendering here
      return ret;
  },
    rerender : function(cmp, helper){
      this.superRerender();
      // do custom rerendering here
  },
    afterRender: function (component, helper) {
      this.superAfterRender();
      // interact with the DOM here
  },
    unrender: function () {
```

```
            this.superUnrender();
            // do custom unrendering here
    }
})
```

Before we dig into each of these functions, let's cover the rendering life cycle of a component.

Understanding the rendering life cycle of a component

The following diagram shows the sequence of events that happens from component instantiation to component rendering:

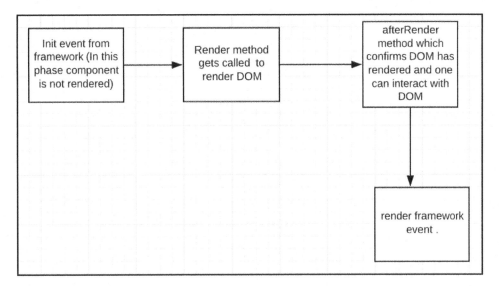

 It's always preferable to use a framework render event to perform custom logic, such as DOM manipulation, instead of overriding the `render` function.

In order to further understand, let's create a Lightning application with the following code, and observe some logs in the console. We'll call the sample application `LifeCycleExampleApp.app`:

```
<aura:application extends="force:slds">
    <aura:handler name="init" value="{!this}" action="{!c.onInit}"/>
```

```
        <aura:handler name="render" value="{!this}" action="{!c.onRender}"/>
        <div aura:id="example">
            <span> 1 </span>
            <span> 2 </span>
            <span> 3 </span>
            <span> 4 </span>
        </div>
    </aura:application>
```

The `LifeCycleExampleAppcontroller.js` file will have to `init` the definition, as follows:

```
({
   onInit : function(component, event, helper) {
     console.log('Inside init event');
         console.log('step1');
         console.log('FIND COMPONENT IN INIT..'+component.find("example"));
         console.log('FIND DOM IN
INIT..'+component.find("example").getElement());
   },
     onRender : function(component, event, helper) {
         console.log('Inside render event');
         console.log('step4');
         console.log('FIND COMPONENT ONCE RENDER EVENT IS
FIRED..'+component.find("example"));
         console.log('FIND DOM ONCE RENDER EVENT IS
FIRED..'+component.find("example").getElement());
     }
})
```

The `RENDERER` file, `LifeCycleExampleApp controllerRender.js`, is as follows:

```
({
   // Your RENDERER method overrides go here
   render : function(component, helper) {
         var ret = this.superRender();
         // do custom rendering here
         console.log('Inside render Function');
         console.log('step2');
         console.log('DOM ELEMENT IN render'
+component.find("example").getElement());
         console.log(ret);
         return ret;
   },
     rerender : function(cmp, helper){
       this.superRerender();
       // do custom rerendering here
   },
```

```
        afterRender: function (component, helper) {
          this.superAfterRender();
            console.log('Inside afterRender Function');
            console.log('step3');
            console.log('COMPONENT IN afterrender' +component.find("example"));
            console.log('DOM ELEMENT IN afterRender'
+component.find("example").getElement());
            // interact with the DOM here
      },
        unrender: function () {
          this.superUnrender();
            // do custom unrendering here
      }
    })
```

The browser console output will be as follows:

```
Inside init event                                                            LifeCycleExampleApp.js:17
step1                                                                        LifeCycleExampleApp.js:18
FIND COMPONENT IN INIT..SecureComponent: markup://aura:html {3:0} {example}{ key: {"namespace":"c"} }    LifeCycleExampleApp.js:19
FIND DOM IN INIT..null                                                       LifeCycleExampleApp.js:20
Inside render Function                                                       LifeCycleExampleApp.js:33
step2                                                                        LifeCycleExampleApp.js:34
DOM ELEMENT IN renderSecureElement: [object HTMLDivElement]{ key: {"namespace":"c"} }    LifeCycleExampleApp.js:35
▶ Proxy {0: div, length: 1}                                                  LifeCycleExampleApp.js:36
Inside afterRender Function                                                  LifeCycleExampleApp.js:45
step3                                                                        LifeCycleExampleApp.js:46
COMPONENT IN afterrenderSecureComponent: markup://aura:html {3:0} {example}{ key: {"namespace":"c"} }    LifeCycleExampleApp.js:47
DOM ELEMENT IN afterRenderSecureElement: [object HTMLDivElement]{ key: {"namespace":"c"} }    LifeCycleExampleApp.js:48
Inside render event                                                          LifeCycleExampleApp.js:23
step4                                                                        LifeCycleExampleApp.js:24
FIND COMPONENT ONCE RENDER EVENT IS FIRED..SecureComponent: markup://aura:html {3:0} {example}{ key:    LifeCycleExampleApp.js:25
{"namespace":"c"} }
FIND DOM ONCE RENDER EVENT IS FIRED..SecureElement: [object HTMLDivElement]{ key: {"namespace":"c"} }    LifeCycleExampleApp.js:26
```

From the logs, the following conclusions can easily be inferred:

- Inside of the init event, the DOM element is not yet created; hence, the element is null.
- The render element creates a secure element.
- The system render event is fired last, and is considered better approach do any DOM manipulation.

Understanding re-rendering the life cycle of a component

Let's take a look at the following diagram, before we dive in deeper with an example:

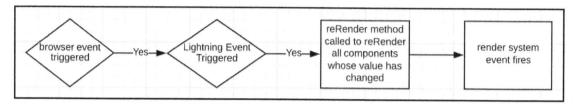

Let's analyze the preceding behavior with an example component, as follows; we have added an input form element and a button to observe the re-rendering cycle:

```
<aura:application extends="force:slds">
    <aura:handler name="init" value="{!this}" action="{!c.onInit}"/>
        <aura:handler name="render" value="{!this}" action="{!c.onRender}"/>
        <aura:attribute name="search" type="string"/>
        <div aura:id="example">
            <span> 1 </span>
            <span> 2 </span>
            <span> 3 </span>
            <span> 4 </span>
        </div>
        <Lightning:input value="{!v.search}" label="search" name="search"
aura:id="searchInput"/>
        <Lightning:button variant="brand" label="Submit" onclick="{!
c.handleClick }" />
</aura:application>
```

Notice that once we bind the attribute, any changes in the value trigger rendering. The controller code is as follows:

```
({
  onInit : function(component, event, helper) {
    console.log('Inside init event');
        console.log('step1');
        console.log('FIND COMPONENT IN INIT..'+component.find("example"));
        console.log('FIND DOM IN
INIT..'+component.find("example").getElement());
    },
      onRender : function(component, event, helper) {
        console.log('Inside render event');
        console.log('step4');
        console.log('FIND COMPONENT ONCE RENDER EVENT IS
```

```
FIRED..'+component.find("example"));
        console.log('FIND DOM ONCE RENDER EVENT IS
FIRED..'+component.find("example").getElement());
    },
    handleClick : function(component, event, helper) {
        component.set("v.search","test");
    }
})
```

Let's add a few `console` objects to the re-render in the RENDERER file, to observe the order of execution:

```
({
  // Your RENDERER method overrides go here
  render : function(component, helper) {
        var ret = this.superRender();
        // do custom rendering here
        console.log('Inside render Function');
        console.log('step2');
        console.log('DOM ELEMENT IN render'
+component.find("example").getElement());
        console.log(ret);
        return ret;
  },
    rerender : function(cmp, helper){
      this.superRerender();
      console.log('Inside rerender');
      console.log('step2');
      // do custom rerendering here
  },
    afterRender: function (component, helper) {
      this.superAfterRender();
        console.log('Inside afterRender Function');
        console.log('step3');
        console.log('COMPONENT IN afterrender' +component.find("example"));
        console.log('DOM ELEMENT IN afterRender'
+component.find("example").getElement());
      // interact with the DOM here
  },
    unrender: function () {
      this.superUnrender();
      // do custom unrendering here
  }
})
```

Type a key on the input, and observe that the component re-renders and calls the `rerender` function. The `console` statements are shown in the following screenshot:

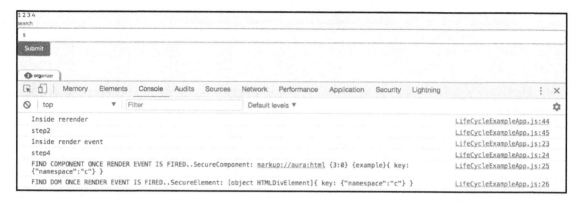

Notice that the `render` system event fires last.

From the preceding example, it can be concluded that one rarely needs to customize the RENDERER JavaScript file, and one can use the render system events to modify the DOM, if required.

Using custom labels in Lightning Components

Custom labels are used to store constants in Salesforce organizations that can be configured by admins. They are completely configurable, and also allow for translation. If you are building a Lightning component to support multiple languages, all of the hardcoded titles need to be inside of labels, so that the platform automatically takes care of displaying the right label, as per the user settings (user-specified language).

The labels in a Salesforce instance can be created by navigating to **Setup** | **User Interface** | **Custom Labels** and then clicking on the **New** button. The following screenshot shows how to create a custom label in Salesforce:

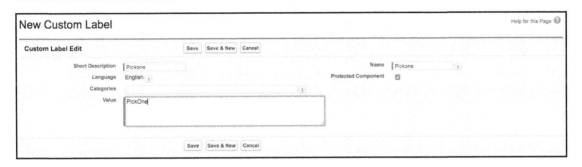

To reference this in a Lightning component, the syntax is as follows:

```
$Label.c.LabelName
```

So, for a label named `Pickone`, the component markup can reference it by using `$Label.c.Pickone`.

In a JavaScript controller, you can get its value by using the following syntax:

```
$A.get("$Label.namespace.labelName")
```

Dynamically populating label parameters

You can provide a string with placeholders, which are replaced by substitute values at runtime.

Let's create a label with the value `Hello {0}` and name it `greeting`. You can dynamically replace `{0}` with an attribute value. The syntax uses the `format` function, as follows:

```
{!format($Label.c.greeting, v.name)} ;//here name is the attribute on the
component
```

ES6 support in Lightning Components

Lightning Components do not fully support ES6 syntax. However, a few important functions, such as `Promise` and array utilities, such as filter, map, and reduce functions, have been found to work, as of the current version.

An introduction to Promises

If you never need the capability to nest callbacks, your code can become difficult to debug and maintain. The following code snippet shows an example of nested callbacks (they are also commonly referred to as `callback` hell):

```
getUsers(function () {
    getUserDetail(function () {
        getProductsPurchasedByUser(function() {
            getRecommendedProducts(function () {

            });
        });
    });
});
```

The `Promise` API (`https://developer.mozilla.Org/en-US/docs/Web/JavaScript/Guide/Using_promises`) in JavaScript solves the problem of `callback` hell by returning the object that can attach callbacks, rather than passing the `callback` a the parameter.

The preceding code snippet for a nested `callback` can be written as follows, using the `Promise` API:

```
getUsers().then(function(userslist) {
  return getUserDetail(userslist);
})
.then(function(userDetail) {
  return getProductsPurchasedByUser(userDetail);
})
.then (function(productsList) {
  return getRecommendedProducts(productsList)){
}
.then(function(product) {
  console.log('Got the final result: ' + product);
})
.catch(failureCallback);//Handle any error
```

In the preceding code snippet, it is assumed that `getUsers()`, `getuserDetail()`, `getProductsPurchasedByUser()`, and `getRecommendedProducts()` are defined as `Promises`. To define a `Promise`, use the following syntax:

```
function getUsers(){
  return new Promise(function(resolve,reject) {
      if(/*resolve state*/){
        resolve();
      }
```

```
      else {
         reject();
      }
   });
}
```

Promise support in Lightning Components

`Promises` are supported in Lightning Components; however, care must be taken, in order to not use them when the action is marked as `storable`; the `callback` function should be wrapped in `$A.getCallback()`. (This is because `Promises` are asynchronous functions. Any asynchronous function, if used in the Lightning component framework, is wrapped in `$A.getCallback()`, to ensure that the framework re-renders the modified component and processes any queued actions.)

The following snippet shows the generic pattern to follow when using `Promises`. Note that the following code assumes that the snippet is part of the `helper` file:

```
({

    getAccounts : function(component,event){
        var fetchaccountAction = component.get("c.getAccounts");
        var params={};
        fetchaccountAction.setParams(params);
        this.promiseAction(fetchaccountAction)
        .then(
            $A.getCallback(function(result){
                // Set attributes
            }),
            $A.getCallback(function(error){
                // Handle any errors
            })
        );
    },

    promiseAction : function(action){
        return new Promise(function(resolve, reject) {
            action.setCallback(this, function(response) {
                var state = response.getState();
                if (state === "SUCCESS") {
                    var response = response.getReturnValue();
                    resolve(response);
                }
                else if (state === "ERROR") {
                }
                  else {
```

```
                    reject(Error("Unknown error"));
                }
            }
        });
        $A.enqueueAction(action);
    }

})
```

You can chain the `Promises` by using the following pattern:

```
firstPromise()
    .then(
        // resolve handler
        $A.getCallback(function(result) {
            return secondPromise();
        }),

        // reject handler
        $A.getCallback(function(error) {
            console.log("Promise was rejected: ", error);
            return errorRecoveryPromise();
        })
    )
    .then(
        // resolve handler
        $A.getCallback(function() {
            return thirdPromise();
        })
    );
```

Summary

In this chapter, we extensively covered the JavaScript API and the Locker Service security model for Lightning Components. Locker Service acts as a virtual browser, with security built into it. Locker Services are an important part of the Salesforce security model, preventing components from accessing data from other components in different namespaces.

In the next chapter, we will look at how to make components talk to each other via events. We will explore application and component events in detail.

5
Events in the Lightning Component Framework

The Lightning Component framework is based on the event-driven model. For two components to talk to each other, the framework recommends using Lightning events. In an event-driven modal, one component acts as a publisher (publisher components register and fire events), and one or more components can subscribe to published events and take action. In the Lightning Component framework, there are two primary types of events: application events and component events. Events are created in a separate file, with an extension of `.evt`. Events in Lightning can also consist of attributes, which allow events to carry data from one component to another.

In this chapter, we will cover the following topics:

- Native browser events, and how they differ from Lightning events
- Application events in Lightning Components
- Component events in Lightning Components
- An example component that illustrates how to use application events

Browser events

Before we dig into how events work in Lightning Components, it is important to briefly touch on JavaScript fundamentals in browser events. In this section, we will explore the bubbling and capturing phases in browser events.

Browser events are signals that are fired on actions (such as page loads, button clicks, key presses, and form submissions). The full list of events supported by browsers can be viewed in the Mozilla developer docs, at `https://developer.mozilla.org/en-US/docs/Web/Events`.

JavaScript provides various ways to attach event handlers. Some of them are as follows:

- Event handler attributes can be attached with an HTML DOM element. Event handler attributes on DOM elements can consist of HTML events, such as onClick, onLoad, onmouseover, onkeyup, onfocus, and many more. The example code for invoking a JavaScript function on a button click is as follows:

```
var btn = document.querySelector('button');

btn.onclick = function() {
 console.log('button clicked!!!');
 }
```

- Inline event handlers are example code for an inline event handler on a button click is as follows:

```
<button onclick="handleclick()">Press me</button>

function handleclick() {
console.log('button clicked!!!');
 }
```

- If you run an inline JavaScript in Lightning Components, you will notice that it is *blocked and not a recommended pattern if used in Lightning Components.*
- You can use the DOM level 2 events format (https://www.w3.org/TR/DOM-Level-2-Events/), leveraging the addEventListener function. The following is example code for handling the click event of a button leveraging DOM level 2 events:

```
var btn = document.querySelector('button');

function handleclick() {
 console.log('Button Clicked!!!!');
 }

btn.addEventListener('click', handleclick);
```

Although you can attach an onclick event to any type of element, for accessibility, consider only applying this event to elements that are actionable in HTML by default, such as the <a>, <button>, or <input> tags in a component markup. You can use an onclick event on a <div> tag, to prevent the event bubbling of a click.

Capturing browser events

The life cycle of an event consists of the capture, target, and bubble phases. The following diagrams show the direction of an event flow for the capture and bubble phases.

The following diagram shows the direction of an event flow during its capturing phase. Observe that the event flows from a parent node to its child node:

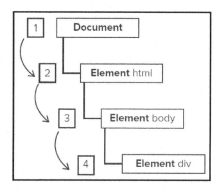

The following diagram shows the direction of an event flow during its bubble phase. During the bubble phase, the events flow from the child node to the parent node:

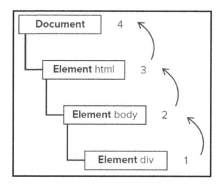

Let's create a Lightning Application bundle using the **Developer Console** (or SFDX project) set up, to help us understand a browser event in a JavaScript application:

```
<aura:application >
 <div onclick="{!c.handleClick}" id="divId">
  <em>If you click on <code>EM</code>, the handler on <code>DIV</code>
runs.</em>
 </div>
</aura:application>
```

The JavaScript controller is as follows:

```
({
 handleClick : function(component, event, helper) {
   console.log(event.target.innerHTML);
   console.log(event.currentTarget.innerHTML);
   var divElement = document.getElementById('divId');
   divElement.addEventListener('click', helper.helperMethod(component,
 event), false);
  }
})
```

The `helper` class code is as follows:

```
({
 helperMethod : function(component, event) {
  console.log('hello');
  }
})
```

When you click the **EM** in the browser, the console logs are as follows:

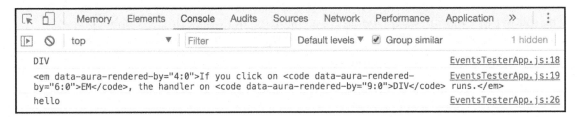

From the preceding content, we can infer the following things about HTML elements in Lightning Components:

- `event.target` gets the proxy object of the object that dispatched the event
- `event.target` gets the deepest element that originated the event
- `event.currentTarget` identifies the element that was bound to the event
- You can add an event listener to the HTML DOM elements, to listen for both the capturing and bubble phases

If you need a visual explanation of the differences between the target and `currentTarget`, refer to `http://joequery.me/code/event-target-vs-event-currenttarget-30-seconds/`.

The event listener, `addEventListener`, has a third parameter as a Boolean, to indicate whether you need to capture the event during its bubble phase or capture phase. `True` indicates that it's the capture phase, and we rarely use them in real applications.

Event handling in Lightning base components

Base components are components with the namespace as Lightning. Some base components are `Lightning:button`, `Lightning:buttonGroup`, `Lightning:input`.

Such components do not expose you to the DOM; hence, using `event.target` or `event.currentTarget` will not work, due to Locker Services (note that the Locker Service prevents accessing the DOM of other components if they are from different namespaces). For such components, you can use the following syntax to get the value of the attribute:

```
event.getSource().get("v.attributename")
```

To set the attributes of the component element, use the following code:

```
event.getSource().set("v.attributename","value")
```

In order to understand how to work with event handling in Lightning base components, let's look at an example of writing a Lightning Application bundle, to highlight a button in a button group when the button is pressed. The challenge here is to highlight only the button that's pressed, and remove the highlight from all other buttons.

Let's create a Lightning Application bundle and name it `ButtonGroupToggle.app`; the code for the application is as follows:

```
<aura:application extends="force:slds">
 <Lightning:buttonGroup>
  <Lightning:button label="Refresh" aura:id="myBtn" variant="Neutral"
onclick="{!c.setActive}"/>
  <Lightning:button label="Edit" aura:id="myBtn" variant="Neutral"
onclick="{!c.setActive}"/>
  <Lightning:button label="Save" aura:id="myBtn" variant="Neutral"
onclick="{!c.setActive}"/>
 </Lightning:buttonGroup>
</aura:application>
```

The JavaScript controller is as follows:

```
({
 setActive : function(component, event, helper) {
 var buttons = component.find("myBtn");
```

```
    buttons.forEach(function(buttonCmp) {
     buttonCmp.set("v.variant","Neutral");
    });
    event.getSource().set("v.variant", "Brand");
  }
})
```

Notice that we have used `event.getSource()` to find the currently clicked button and change the variant to `Brand`. Also, notice that we used the same ID across all of the buttons, so that it will be easier to get all of the buttons using `component.find()`.

The output, rendered on the screen, is as follows:

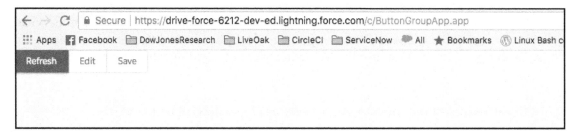

Lightning Component events are of two types:

- Application events
- Component events

Application events

Application events are fired from a component, and any other component can handle the event. The event propagation is very similar to browser events; both have capture and bubble phases, as we discussed in the previous section. However, there are some differences in the rules, which we will cover later in this section.

Apart from the capture and bubble phases, there is a default phase. The default phase is useful for handling application events that affect components in different sub-trees of your app. Note that the default phase does not have propagation rules to follow in a hierarchy, such as a capture and bubble phase.

The framework executes the default phase from the root node unless `preventDefault()` was called in the capture or bubble phases.

Let's look at a few code snippets, to understand how you can fire the application events, and how components can listen to the events.

Creating application events

To create an application event, you need to define the `a.evt` file, as follows. Let's name the file `appEvent`:

```
<aura:event type="APPLICATION" description="Event template">
 <aura:attribute name="message" type="String"/>
</aura:event>
```

Notice that we have `type="APPLICATION"`; you can also define as many attributes as you like, for sending data via the events. Note that when fired, attributes carry payload data along with the event, and the listener component can read the payload.

Registering application events

To register an application event, the notifier (or the publisher component) should have the following snippet in the markup:

```
<aura:registerEvent name="appEvent" type="c:appEvent"/>
```

Notice that we need the `name` attribute here, but it is not used anywhere else. Also, notice that for the type of the event, we specify the event filename, prefixed with a colon `:`, and the namespace (for an application with no namespace, we always use `c:`).

Firing an application event

You can fire an event from the controller or `helper` file by using the following code snippet:

```
var appEvent = $A.get("e.c:appEvent");
// Optional: set some data for the event (also known as event shape)
// A parameter's name must match the name attribute
// of one of the event's <aura:attribute> tags
```

```
//appEvent.setParam({ "message" : myValue });
appEvent.fire();
```

Notice that we have used a global $A variable, and we obtain the instance of the application event using the type of the application. Also, use setParam (for only one parameter) or setParams() (for multiple parameters) to provide the ability to set the event attributes.

Handling application events

The component handling the event should have the following code in the markup:

```
<aura:handler event="c:appEvent" action="{!c.handleApplicationEvent}"/>
```

Note that we have used the event type as the event filename, prefixed with the namespace and a colon (:). Also, there is an action attribute to invoke the controller action, once the event is handled.

The handler for an application event won't work if you set the name attribute in <aura:handler>. Use the name attribute only when you're handling component events.

Getting event attributes from a handled event

To extract event values, the code snippet is as follows:

```
{
  handleApplicationEvent : function(component, event) {
    var message = event.getParam("message");
}
```

Note the use of event.getParam(), to extract the parameter from the attributes of the fired event.

Handling capturing and bubbling events

A containment hierarchy is a component tree hierarchy, from its top-level parent to its child. The bubble phase and the capture phase do not follow the rule that every parent component can handle the event. By default, the owner of the component can handle an event raised during the bubble or capture phase. Note that we are only referring to the bubble or capture phase here; for the default phase, this rule does not apply.

For declaratively created components, the owner is the outermost component containing the markup that references the component firing the event. For programmatically created components, the owner component is the component that invoked $A.createComponent to create the component.

To understand what *the owner* means, let's consider the following example. In this example, c:owner contains c:container, which in turn contains c:eventSource. For the eventSource component, the outermost component is the c:owner component, and hence, that is the owner:

```
<!--c:owner-->
<aura:component>
 <c:container>
  <c:eventSource />
 </c:container>
</aura:component>
```

The event flow direction for the bubble phase is illustrated in the following diagram:

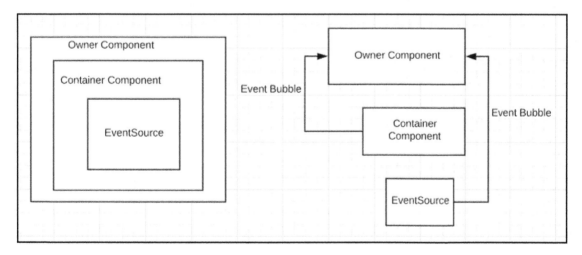

Clearly, from the preceding diagram, the event raised from the `EventSource` component can be handled only by the **Owner Component** by default, since it is the owner.

By default, the handler assumes that the event phase is a bubble phase. To explicitly indicate the capture phase of the event, use the following syntax:

```
<aura:component>
 <aura:handler event="c:appEvent" action="{!c.handleCapture}"
  phase="capture" />
</aura:component>
```

You can force the event to flow to every parent component by adding `includeFacets="true"` to the `<aura:handler>` tag of the parent component.

For example, if, in the preceding example, we wanted the container component to receive the event, we would add the following handler to the container component:

```
<aura:handler event="c:appEvent" action="{!c.handleBubbling}"
 includeFacets="true" />
```

Component events

The primary difference between component events and application events is that a component event does not have the default phase, and hence, it cannot be used if two components are not part of the same tree.

Syntactically, they defer from an application by requiring a name for the handler, and they do not use the `$A` global provider.

Also, note that the default event propagation rules for capture and bubbling are exactly the same as those we discussed in the previous section. A default handler without a phase parameter in `aura:handler` indicates the bubble phase.

Component events are more performant; unless you need application events, you should always use component events.

Creating a component event

To create a component event, create a `a.evt` file using the **Developer Console**; the type is specified as the `COMPONENT`:

```
<!--c:compEvent-->
```

```
<aura:event type="COMPONENT">
 <!-- Add aura:attribute tags to define event shape.
   One sample attribute here. -->
 <aura:attribute name="message" type="String"/>
</aura:event>
```

Registering a component event

Registering a component is similar to registering an application event. The code snippet is as follows:

```
<aura:registerEvent name="sampleComponentEvent" type="c:compEvent"/>
```

Firing the component event

To fire a component event, the syntax is a bit different from an application event, and uses the name identifier to identify the event:

```
var compEvent = component.getEvent("sampleComponentEvent");
// Optional: set some data for the event (also known as event shape)
// A parameter's name must match the name attribute
// of one of the event's <aura:attribute> tags
// compEvent.setParams({"myParam" : myValue });
compEvent.fire();
```

Handling component events

To handle a component event, declare an aura:handler in the handling component. Note that you will need to specify the exact name of the handler, equal to the name used when registering the event:

```
<aura:handler name="sampleComponentEvent" event="c:compEvent"
 action="{!c.handleComponentEvent}"/>
```

Note that a component can also self-handle an event raised by itself. In that case, both the register and handler tags are present on the component. The syntax is as follows:

```
<aura:registerEvent name="sampleComponentEvent" type="c:compEvent"/>
<aura:handler name="sampleComponentEvent" event="c:compEvent"
 action="{!c.handleSampleEvent}"/>
```

Alternate syntax to handle events raised by child components

There is an alternate syntax to handle an event raised by a child component in a parent component. Let's take a look at the syntax:

```
<!-- parent.cmp -->
<aura:component>
 <c:child sampleComponentEvent="{!c.handleChildEvent}"/>
</aura:component>
```

In this case, the child component has registered and fired an event named `sampleComponentEvent`. Notice that in the parent component, we used an attribute name the same as that of the event name registered by the child component. This is a shorthand notation of the following syntax:

```
<!-- parent.cmp -->
<aura:component>
 <aura:handler name="sampleComponentEvent" event="c:compEvent"
  action="{!c.handleSampleEvent}"/>
 <c:child />
</aura:component>
```

Getting event attributes from handled events

Getting event attributes from handled events is similar to how we got the parameter value from the application event variable, using `getParam()`. The same syntax is as follows:

```
{
 handleSampleEvent : function(component, event) {
  var message = event.getParam("message");
}
```

Creating a sales LeaderBoard Lightning Application using events

The aim of this section is to build a Lightning Application to display a sales LeaderBoard and to launch a modal using the events. We will pass data to the modal component using the application event.

A diagram of the component that we will be building is as follows:

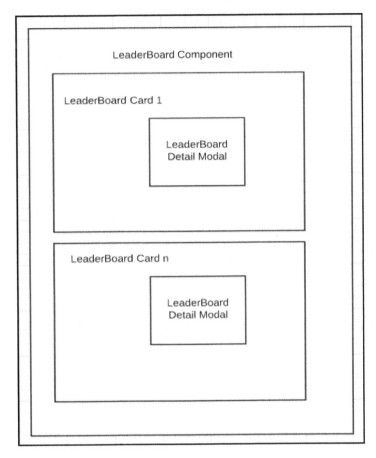

The following screenshot displays the **LeaderBoard** card component:

Once the card is clicked on, the modal displays the details as follows:

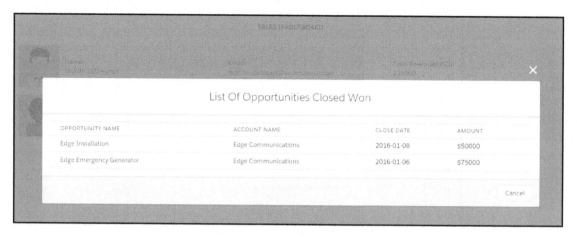

Let's start with the backend Apex code needed for the frontend markup. The `SalesLeader` class creates the data structure that we need for each card on the UI. Each card shows data from the Salesforce user table. Notice that we have implemented an Apex comparable interface, to allow for the capability to sort the list:

```
public class SalesLeader implements Comparable{

    @AuraEnabled
    public String fullname {get;set;}
    @AuraEnabled
    public String email {get;set;}
    @AuraEnabled
    public String userId {get;set;}
    @AuraEnabled
    public Decimal netsales {get;set;}
    @AuraEnabled
    public String photoURL {get;set;}

    public SalesLeader(String fullName,String email,String userId,decimal
    netsales,string photourl){
      this.fullname = fullname;
      this.email = email;
      this.userId = userId;
      this.netsales = netsales;
      this.photoURL = photourl;
    }

    // Implement the compareTo() method
    public Integer compareTo(Object compareTo) {
```

```
      SalesLeader compareTonetrevenue = (SalesLeader)compareTo;
      if (netsales == compareTonetrevenue.netsales) return 0;
      if (netsales < compareTonetrevenue.netsales) return 1;
      return -1;
    }

  }
```

The following is the Apex class to return the list of users in the Salesforce, and to use the Salesforce user ID to return the opportunity they own:

```
public with sharing class SalesLeaderBoardController {

  @AuraEnabled
  public static list<SalesLeader> getSLDashboardData(){
    list<SalesLeader> lstsalesleader = new list<SalesLeader>();
    Integer THIS_YEAR = System.date.today().year();
    map<String,decimal> mapUserIdByamount = new map<String,decimal>();
    for(AggregateResult ag:[SELECT SUM(Amount)sum,
        ownerId
        FROM Opportunity
        WHERE stageName='Closed Won'
        AND CALENDAR_YEAR(CloseDate) = :THIS_YEAR
        GROUP BY OwnerId
        ORDER BY SUM(Amount) DESC
        LIMIT 10]){
      mapUserIdByamount.put((String)ag.get('ownerId'),(Decimal)ag.get('sum'));
    }
    for(User u :[Select Id,Name,Email,FullPhotoUrl from User where ID IN
:mapUserIdByamount.keyset()]){
      SalesLeader sleader = new
SalesLeader(u.Name,u.Email,u.Id,mapUserIdByamount.get(u.Id),u.FullPhotoUrl)
;
      lstsalesleader.add(sleader);
    }
    lstsalesleader.sort();
    return lstsalesleader;
    }

  @AuraEnabled
  public static list<Opportunity> getlstopportunities(String ownerId){

    Integer THIS_YEAR = System.date.today().year();

    return [Select Id,
      Name,
      Account.Name,
      CloseDate,
```

```
        Amount
        FROM Opportunity
        WHERE ownerId =:ownerId
        AND stageName='Closed Won'
        AND CALENDAR_YEAR(CloseDate) = :THIS_YEAR
        ORDER BY CloseDate DESC LIMIT 100];
    }

    }
```

The `getSLDashboardData()` method gets the array of users with the sales amount they had closed by the current year, and the `getlstopportunities()` method takes the `userId` (the ID of the sales user that owns the opportunity record in Salesforce) and lists all of the opportunities for the selected user in a modal.

Before we look into the component markup, let's take a look at the following diagram, which shows the component architecture:

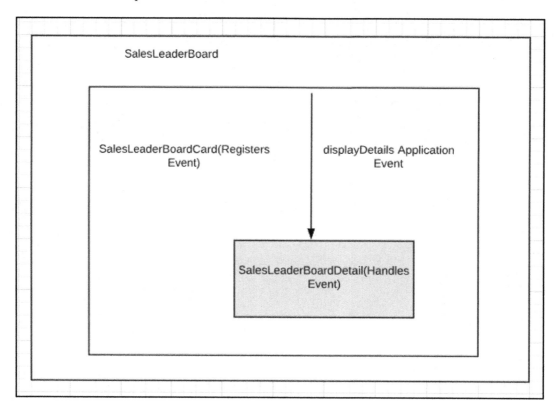

For the component to work properly, we will need to accomplish the following in the component markup and JavaScript code:

- We need three different Lightning Components: **SalesLeaderBoard** is the topmost component, consisting of 1 to *n* of the **SalesLeaderBoardCard** components.
- The **SalesLeaderBoardCard** component comprises a child component and a **SalesLeaderBoardDetail** component.
- When the user clicks on a SalesLeaderBoardComponent, it fires an application event that comprised of the `userId` of the clicked element. This component needs to register an event, and, upon a click, it needs to fire that event.
- The SalesLeaderBoardDetail component handles the event and uses the `userId` obtained from the event to call the Apex controller, to get the opportunity details. This component also performs the client-side action, to toggle CSS elements that show and hide the modal upon event handling.
- The click event is on the **SalesLeaderBoardCard**, and the **SalesLeaderBoardDetail** (it has markup to pop up as a modal) is a child component of the **SalesLeaderBoardCard** component. Hence, a component event cannot be used, because the event bubbles up in the component event, and here, the direction of communication is from the parent to the child component.
- An application event is a great choice if we need these components to be decoupled. That means that we can independently use any of the components, without them depending on each other. For this example, we use application events, assuming that we wanted these components to be decoupled.

We can use `aura:method`, covered in the next section, to keep the code clean and to pass data from the parent to the child component.

Note that there are multiple ways to trigger the modal. You can also use the `$A.createComponent` method, which we explored in previous chapters, to dynamically create the modal component.

For this example, let's assume that we will apply the application event concept learned in this chapter and use the $A.util toggle function to change the CSS class, for modal creation and destruction.

Let's start by creating the last child component: c:SalesLeaderBoardDetail. This component comprises HTML markup to render it as a modal (we will use the SLDS modal, available at https://www.Lightningdesignsystem.com/components/modals/). To create the modal, we will use $A.util to add and remove CSS classes, to hide or show the modal. This component listens for the event and fetches the closed won opportunity records for the current user.

The component markup for c:SalesLeaderBoardDetail is as follows:

```
<aura:component controller="SalesLeaderBoardController">
 <!--ATTRIBUTES DECLARATION -->
 <aura:attribute name="lstopps" type="Opportunity[]"/>
 <!--PUBLISHER -->

 <!--EVENT LISTENER -->
 <aura:handler event="c:displayDetails" action="{!c.showOppmodal}"/>

 <div class="slds">
  <div aria-hidden="true" role="dialog" class="slds-modal slds-modal-large
slds-fade-in-hide" aura:id="modaldialog">
    <div class="slds-modal__container">
    <div class="slds-modal__header">
     <h2 class="slds-text-heading-medium">List Of Opportunities Closed
Won</h2>
     <button class="slds-button slds-button-icon-inverse slds-modal__close"
onclick="{!c.hideModal}">
     <Lightning:icon iconName="utility:close" size="medium"
alternativeText="Indicates approval"/>
     <span class="slds-assistive-text">Close</span>
     </button>
    </div>
    <div class="slds-modal__content">
    <div>
     <table class="slds-table slds-table-bordered slds-max-medium-table-
stacked">
      <thead>
      <tr class="slds-text-heading-label">
       <th class="slds-is-sortable" scope="col">
        <span class="slds-truncate">Opportunity Name</span>
       </th>
       <th scope="col">
        <span class="slds-truncate">Account Name</span>
       </th>
```

```
     <th scope="col">
      <span class="slds-truncate">Close Date</span>
     </th>
     <th scope="col">
      <span class="slds-truncate">Amount</span>
     </th>
    </tr>
    </thead>
    <tbody>
    <aura:iteration items="{!v.lstopps}" var="opp">
     <tr class="slds-hint-parent">
     <th data-label="opportunity-name" role="row"><a href="#"
class="slds-truncate">{!opp.Name}</a></th>
        <td data-label="account"><a href="#" class="slds-
truncate">{!opp.Account.Name}</a></td>
        <td data-label="Close Date">
         <span class="slds-truncate">{!opp.CloseDate}</span>
        </td>
        <td data-label="amount">
         <span class="slds-truncate">${!opp.Amount}</span>
        </td>
       </tr>
     </aura:iteration>
     </tbody>
    </table>
   </div>
  </div>
  <div class="slds-modal__footer">
   <div class="slds-x-small-buttons-horizontal">
    <button class="slds-button slds-button-neutral"
onclick="{!c.hideModal}">Cancel</button>
   </div>
  </div>
  </div>
 </div>
<!-- This is the magic code for the Modal -->
  <div class="slds-backdrop slds-backdrop-hide" aura:id="backdrop">
  </div>
 </div>
</aura:component>
```

The controller code is as follows. It calls the `helper` files that handle the creation of the modal, and uses the `UserId` (obtained by) gets all closed-won opportunities for the user. This is achieved by toggling the CSS classes on elements by removing hide CSS class when we need to show the modal and adding the CSS class to hide the modal when we need to close the modal pop-up:

```
({
 showOppmodal: function(component, event, helper) {
   //Toggle CSS styles for opening Modal
  helper.toggleClass(component,'backdrop','slds-backdrop--');
  helper.toggleClass(component,'modaldialog','slds-fade-in-');
  helper.getopportunitylst(component,event);
 },

 hideModal : function(component, event, helper) {
   //Toggle CSS styles for hiding Modal
  helper.toggleClassInverse(component,'backdrop','slds-backdrop--');
  helper.toggleClassInverse(component,'modaldialog','slds-fade-in-');
 }
})
```

The `helper` file that the controller code calls is as follows:

```
({
 toggleClass: function(component,componentId,className) {
  var modal = component.find(componentId);
  $A.util.removeClass(modal,className+'hide');
  $A.util.addClass(modal,className+'open');
 },

 toggleClassInverse: function(component,componentId,className) {
  var modal = component.find(componentId);
  $A.util.addClass(modal,className+'hide');
  $A.util.removeClass(modal,className+'open');
 },

 getopportunitylst : function(component,event){
  var action = component.get("c.getlstopportunities");
  var self = this;
  var ownerId = event.getParam("userId");
  console.log(ownerId);
  action.setParams({
   "ownerId": ownerId
  });
  action.setCallback(this, function(response) {
  var state = response.getState();
  console.log('STATE'+response.getReturnValue());
```

```
      if (component.isValid() && state === "SUCCESS") {
       component.set("v.lstopps",response.getReturnValue());
      }else if (state === "ERROR") {
      var errors = response.getError();
      if (errors) {
      } else {
      }
      }
    });
    $A.enqueueAction(action);
  }
})
```

The card component (c:SalesLeaderBoardCard) markup is as follows:

```
<aura:component >
 <!--ATTRIBUTES DECLARATION -->
 <aura:attribute name="salesUser" type="SalesLeader"/>

 <!--REGISTER EVENT -->
 <aura:registerEvent name="openDetailModal" type="c:displayDetails"/>

  <div class="slds-card" onclick="{!c.displayOpportunities}">
    <div class="slds-media slds-media-center">
     <div class="slds-media__figure">
      <a aura:id="leadercard" >
      <img src="{!v.salesUser.photoURL}" style="height:90px;"
alt="Placeholder" />
      </a>
     </div>
     <div class="slds-media__body">
      <div class="slds-tile__detail">
       <dl class="slds-dl_horizontal slds-text-body-large">
       <dt class="slds-dl-horizontal__label">
        <p class="slds-truncate">Name:</p>
        <p class="slds-truncate">{!v.salesUser.fullname}</p>
       </dt>
       <dt class="slds-dl-horizontal__label">
        <p class="slds-truncate">Email:</p>
        <p class="slds-truncate">{!v.salesUser.email}</p>
       </dt>
       <dt class="slds-dl-horizontal__label">
        <p class="slds-truncate">Total Revenue(USD):</p>
        <p class="slds-truncate">{!v.salesUser.netsales}</p>
       </dt>
       </dl>
      </div>
     </div>
```

```
      </div>
     </div>
    <!-- Detail Component -->
    <c:SalesLeaderBoardDetail />
   </aura:component>
```

Notice that this component registers the application event. The controller code handles the click event and fires the event:

```
({
  displayOpportunities: function(component, event, helper) {
    var appEvent = $A.get("e.c:displayDetails");
    appEvent.setParams({ "userId": component.get('v.salesUser.userId')});
    appEvent.fire();
  }
})
```

The component code for the topmost parent component (c:SalesLeaderBoard) is as follows:

```
<aura:component
implements="force:appHostable,flexipage:availableForAllPageTypes"
controller="SalesLeaderBoardController">

  <aura:handler name="init" value="{!this}" action="{!c.getData}" />

  <!--ATTRIBUTES DECLARATION -->
  <aura:attribute name="lstsalesUser" type="SalesLeader[]" />

  <Lightning:layout verticalAlign="start" multipleRows="true">
   <Lightning:layoutItem flexibility="auto" padding="around-small">
     <aura:iteration items="{!v.lstsalesUser}" var="usr">
  <c:SalesLeaderBoardCard salesUser="{!usr}"/>
     </aura:iteration>
   </Lightning:layoutItem>
  </Lightning:layout>
</aura:component>
```

The `init` method is invoked to bring a user list, sorted by a user summation of the closed-won opportunity amounts (the salesperson who closed the maximum deals and brought the most revenue to the firm is placed at the top). We will use a `helper` to do the heavy lifting of calling the controller action. The controller and `helper` code is as follows:

```
({
 getData: function(component, event, helper) {
  helper.setdashboard(component);
 }
})
```

The `helper` file is as follows. It fetches the list of users using the Apex controller:

```
({
 setdashboard: function(component) {
  var action = component.get("c.getSLDashboardData");
   var self = this;
   action.setCallback(this, function(response) {
   var state = response.getState();
   console.log(response.getReturnValue());
    if (component.isValid() && state === "SUCCESS") {
     component.set("v.lstsalesUser", response.getReturnValue());
    }else if (state === "ERROR") {
     var errors = response.getError();
     if (errors) {
     } else {
     }
    }
   });
  $A.enqueueAction(action);
 }
})
```

> We have skipped error handling for simplicity, and we will cover it in later chapters.

Let's declare the event file to handle the click and display the details, as follows:

```
<aura:event type="APPLICATION" description="Event template">
 <aura:attribute name="userId" type="String"/>
</aura:event>
```

Communicating between components

This section will highlight some of the recommended patterns to follow to communicate between parent and child components.

Passing data down the component hierarchy

To pass data down the hierarchy, you need to define attributes in child components, and then pass the attribute values from the parent component.

The parent component code is as follows:

```
<aura:component>
 <aura:attribute name="parentAttribute" type="String"/>
 <c:childComponent childAttribute="{!v.parentAttribute}"/>
</aura:component>
```

The child component code is as follows:

```
<aura:component>
 <aura:attribute name="childAttribute" type="String"/>
</aura:component>
```

This way of passing data from the child to the parent is expensive when it comes to performance. Leverage the aura methods covered in the next section.

Using aura:method to call child methods from parent methods

The `aura:method` command is a very useful utility that allows for defining methods in the child component API, so that a parent component can call the method directly, without having to create event files.

Let's look at the following sample code to understand the syntax.

Let's create a child component with the `aura` method, as follows, and name the component `childMethodCmp`:

```
<aura:method name="sampleMethod" action="{!c.doAction}"
 description="Sample method with parameters">
```

```
 <aura:attribute name="param1" type="String" default="parameter 1"/>
 <aura:attribute name="param2" type="Object" />
</aura:method>
/* auraMethodController.js */
({
 doAction : function(cmp, event) {
  var params = event.getParam('arguments');
  if (params) {
   var param1 = params.param1;
   var param2 = params.param2
   return param2;
  }
 },
})
```

Now, let's create `Parent component`, with the following code:

```
<!-- c:auraMethodCaller.cmp -->
<aura:component >
 <p>Parent component calls aura:method in child component</p>
 <c:childMethodCmp aura:id="child" />

 <Lightning:button label="Call aura:method in child component"
  onclick="{! c.callAuraMethod}" />
</aura:component>
```

The controller code for the parent component is shown as follows. Notice that upon the button click action, we invoke the `sampleMethod` method of the child component. Carefully observe how we also pass parameters to the function in the child component:

```
/* auraMethodCallerController.js */
({
 callAuraMethod : function(component, event, helper) {
  var childCmp = component.find("child");
  // call the aura:method in the child component
  var param = {'name' : 'Mohith'};
  var auraMethodResult = childCmp.sampleMethod("1",param);
  console.log("auraMethodResult: " + auraMethodResult);
 },
})
```

Using the aura method asynchronously

The `aura` method discussed in the preceding section has return statements and is synchronous. Most often, when you are working with server-side code to fetch values using `@AuraEnabled` methods, it's asynchronous. If you use return statements, you will notice that `aura` methods run before the server returns the value; so, it's important to pass the function and use `callback` (https://developer.mozilla.org/en-US/docs/Glossary/Callback_function).

Let's demonstrate how `callback` works, with the help of the following example code.

Let's create a child component (we will assume it's a component API, which can be reused across various components). The controller code to fetch the contacts is as follows:

```
public with sharing class ContactController {

 @AuraEnabled
 public static list<Contact> getServerContacts(){
   return [Select Id, Name, Email, Phone From Contact ORDER BY CREATEDDATE
DESC limit 10];
 }
}
```

The child component markup that calls the Apex controller code is as follows:

```
<!-- GetContacts.cmp -->
<aura:component controller="ContactController">
 <aura:method name="getContacts"
description="Sample method with server-side call">
  <aura:attribute name="callback" type="Function" />
 </aura:method>
</aura:component>
```

Notice that the name `getContacts` function in the JavaScript controller has the same name as the `name` used in the `aura:method` component markup. The controller code is shown as follows, invoking the Apex controller method, `getServerContacts`:

```
/* auraMethodController.js */
({
 getContacts : function(cmp, event) {
  var params = event.getParam('arguments');
  var callback;
  if (params) {
   callback = params.callback;
  }
```

```
 var action = cmp.get("c.getServerContacts");
 action.setCallback(this, function(response) {
  var state = response.getState();
  if (state === "SUCCESS") {
   console.log("From server: " + response.getReturnValue());
   //return doesn't work for async server action call
   //return response.getReturnValue();
   // call the callback passed into aura:method
   if (callback) callback(response.getReturnValue());
  }
  else if (state === "INCOMPLETE") {
   // do something
  }
  else if (state === "ERROR") {
   var errors = response.getError();
   if (errors) {
    if (errors[0] && errors[0].message) {
     console.log("Error message: " +
      errors[0].message);
    }
   } else {
    console.log("Unknown error");
   }
  }
 });
 $A.enqueueAction(action);
 },
})
```

The child component is almost an API for a parent component to use this. Let's assume that the parent component is a button and invokes the child component controller in an asynchronous way.

The parent component markup is as follows:

```
<aura:component>
 <aura:attribute type="Contact[]" name="contactList"/>
 <c:GetContacts aura:id="child" />
 <Lightning:layout multipleRows="true" horizontalAlign="center"
verticalAlign="center">
   <Lightning:layoutItem flexibility="auto" padding="horizontal-small"
size="8">
   <aura:iteration items="{!v.contactList}" var="contact">
    <Lightning:card title="{!contact.Name}">
     <p class="slds-p-horizontal_small">
      {!contact.Email}
     </p>
    </Lightning:card>
```

```
      </aura:iteration>
      </Lightning:layoutItem>
   </Lightning:layout>
   <Lightning:button label="Get Contacts From Server"
    onclick="{!c.fetchContacts}"/>
 </aura:component>
```

The controller code is as follows:

```
({
 fetchContacts : function(component, event, helper) {
  var childCmp = component.find("child");
  // call the aura:method in the child component
  childCmp.getContacts(function(result) {
   console.log("callback for aura:method was executed");
   console.log("result: " + result);
   component.set("v.contactList",result);
  });
 }
})
```

The final component is as follows, fetching the contact with the email from the server:

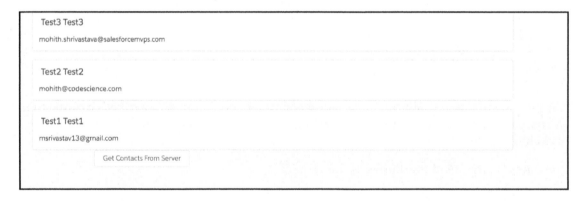

Optimal event architecture design pattern

Adding a high number of component events and application events can not only add more files to your project but can also make debugging your application more difficult.

Keep it simple by using the following patterns:

1. Use only one component file throughout the application. The component event
   has the attribute `name`, where can define different names. This will enable us to
   distinguish them without creating a separate file for each component event. To
   further understand this, let's take a look at the following code snippet, as an
   example that defines a component event. Let's name the event file `genericEvt`:

   ```
   <aura:event type="COMPONENT" description="Generic Component Event"
   >
    <aura:attribute name="cmpData" type="Object"/>
   </aura:event>
   ```

2. Let's create a parent component, as follows:

   ```
   <aura:component>
    <aura:handler name="cmp1" event="c:genericEvt"
   action="{!c.handlecmp1}"/>
    <aura:handler name="cmp2" event="c:genericEvt"
   action="{!c.handlecmp2}"/>
    <c:childCmpOne/>
    <c:childCompTwo/>
   </aura:component>
   ```

3. The child component's code that registers these events is as follows, in
   the `childCmpOne` code snippet:

   ```
   <aura:component>
    <aura:registerEvent name="cmp1" type="c:genericEvt"/>
   </aura:component>
   ```

   The `childCmpTwo` code snippet is as follows:

   ```
   <aura:component>
    <aura:registerEvent name="cmp2" type="c:genericEvt"/>
   </aura:component>
   ```

4. Use only one application event throughout the Lightning Application. Let's
   create an application event named `genericAppEvt`, as follows:

   ```
   <aura:event type="APPLICATION" description="Generic Component
   Event" >
    <aura:attribute name="appData" type="Object"/>
   </aura:event>
   ```

5. Now, you can use a key named `type` to define its various types. An example code snippet to fire an event with different types is as follows:

```
<!--c:aeNotifier-->
<aura:component>
 <aura:registerEvent name="appEvent" type="c:genericAppEvt"/>

 <h1>Simple Application Event Sample</h1>
 <p><Lightning:button
  label="Search"
  onclick="{!c.search}" />
 </p>
<p><Lightning:button
  label="Filter"
  onclick="{!c.filter}" />
 </p>

</aura:component>
```

6. The controller fire event is as follows:

```
/* aeNotifierController.js */
{
 search : function(cmp, event) {
  var searchEvent = $A.get("e.c:genericAppEvt");
  var appData = {
   "type" : "search"
  }
  searchEvent.setParams({
   "appData" : appData
  });
  searchEvent.fire();
 },

 filter : function(cmp, event) {
  var filterEvent = $A.get("e.c:genericAppEvt");
  var appData = {
   "type" : "filter"
  }
  filterEvent.setParams({
   "appData" : appData
  });
  filterEvent.fire();
 }

}
```

7. You can implement a generic handler. The following code snippet illustrates how to handle and distinguish various types in the event:

```
<aura:handler event="c:genericAppEvt"
action="{!c.handleApplicationEvent}"/>
```

8. The controller method uses `switch` statements from JavaScript to write the logic to branch and call different methods, based on the type parameters:

```
handleApplicationEvent : function handleApplicationEvent(component,
event, helper){
 var params = event.getParam("appData");
 if (params && params.type) {
  switch(params.type){
  case 'search':
   helper.search();
   break;
  case 'filter':
   helper.filter();
   break;
  default:
   break;
  }
 }
}
```

- To pass parameters from the parent component to the child component, leverage `aura:methods`, and not events.
- Prefer component events over application events. A component event can be used to pass data from the child component to the parent component.
- Application events should be used only if you have decoupled components. Application events consume more resources, and may degrade the performance of the application.

- The following diagram shows how you can communicate from the parent to the child, and vice versa, using `aura:methods` and component events, respectively:

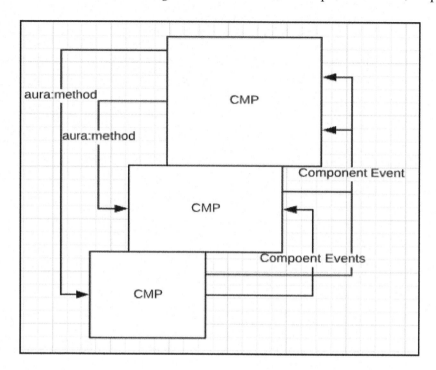

Adding custom events to components dynamically

You can add custom events to the components dynamically by using the `addEventHandler()` method in the component object.

The syntax for a custom event is as follows:

```
addEventHandler(String event, Function handler, String phase, String
includeFacets)
```

The following provides a description for each of the parameters of the `addEventHandler` component method:

- The first argument is the name of the event that triggers the handler. The `<aura:registerEvent>` tag in a component's markup declares the event that the component fires.

> For a component event, set this argument to match the name attribute of the `<aura:registerEvent>` tag. For an application event, set this argument to match the event descriptor in the format `namespace:eventName`.

- The second argument is the action that handles the event. The format is similar to the value that you would put in the action attribute in the `<aura:handler>` tag, if the handler was statically defined in the markup. There are two options for this argument.
- To use a controller action in the handler, use the following format:

```
cmp.getReference("c.actionName")
```

- To use an anonymous function, use the following format:

```
function(auraEvent) {
// handling logic here
}
```

Summary

In this chapter, we explored events in the Lightning Component framework. Conceptually, events are hard to grasp. However, once you understand them, they can help you to write code to communicate between different components. Care must be taken to document these events, and to follow a well-defined pattern, so that it will be easy to maintain the application.

In the next chapter, we will explore Lightning base components and Lightning Data Service, and we will look at how they can simplify building Lightning Components.

6
Lightning Data Service and Base Components

Lightning Data Service provides the ability to listen to data updates that occur in the UI layer and to react and refresh itself with current data. It has a built-in caching ability, and it takes care of **create, read, update, delete (CRUD)** / **Field Level Security (FLS)** (security settings configured by the Salesforce system administrator), based on the user context. In this chapter, we will explore Lightning base components. Lightning base components have built-in JavaScript and SLDS support, to accelerate development and prototyping.

In this chapter, we will cover the following:

- Lightning Data Service
- Example Lightning components using Lightning Data Service
- Lightning base components

Lightning Data Service

If we have multiple custom components on a page with its own Apex controller, we can easily repeat SOQL queries.

Let's take a look at a scenario wherein multiple components have their own SOQL query, and there is no data sharing between components, as illustrated in the following diagram:

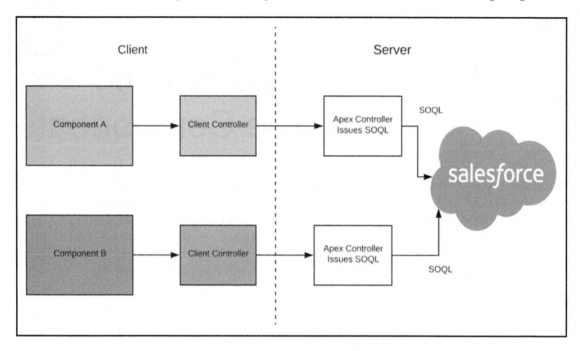

Lightning Data Service provides the following advantages:

- Introduces the sharing of data via a common cache implementation.
- Avoids the need to write Apex, and also takes care of CRUD/FLS and DML security settings configured by the administrator.

The following diagram shows how the data flow is simplified with Lightning Data Service, with the ability to cache and share the data:

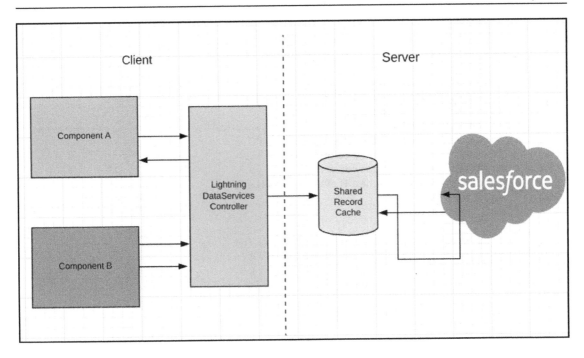

Loading Salesforce record context data using force:recordData

The `force:recordData` component allows us to load the record from the Salesforce object, using `recordId`. `recordId` on the standard record page can be obtained by implementing the `force:hasRecordId` interface, shown as follows:

```
<aura:component implements="force:hasRecordId">
<!-- The following is an attribute that automatically holds the Id if the
component implements the force:hasRecordId -->
<aura:attribute name="recordId" type="String" />

    <!--... -->
</aura:component>
```

The syntax for loading the data for the record using `force:recordData` is as follows:

```
<aura:component
implements="flexipage:availableForRecordHome,force:hasRecordId">

    <aura:attribute name="record" type="Object"/>
```

```
<aura:attribute name="simpleRecord" type="Object"/>
<aura:attribute name="recordError" type="String"/>
<aura:attribute name="recordId" type="String"/>


<force:recordData aura:id="recordLoader"
  recordId="{!v.recordId}"
  layoutType="FULL"
  targetRecord="{!v.record}"
  targetFields="{!v.simpleRecord}"
  targetError="{!v.recordError}"
  recordUpdated="{!c.handleRecordUpdated}"
  mode = "VIEW"
  />


<!-- Display Lightning Data Service errors, if any -->
<aura:if isTrue="{!not(empty(v.recordError))}">
    <div class="recordError">
        <ui:message title="Error" severity="error" closable="true">
            {!v.recordError}
        </ui:message>
    </div>
</aura:if>
</aura:component>
```

You will notice that we have `targetRecord` and `targetFields` attributes, both of type object. They are almost identical, and they hold `recordData`, with a key as the field name. Using `targetRecord`, the syntax was too long, and `targetFields` simplified it.

With `targetRecord`, the syntax to get the field value will be `v.targetRecord.fields.Name.value`, while for `targetFields`, the syntax to extract the value of the field is simplified to `v.targetFields.Name`. Note that `Name` is the field's name.

Also, notice that we have `layoutType`, which can have one of two options: `FULL` or `COMPACT`.

With `FULL`, the fields configured by the Salesforce administrator for the page layout are automatically queried. `COMPACT` queries for fields in the `COMPACT` layout.

You can also specify fields explicitly by using the `fields` attribute and specifying the list of fields, separated by commas.

The mode attribute is always `view` by default, but for edit layouts, you can specify `EDIT`.

The `recordUpdate` object provides the ability to hook the event to the component, to handle any data changes.

The controller code to handle record changes for various use cases is shown as follows. Notice that the event automatically has a property named `changeType`, to help identify the type of operation that happened on the record:

```
({
    handleRecordUpdated: function(component, event, helper) {
        var eventParams = event.getParams();
        if(eventParams.changeType === "LOADED") {
            // record is loaded (render other component which needs record
data value)
            console.log("Record is loaded successfully.");
        } else if(eventParams.changeType === "CHANGED") {
            // record is changed
        } else if(eventParams.changeType === "REMOVED") {
            // record is deleted
        } else if(eventParams.changeType === "ERROR") {
            // there's an error while loading, saving, or deleting the
record
        }
    }
})
```

Functions available for CRUD records

The Lightning Data Service component `force:recordData` provides utility functions to create a new record, save an existing record, delete a record, and detect changes on a Salesforce object. This makes it very easy to build the components used on Salesforce record pages.

Let's suppose that we have a Lightning component with an `aura:id` attribute, illustrated as `recordComponent` in the following code:

```
<force:recordData aura:id="recordComponent"
        recordId="{!v.recordId}"
        layoutType="FULL"
        targetRecord="{!v.record}"
        targetFields="{!v.simpleRecord}"
        targetError="{!v.recordError}"
        recordUpdated="{!c.handleRecordUpdated}"
        mode = "VIEW"
        />
```

The following section will describe code snippets for various operations that perform data manipulation.

Saving existing records

To save existing records, use EDIT mode in the force:recordData component. The controller markup is as follows:

```
<force:recordData aura:id="recordComponent"
        recordId="{!v.recordId}"
        layoutType="FULL"
        targetRecord="{!v.record}"
        targetFields="{!v.simpleRecord}"
        targetError="{!v.recordError}"
        recordUpdated="{!c.handleRecordUpdated}"
        mode = "EDIT"
        />
```

The controller function is as follows:

```
component.find("recordComponent").saveRecord($A.getCallback(function(saveRe
sult) {
        // NOTE: If you want a specific behavior(an action or UI
behavior) when this action is successful
        // then handle that in a callback (generic logic when record is
changed should be handled in recordUpdated event handler)
        if (saveResult.state === "SUCCESS" || saveResult.state ===
"DRAFT") {
            // handle component related logic in event handler
        } else if (saveResult.state === "INCOMPLETE") {
            console.log("User is offline, device doesn't support
drafts.");
        } else if (saveResult.state === "ERROR") {
            console.log('Problem saving record, error: ' +
JSON.stringify(saveResult.error));
        } else {
            console.log('Unknown problem, state: ' + saveResult.state +
', error: ' + JSON.stringify(saveResult.error));
        }
    }));
```

It is important to use `aura:id` to find the target component. The syntax to find the component with the `aura:id` value `recordComponent` is as follows:

```
component.find("recordComponent")
```

The `force:recordData` component consists of a function, `saveRecord`, that saves the data and provides a `callback` function to handle SUCCESS and failures. The following lines of code save the record, using `saveRecord`:

```
component.find("recordComponent").saveRecord($A.getCallback(function(saveRe
sult) {
}
```

> For saving existing records, you will need to make sure that the `recordId` is provided in the `force:recordData` component.

Creating a new record

To create a new record, find the `force:recordData` component and use the `getNewRecord()` function to initialize `sObject`. It is usually better to initialize the object in the `init` handler of the component.

The component code and controller to initialize the `sObject` for the `force:recordData` is shown as follows. The following example assumes that we are creating a simple `Lead` record in Salesforce:

```
<aura:component implements="flexipage:availableForRecordHome,
force:hasRecordId">

<aura:handler name="init" value="{!this}" action="{!c.doInit}"/>


<aura:attribute name="newLead" type="Object"/>
<aura:attribute name="recordError" type="String"/>

    <force:recordData aura:id="recordComponent"
        layoutType="FULL"
        targetFields="{!v.newLead}"
        targetError="{!v.recordError}"
    />

    <!-- Display the new Lead form -->
    <div class="slds-form_stacked">
```

```
                <Lightning:input aura:id="leadField" name="firstName" label="First
Name"
                            value="{!v.newLead.FirstName}" required="true"/>
            <Lightning:input aura:id="leadField" name="lastname" label="Last
Name"
                        value="{!v.newLead.LastName}" required="true"/>
            <Lightning:input aura:id="leadField" name="title" label="Title"
                        value="{!v.newLead.Company}" />
            <Lightning:button label="Save Lead" onclick="{!c.handleSaveLead}"
                    variant="brand" class="slds-m-top_medium"/>
    </div>
</aura:component>
```

The controller code snippet is as follows:

```
({
    doInit: function(component, event, helper) {
        // Prepare a new record from template
        component.find("recordComponent").getNewRecord(
            "Lead", // sObject type (objectApiName)
            null, // recordTypeId
            false, // skip cache?
            $A.getCallback(function() {
                var rec = component.get("v.newLead");
                var error = component.get("v.recordError");
                if(error || (rec === null)) {
                    console.log("Error initializing record template: " +
error);
                    return;
                }
                console.log("Record template initialized: " +
rec.sobjectType);
            })
        );
    },

    handleSaveLead: function(component, event, helper) {
    component.find("recordComponent").saveRecord(function(saveResult) {
            if (saveResult.state === "SUCCESS" || saveResult.state ===
"DRAFT") {
                // record is saved successfully
                var resultsToast = $A.get("e.force:showToast");
                resultsToast.setParams({
                    "title": "Saved",
                    "message": "The record was saved."
                });
                resultsToast.fire();
```

```
            } else if (saveResult.state === "INCOMPLETE") {
                // handle the incomplete state
                console.log("User is offline, device doesn't support
drafts.");
            } else if (saveResult.state === "ERROR") {
                // handle the error state
                console.log('Problem saving Lead, error: ' +
JSON.stringify(saveResult.error));
            } else {
                console.log('Unknown problem, state: ' +
saveResult.state + ', error: ' + JSON.stringify(saveResult.error));
            }
        });
    }
})
```

Notice that to create a new record, we must first initialize it, as follows:

```
getNewRecord(objectAPIname, recordTypeId, skipcache, callback)
```

The parameter definitions are listed as follows, for reference:

Attribute Name	Type	Description
objectApiName	String	The object API name for the new record.
recordTypeId	String	The 18-character ID of the record type for the new record. If not specified, the default record type for the object is used, as defined in the user's profile.
skipCache	Boolean	Whether to load the record template from the server instead of the client-side Lightning Data Service cache. Defaults to false.
callback	Function	A function invoked after the empty record is created. This function receives no arguments.

The save function will be similar to the one we explored in the *Saving existing records* section. The code snippet that handles saving a record upon a button click is as follows:

```
component.find("recordComponent").saveRecord(function(saveResult) {

}
```

Deleting records

The `force:recordData` component also provides a `delete` function, for the ability to delete records. Note that you will need to have `recordId` populated in order to delete the record.

The component code is as follows:

```
<aura:component
implements="flexipage:availableForRecordHome,force:hasRecordId">

    <aura:attribute name="recordError" type="String" access="private"/>
    <force:recordData aura:id="recordHandler"
        recordId="{!v.recordId}"
        fields="Id"
        targetError="{!v.recordError}"
        recordUpdated="{!c.handleRecordUpdated}" />

    <!-- Display Lightning Data Service errors, if any -->
    <aura:if isTrue="{!not(empty(v.recordError))}">
        <div class="recordError">
            <ui:message title="Error" severity="error" closable="true">
                {!v.recordError}
            </ui:message>
        </div>
    </aura:if>

    <div class="slds-form-element">
        <Lightning:button
            label="Delete Record"
            onclick="{!c.handleDeleteRecord}"
            variant="brand" />
    </div>
</aura:component>
```

The controller code snippet with the `deleteRecord()` function is as follows:

```
({
    handleDeleteRecord: function(component, event, helper) {
component.find("recordHandler").deleteRecord($A.getCallback(function(delete
Result) {
            // NOTE: If you want a specific behavior(an action or UI
behavior) when this action is successful
            // then handle that in a callback (generic logic when record is
changed should be handled in recordUpdated event handler)
            if (deleteResult.state === "SUCCESS" || deleteResult.state ===
"DRAFT") {
                // record is deleted
```

```
                    console.log("Record is deleted.");
            } else if (deleteResult.state === "INCOMPLETE") {
                console.log("User is offline, device doesn't support
drafts.");
            } else if (deleteResult.state === "ERROR") {
                console.log('Problem deleting record, error: ' +
JSON.stringify(deleteResult.error));
            } else {
                console.log('Unknown problem, state: ' + deleteResult.state
+ ', error: ' + JSON.stringify(deleteResult.error));
            }
        }));
    },

    /**
     * Control the component behavior here when record is changed (via any
component)
     */
    handleRecordUpdated: function(component, event, helper) {
        var eventParams = event.getParams();
        if(eventParams.changeType === "CHANGED") {
            // record is changed
        } else if(eventParams.changeType === "LOADED") {
            // record is loaded in the cache
        } else if(eventParams.changeType === "REMOVED") {
            // record is deleted, show a toast UI message
            var resultsToast = $A.get("e.force:showToast");
            resultsToast.setParams({
                "title": "Deleted",
                "message": "The record was deleted."
            });
            resultsToast.fire();

        } else if(eventParams.changeType === "ERROR") {
            // there's an error while loading, saving, or deleting the
record
        }
    }
})
```

Notice that upon successful deletion, the `changeType` in the event parameters handled on the record update will include the `REMOVED` keyword.

Using SaveRecordResult

You will have noticed that the `saveRecord` and `deleteRecord` functions of Lightning Data Service return a `SaveRecordResult` object in the `callback`.
The `SaveRecordResult` object has information related to the context ID of the record and the error details. The following table describes the various properties available in the `SaveRecordResult` object:

Attribute Name	Type	Description
`objectApiName`	String	The object API name for the record.
`entityLabel`	String	The label for the name of the `sObject` of the record.
`error`	String	The error can be one of the following: • A localized message indicating what went wrong. • An array of errors, including a localized message indicating what went wrong. It might also include further data to help handle the error, such as the field or page-level errors. An error is undefined if the save state is SUCCESS or DRAFT.
`recordId`	String	The 18-character ID of the record affected.
`state`	String	The result state of the operation. Possible values are: • SUCCESS: The operation completed on the server successfully. • DRAFT: The server wasn't reachable, so the operation was saved locally, as a draft. The change is applied to the server when it's reachable. • INCOMPLETE: The server wasn't reachable, and the device doesn't support drafts. (Drafts are supported only in the Salesforce app.) Try this operation again later. • ERROR: The operation couldn't be completed. Check the `error` attribute for more information.

Lightning Data Service does not support all of the objects, and a comprehensive list of considerations and limitations can be found in the official documents at `https://developer.Salesforce.com/docs/atlas.en-us.Lightning.meta/Lightning/data_service_considerations.htm`.

Example components using Lightning Data Service

The Lightning Data Service components that we explored in the previous section can be combined with custom components to achieve various functionalities without writing excessive code. In the next section, we will cover some base components. With Lightning Data Service and base components, we can rapidly build components, to achieve various functionalities.

In this section, we will build a path component that changes based on the Lead status. Note that this component may be available out of the box in Salesforce, but our aim is to demonstrate how to leverage Lightning Data Service in custom components:

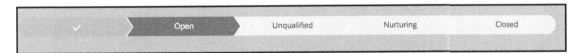

Let's use the data service `force:recordData` on the lead layout, in order to build this. The Lightning base components library provides a component to make this easier; the code snippet for it is as follows:

```
<aura:component>
    <Lightning:progressIndicator currentStep="3" type="path"
variant="base">
        <Lightning:progressStep label="Contacted" value="1"/>
        <Lightning:progressStep label="Open" value="2"/>
        <Lightning:progressStep label="Unqualified" value="3"/>
        <Lightning:progressStep label="Nurturing" value="4"/>
        <Lightning:progressStep label="Closed" value="5"/>
    </Lightning:progressIndicator>
</aura:component>
```

Before you proceed, make sure that you have the same values in the **Lead Status** field, using the Salesforce standard interface. Navigate to **Object Manager | Fields and Relationships | Lead | Status**, and add and remove **Picklist**. The following screenshot shows the **Status** field **Picklist** values:

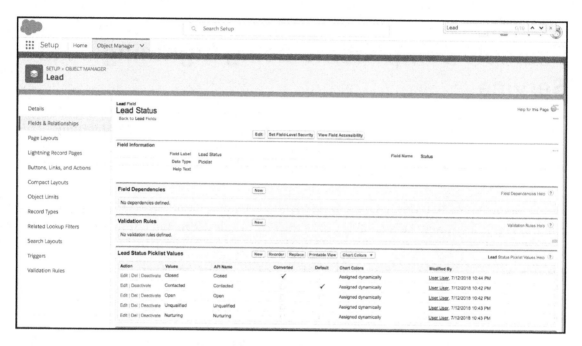

Our goal is to create a functional component that automatically moves to the next stage when the Lead status is changed in the Salesforce **Detail View**. We will use Lightning Data Service to detect when the user changes the status in the Lead, and will then update the attribute currentStep.

The component code for the LeadPath is as follows:

```
<aura:component
implements="force:hasRecordId,flexipage:availableForRecordHome">

    <aura:attribute name="currentStep" type="String" />
    <aura:attribute name="recordId" type="String" />
    <aura:attribute name="record" type="Object"/>
    <aura:attribute name="recordError" type="String"/>

    <aura:handler name="init" value="{!this}" action="{!c.onInit}"/>

    <!--Add Lighnting Data Service Here-->
```

```
<force:recordData aura:id="recordComponent"
  recordId="{!v.recordId}"
  layoutType="FULL"
  targetFields="{!v.record}"
  targetError="{!v.recordError}"
  recordUpdated="{!c.handleRecordUpdated}"
  mode = "VIEW"
  />

  <!-- Display Lightning Data Service errors, if any -->
<aura:if isTrue="{!not(empty(v.recordError))}">
    <div class="recordError">
        <ui:message title="Error" severity="error" closable="true">
            {!v.recordError}
        </ui:message>
    </div>
</aura:if>

<div class="slds-p-around_x-small">
    <Lightning:progressIndicator currentStep="{!v.currentStep}"
type="path" variant="base">
        <Lightning:progressStep label="Contacted" value="1"/>
        <Lightning:progressStep label="Open" value="2"/>
        <Lightning:progressStep label="Unqualified" value="3"/>
        <Lightning:progressStep label="Nurturing" value="4"/>
        <Lightning:progressStep label="Closed" value="5"/>
    </Lightning:progressIndicator>
</div>
</aura:component>
```

Notice that we have the `force:RecordData` component, which gets the context data, including the `status` field. Also, we created an attribute named `currentStep`, for the current step.

Also, notice that we have a handler that invokes the controller function; the controller code invokes the helper to set the path on the custom Lightning component. We used the Lightning helper to keep the logic reusable.

The `LeadPathController.js` code is as follows:

```
({
    onInit:function(component, event, helper) {
    },
    handleRecordUpdated : function(component, event, helper) {
        var eventParams = event.getParams();
        if(eventParams.changeType === "LOADED") {
            // record is loaded (render other component which needs record
    data value)
            console.log("Record is loaded successfully.");
            helper.setPathValue(component, event);
        } else if(eventParams.changeType === "CHANGED") {
            // record is changed
            helper.setPathValue(component, event);
        } else if(eventParams.changeType === "REMOVED") {
            // record is deleted
        } else if(eventParams.changeType === "ERROR") {
            // there's an error while loading, saving, or deleting the
    record
        }
    }
})
```

The `helper` JavaScript code is as follows:

```
({
    setPathValue : function(component,event) {
        var mapStatus = {"Contacted" : "1" , "Open" : "2" , "Unqualified" :
"3" ,"Nurturing" : "4", "Closed" : "5" };
        var status = component.get("v.record").Status;
        component.set("v.currentStep",mapStatus[status]);
    }
})
```

Notice that we used the JavaScript object to keep the mappings for the status on `Lead` and the value that the out-of-the-box path component uses.

Once we have these, we can drag and drop our custom component and change the path values that are automatically reflected in the lead status. The following screenshot shows the results:

Screenshot shows the LeadPatch custom component that changes its values based on Data changes to the Lead Record From Standard Record Detail view

Now that we have explored Lightning Data Service, we will move on to the Lightning base components. Base components provide pre-built components, making it a breeze to prototype business requirements. They provide various pre-built components, without having to build a lot of code from scratch.

Lightning base components

The idea behind Lightning base components is to accelerate development by providing out-of-the-box components that have built-in design patterns, found in the Salesforce Lightning Design System (`https://www.Lightningdesignsystem.com/`). The components also have JavaScript functions built in, and include attributes to ease customization. These components may not provide all of the flexibility that we need, and they may not fit for all business requirements, but they can be used for most common use cases. The library is rich, and is getting better with every release. You will find components such as `carousel`, tree, `datatable`, input forms, and more.

In this section, we will briefly discuss a few of the important components, with examples. For a comprehensive listing, always refer to the Salesforce release notes and the component library. Note that these components have the Lightning namespace.

 To explore the component library, refer to the standard component library at `https://developer.Salesforce.com/docs/component-library`.

An introduction to Lightning input field components

The Lightning `Input` field allows us to create a form (using `Lightning:recordEditForm`) to insert/update records. For update scenarios, specify the `recordId` and `recordTypeId` attributes. The advantage of this component depends on the field data type the form fields widgets appear appropriately. For example, if you have a dependent **Picklist**, the **Picklist** selector is rendered; for a date type field, a date picker is rendered.

Creating an input form using the RecordEdit and Lightning input field components

The following component demonstrates an example of how you can use the `Lightning:inputfield` to collect user input and create a record in Salesforce. This component does not require Data Service or Apex controllers, as it can be obtained by using base components. Note that base components respect security settings configured by the Salesforce system administrator for fields and objects.

The component code for the `recordEdit` form is as follows:

```
<aura:component
implements="force:hasRecordId, flexipage:availableForRecordHome">
<aura:attribute name="companyName" type="String"/>
    <Lightning:layout verticalAlign="start" multipleRows="true">
        <Lightning:layoutItem flexibility="auto" padding="around-small">
            <Lightning:recordEditForm aura:id="recordEditForm"
                            objectApiName="Lead"
onsuccess="{!c.handleSuccess}" onsubmit="{!c.handleSubmit}"
onload="{!c.handleOnload}">
                <Lightning:messages />
                <Lightning:inputField fieldName="Name" />
```

```
                <Lightning:inputField fieldName="Company" />
                <Lightning:inputField fieldName="Phone" />
                <Lightning:button variant="brand" class="btn" type="submit"
label="Create new lead" />
            </Lightning:recordEditForm>
        </Lightning:layoutItem>
    </Lightning:layout>
</aura:component>
```

In the preceding code, the component requires a recordEditForm component and an input field for your user to enter into, followed by a Lightning:button of the type submit.

The controller code illustrates how to handle various events, such as submitting actions (onsubmit) and after successful actions (onsuccess):

```
({
    handleSuccess : function(component, event, helper) {
        console.log(event.getParams().response);
        for (let key of Object.keys(event.getParams().response)) {
            console.log(key + event.getParams().response[key]);
        }
        console.log(event.getParams().response.id);
        //console.log(component.find("name").get("v.value"));
        var toastEvent = $A.get("e.force:showToast");
        toastEvent.setParams({
            "title": "Success!",
            "message": "The record has been created successfully.",
            "type": "success"
        });
        toastEvent.fire();
    },

    handleSubmit : function(component, event, helper) {
        console.log('Submit Event' + JSON.stringify(event.getParams()));
        console.log(component.find("company"));
        //The following is useful if you want to overwrite.Notice you need
    to specify both the values.This also assumes you have aura:id on the
    company field.
        //component.find("company").set("v.fieldName","Company");
        //component.find("company").set("v.value","value");
    },

    handleOnload : function(component, event, helper) {
        console.log('Load Event' + JSON.stringify(event.getParams()));
    },
})
```

The following screenshot shows the screen for the component that we created using
`Lightning:recordEditForm`:

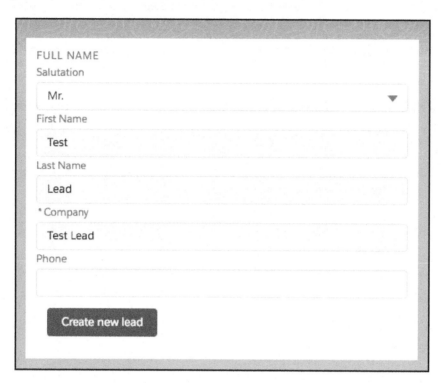

Introducing events and attributes in Lightning record edit form and input field

The `onerror` action returns the following parameter:

Parameter	Type	Description
error	Object	`error`: Data returned by the form submission. `errorCode`: An error code with information about the error; for example, `INSUFFICIENT_PRIVILEGES`. `message`: Description of error; we recommend using `Lightning:messages` to display your error messages in the UI.

The `onload` action returns the following parameter:

Parameter	Type	Description
recordUi	Object	The object's metadata. For more information, see the *User Interface API Developer Guide* at `https://developer.Salesforce.com/docs/atlas.en-us.212.0.uiapi.meta/uiapi/ui_api_get_started_supported_objects.htm`.

The `onsubmit` action returns the following parameter:

Parameter	Type	Description
fields	Object	The fields that are provided for submission during a record creation. For example, if you include a `Lightning:inputField` component with the `Name` field, it returns `FirstName`, `LastName`, and `Salutation`.

The `onsuccess` action returns the following parameter:

Parameter	Type	Description
response	Object	The response data associated with the record during a record creation or edit: • `apiName`: The record's API name, such as `Contact`. • `childRelationships`: The child relationship data for this record. • `fields`: The field data for this record, matching the requested layout. • `id`: The ID of this record. • `recordTypeInfo`: The record type info for this record, if any.

The `attribute` definitions for `Lightning:recordEditForm` are as follows:

Attribute Name	Attribute Type	Description	Required?
body	Component	The body of the component. In markup, this is everything in the body tag.	
class	String	The API name of the object.	
objectApiName	String	The API name of the object.	Yes
onerror	Action	The action triggered when there is an error upon form submission.	
onload	Action	The action triggered when the form data is loaded.	
onsubmit	Action	The action triggered when the form is submitted.	
onsuccess	Action	The action triggered when the form is saved.	
recordId	String	The ID of the record to be displayed.	
recordTypeId	String	The ID of the record type, which is required if you created multiple record types but don't have a default.	

The attribute definitions for `Lightning:inputfield` are as follows:

Attribute Name	Attribute Type	Description
body	Component[]	The body of the component. In markup, this is everything in the body of the tag.
class	String	A CSS class for the outer element, in addition to the base class.
fieldName	String	The API name of the field to be displayed.
value	String	The field value that overrides the existing value.
onchange	Action	The action triggered when the input value changes.

Creating a contact edit form using the Lightning input field and RecordEditForm components

For a contact edit form, you will need to provide the ID of the record that needs updating. The following example shows how to use the `RecordEditForm` component to edit a contact record:

```
<aura:component
implements="force:hasRecordId, flexipage:availableForRecordHome">
```

```
        <div class="slds-p-bottom_large slds-p-left_large" style="width:500px">
   <Lightning:recordEditForm aura:id="recordViewForm"
                                recordId="{!v.recordId}"
                                recordTypeId="012R00000000000000"
                                objectApiName="Contact">
            <Lightning:messages />
            <Lightning:inputField fieldName="FirstName" />
            <Lightning:inputField fieldName="LastName" />
            <Lightning:inputField fieldName="Birthdate" />
            <Lightning:inputField fieldName="Phone" />
            <!--Picklist-->
            <Lightning:inputField fieldName="Level__c" />
             <Lightning:inputField fieldName="LeadSource" />
       <Lightning:inputField fieldName="Level__c" />
            <Lightning:button aura:id="submit" type="submit" label="Update
record" class="slds-m-top_medium" />
            </Lightning:recordEditForm>
        </div>
</aura:component>
```

Using the Lightning output field component

The Lightning output field component allows us to display the record view using the
provided fields. You will need to enclose `Lightning:outputfield` in a wrapper
component: `Lightning:recordViewForm`. The mandatory attributes for the
`recordViewForm` are the `recordId` and the `objectAPIName`.

The syntax for the record view form is as follows:

```
<aura:component
implements="force:hasRecordId,flexipage:availableForRecordHome">
    <Lightning:recordViewForm recordId="{!v.recordId}"
objectApiName="Contact">
    <div class="slds-grid">
        <div class="slds-col slds-size_1-of-2">
            <!-- Your Lightning:outputField components here -->
        </div>
        <div class="slds-col slds-size_1-of-2">
            <!-- More Lightning:outputField components here -->
        </div>
    </div>
</Lightning:recordViewForm>
</aura:component>
```

Note that in the real world, it is not recommended to use hardcoded ID values; instead, use the `force:hasrecordId` interface to provide the record ID.

The list view component

The list view component allows us to display the list view in a custom component. The following example shows the code for the list view component, using a design file to make it generic enough to adopt for any object and any list view:

```
<aura:component
implements="flexipage:availableForRecordHome,flexipage:availableForAllPageT
ypes">

    <aura:attribute name="ObjectName" type="String" default="Account"/>
    <aura:attribute name="ListViewName" type="String"
default="My_Accounts"/>

    <Lightning:listView aura:id="listViewAccounts"
    objectApiName="{!v.ObjectName}"
    listName="{!v.ListViewName}"
    rows="15"
    showActionBar="false"
    enableInlineEdit="true"
    showRowLevelActions="false"/>

</aura:component>
```

The design file for the preceding component is as follows:

```
<design:component >
    <design:attribute name="ObjectName" label="Object Name"
description="Enter Object Name" />
    <design:attribute name="ListViewName" label="ListView Name"
description="Enter Name of the List View" />
</design:component>
```

The following screenshot shows how one can configure this component, by providing the object name and the list view name. Note that you will need the API name of the list view:

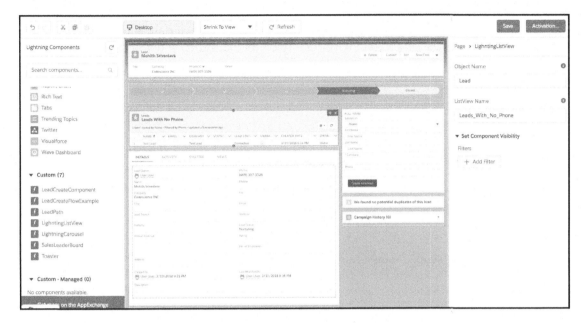

To learn more about considerations and supported features, explore the documents at `https://developer.Salesforce.com/docs/component-library?page=Lightning:listView`.

Creating a tree view using the tree and tree grid components

The tree grid component allows us to create a tree view along with a grid. A sample code snippet is as follows:

```
<aura:application extends="force:slds">
<aura:handler name="init" value="{!this}" action="{!c.init}" />
<aura:attribute name="gridColumns" type="List" />
<aura:attribute name="gridData" type="Object" />
<aura:attribute name="gridExpandedRows" type="Object" />
<Lightning:treeGrid
columns="{! v.gridColumns }"
data="{! v.gridData }"
expandedRows="{! v.gridExpandedRows }"
keyField="name"
```

```
    aura:id="mytree"
    />
</aura:application>
```

The JavaScript controller code for this component generates mock data, shown as follows. You can easily substitute mock data with data from the backend by using Apex code:

```
({
    init: function(cmp) {
        var columns = [{
                type: 'text',
                fieldName: 'accountName',
                label: 'Account Name'
            },
            {
                type: 'number',
                fieldName: 'employees',
                label: 'Employees'
            },
            {
                type: 'phone',
                fieldName: 'phone',
                label: 'Phone Number'
            },
            {
                type: 'url',
                fieldName: 'accountOwner',
                label: 'Account Owner',
                typeAttributes: {
                    label: {
                        fieldName: 'accountOwnerName'
                    }
                }
            }
        ];
        cmp.set('v.gridColumns', columns);
        var nestedData = [{
                "name": "123555",
                "accountName": "Rewis Inc",
                "employees": 3100,
                "phone": "837-555-1212",
                "accountOwner": "http://sfdc.co/jane-doe",
                "accountOwnerName": "Jane Doe"
            },
            {
                "name": "123556",
                "accountName": "Acme Corporation",
                "employees": 10000,
```

```
                    "phone": "837-555-1212",
                    "accountOwner": "http://sfdc.co/john-doe",
                    "accountOwnerName": "John Doe",
                    "_children": [{
                        "name": "123556-A",
                        "accountName": "Acme Corporation (Bay Area)",
                        "employees": 3000,
                        "phone": "837-555-1212",
                        "accountOwner": "http://sfdc.co/john-doe",
                        "accountOwnerName": "John Doe",
                        "_children": [{
                            "name": "123556-A-A",
                            "accountName": "Acme Corporation (Oakland)",
                            "employees": 745,
                            "phone": "837-555-1212",
                            "accountOwner": "http://sfdc.co/john-doe",
                            "accountOwnerName": "John Doe"
                        },
                        {
                            "name": "123556-A-B",
                            "accountName": "Acme Corporation (San
Francisco)",
                            "employees": 578,
                            "phone": "837-555-1212",
                            "accountOwner": "http://sfdc.co/jane-doe",
                            "accountOwnerName": "Jane Doe"
                        }
                        ]
                    }]
                },
            ];
            cmp.set('v.gridData', nestedData);
            var expandedRows = ["123556"];
            cmp.set('v.gridExpandedRows', expandedRows);
        }
    })
```

The following screenshot shows the tree grid component:

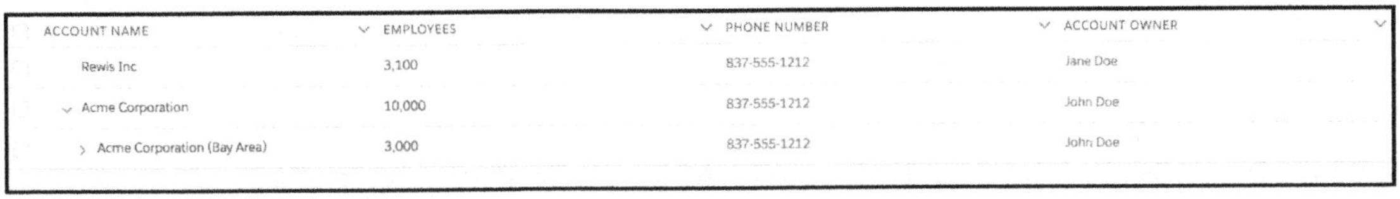

ACCOUNT NAME	EMPLOYEES	PHONE NUMBER	ACCOUNT OWNER
Rewis Inc	3,100	837-555-1212	Jane Doe
⌄ Acme Corporation	10,000	837-555-1212	John Doe
⟩ Acme Corporation (Bay Area)	3,000	837-555-1212	John Doe

To learn more about the tree grid component, explore `https://developer.Salesforce.com/docs/component-library/bundle/Lightning:treeGrid/example`. If you do not need a grid view, there is a tree component illustrated at `https://developer.Salesforce.com/docs/component-library/bundle/Lightning:tree/example`.

Formatting output data using Lightning base components

The Lightning base components for formatting allow us to format emails, addresses, dates, URLs, and much more.

The following screenshot from the component library shows various format options:

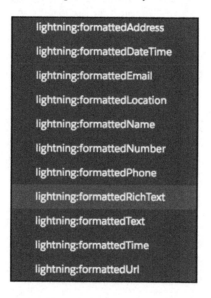

The following component demonstrates a working example of how to use these components. Note that we also use some of the base input components for the addresses and names input:

```
<aura:application extends="force:slds">

<aura:attribute name="street" type="string"/>
<aura:attribute name="city" type="string"/>
<aura:attribute name="country" type="string"/>
<aura:attribute name="province" type="string"/>
<aura:attribute name="postalCode" type="string"/>
```

```
<aura:attribute name="provinceOptions" type="List" default="[
{'label': 'California', 'value': 'CA'},
{'label': 'Texas', 'value': 'TX'},
{'label': 'Washington', 'value': 'WA'},
{'label': 'Tennesse', 'value': 'TN'},
]"/>
<aura:attribute name="countryOptions" type="List" default="[
{'label': 'United States', 'value': 'US'},
{'label': 'Japan', 'value': 'JP'},
{'label': 'China', 'value': 'CN'},
{'label': 'India', 'value': 'IN'},
]"/>

<aura:attribute name="salutationOptions" type="List" default="[
{'label': 'None', 'value': 'None'},
{'label': 'Mr.', 'value': 'Mr.'},
{'label': 'Ms.', 'value': 'Ms.'},
{'label': 'Mrs.', 'value': 'Mrs.'},
{'label': 'Dr.', 'value': 'Dr.'},
{'label': 'Prof.', 'value': 'Prof.'}
]"/>

<aura:attribute name="fields" type="List" default="['firstName',
'lastName']"/>

<aura:attribute name="firstName" type="string"/>
<aura:attribute name="middleName" type="string"/>
<aura:attribute name="lastName" type="string"/>
<aura:attribute name="informalName" type="string"/>
<aura:attribute name="suffix" type="string"/>
<aura:attribute name="salutation" type="string"/>

<Lightning:layout verticalAlign="start" multipleRows="true">
<Lightning:layoutItem flexibility="auto" padding="around-small" size="12">
<Lightning:inputAddress
aura:id="myaddress"
addressLabel="Address"
streetLabel="Street"
cityLabel="City"
countryLabel="Country"
provinceLabel="State"
postalCodeLabel="PostalCode"
street="{!v.street}"
city="{!v.city}"
country="{!v.city}"
province="{!v.province}"
postalCode="{!v.postalCode}"
countryOptions="{!v.countryOptions}"
```

```
            provinceOptions="{!v.provinceOptions}"
            required="true"
            />
            </Lightning:layoutItem>
            <Lightning:layoutItem flexibility="auto" padding="around-small" size="12">
            Formatted Address :<Lightning:formattedAddress
            street="{!v.street}"
            city="{!v.city}"
            country="{!v.country}"
            province="{!v.province}"
            postalCode="{!v.postalCode}"
            />
            </Lightning:layoutItem>
            </Lightning:layout>
            <Lightning:layoutItem flexibility="auto" padding="around-small" size="6">
            <Lightning:inputName
            aura:id="myname"
            label="Contact Name"
            firstName="{!v.firstName}"
            middleName="{!v.middleName}"
            lastName="{!v.lastName}"
            informalName="{!v.informalName}"
            suffix="{!v.suffix}"
            salutation="{!v.salutation}"
            options="{!v.salutationOptions}"
            fieldsToDisplay="{!v.fields}"
            />
            </Lightning:layoutItem>
            <Lightning:layoutItem flexibility="auto" padding="around-small" size="12">
            Formatted Name : <Lightning:formattedName
            firstName="{!v.firstName}"
            middleName="{!v.middleName}"
            lastName="{!v.lastName}"
            informalName="{!v.informalName}"
            suffix="{!v.suffix}"
            salutation="{!v.salutation}"
            />
            </Lightning:layoutItem>
            </aura:application>
```

The following screenshot shows the output for the preceding component:

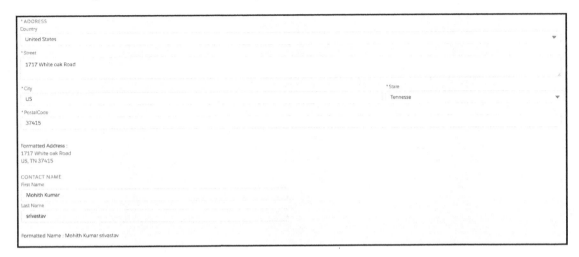

Using the datatable component

The `datatable` component allows us to create a data table from an array of objects. The component sample code is shown as follows. The component creates a simple table, with the columns name ID, opportunity name, confidence, amount, email, and phone:

```
<aura:component>
  <aura:attribute name="mydata" type="Object"/>
  <aura:attribute name="mycolumns" type="List"/>
  <aura:handler name="init" value="{! this }" action="{! c.init }"/>
  <Lightning:datatable data="{! v.mydata }" columns="{! v.mycolumns }"
keyField="id" onrowselection="{! c.getSelectedName }"/>
</aura:component>
```

The controller code illustrates an example with some mock data, as follows:

```
({

    init: function(cmp, event, helper) {

        cmp.set('v.mycolumns',

            [{
                    label: 'Opportunity name',
                    fieldName: 'opportunityName',
                    type: 'text'
```

```
                },

                {
                    label: 'Confidence',
                    fieldName: 'confidence',
                    type: 'percent',
                    cellAttributes: {
                        iconName: {
                            fieldName: 'trendIcon'
                        },
                        iconPosition: 'right'
                    }
                },

                {
                    label: 'Amount',
                    fieldName: 'amount',
                    type: 'currency',
                    typeAttributes: {
                        currencyCode: 'EUR'
                    }
                }, {
                    label: 'Contact Email',
                    fieldName: 'contact',
                    type: 'email'
                }, {
                    label: 'Contact Phone',
                    fieldName: 'phone',
                    type: 'phone'
                }
            ]);
        cmp.set('v.mydata', [{
            id: 'a',
            opportunityName: 'Cloudhub',
            confidence: 0.2,
            amount: 25000,
            contact: 'jrogers@cloudhub.com',
            phone: '2352235235',
            trendIcon: 'utility:down'
        }, {
            id: 'b',
            opportunityName: 'Quip',
            confidence: 0.78,
            amount: 740000,
            contact: 'quipy@quip.com',
            phone: '2352235235',
            trendIcon: 'utility:up'
        }]);
```

```
        },
        getSelectedName: function(cmp, event) {
            var selectedRows = event.getParam('selectedRows'); // Display
    that fieldName of the selected rows
            for (var i = 0; i < selectedRows.length; i++){
                alert("You selected: " + selectedRows[i].opportunityName);
            }
        }
    }
})
```

You can learn more about Lightning `datatable` at `https://developer.Salesforce.com/docs/component-library/bundle/Lightning:datatable/example`. The Lightning `datatable` allows you to lazily load data, take actions from the selected data rows (selected using inline checkboxes provided by the component), infinite list load, select data rows, and add static and dynamic actions.

Using Lightning input components

Lightning input components allow you to create input for the form elements. They have built-in validations, based on the type of field, and can be used with various data types. To learn more about `Lightning: input`, refer to the standard component library at `https://developer.Salesforce.com/docs/component-library/bundle/Lightning:input/example`.

The following snippet shows a working example of the code for the `Lightning:input` component. The component markup creates a simple form for lead capture. Notice that we have made all of the fields mandatory by using the `required` attribute on `lighnting:input`:

```
<aura:component access="global" >

    <aura:attribute name="lastName" type="String"/>
    <aura:attribute name="email" type="String" />
    <aura:attribute name="company" type="String" />
    <aura:attribute name="phone" type="String" />

    <aura:handler name="init" value="{!this}" action="{!c.onInit}"/>

    <aura:if isTrue="{!v.isSpinner}">
        <Lightning:spinner variant="brand" size="small" />
    </aura:if>

    <Lightning:messages />

    <div class="slds-grid slds-gutters">
```

```
                <div class="slds-col slds-size_1-of-2">
                        <Lightning:input aura:id="field" name="LastName"
label="LastName" value="{!v.lastName}" required="true"/>
                        <Lightning:input aura:id="field" name="Email" label="Email"
type="email" value="{!v.email}" required="true"/>
                        <Lightning:input aura:id="field" name="Phone" type="tel"
label="Phone" value="{!v.phone}" required="true"/>
                        <Lightning:input aura:id="field" name="Company" type="text"
label="Company" value="{!v.company}" required="true"/>
                </div>
        </div>

        <div class="wrapper">
                <Lightning:button variant="brand" class="slds-m-top_small"
onclick="{!c.handleSubmit}" label="Let's Talk" />
        </div>
</aura:component>
```

The controller code shows how to add validation checks using the out-of-the-box attributes provided and the reduce JavaScript function:

```
({
    handleSubmit : function(component, event, helper) {
        var allValid = component.find('field').reduce(function (validSoFar,
inputCmp) {
                inputCmp.showHelpMessageIfInvalid();
                return validSoFar && inputCmp.get('v.validity').valid;
        }, true);
        if (allValid) {
            component.set("v.isSpinner",true);
            //call apex here
        } else {
            component.set("v.isSpinner",false);
            var toastEvent = $A.get("e.force:showToast");
            toastEvent.setParams({
                "title": 'Error',
                "message": 'Please update the invalid form entries and try
again.',
                "type": "error",
                "mode": "sticky"
            });
            toastEvent.fire();
        }
    },
})
```

Using the carousel component

The `carousel` component allows you to display the `carousel`. The component expects image URLs for the image source (prefer the URL from the static resources or the content version object). The following is a sample code snippet for the `carousel` component. Notice that it has an attribute named `src`, which accepts the URL of the image and the attributes for the header and description.

The following code illustrates how to use a Lightning `carousel` component, using images stored in the Salesforce static resource:

```
<aura:component
implements="flexipage:availableForRecordHome,flexipage:availableForAllPageT
ypes" access="global">
   <Lightning:carousel>
        <Lightning:carouselImage src = "{!$Resource.Module1}" header =
"Trailhead Module 1" description = "Trailhead Module 1" alternativeText =
"Trailhead Module 1">
    </Lightning:carouselImage>
     <Lightning:carouselImage
        src = "{!$Resource.Module2}"
        header = "Trailhead Module 2"
        description = "Trailhead Module 1"
        alternativeText = "Trailhead Module 1">
        </Lightning:carouselImage>
     <Lightning:carouselImage
        src = "{!$Resource.Module3}"
        header = "Trailhead Module 3"
        description = "Trailhead Module 3"
        alternativeText = "Trailhead Module 3">
     </Lightning:carouselImage>
   </Lightning:carousel>
  </aura:component>
```

Summary

Lightning Data Service and Lightning base components allow designers and developers to accelerate the development cycle. You must look into the base component library carefully, to see if there are any out-of-the-box components that you can leverage to achieve your business requirements, before deciding on a completely customized approach. Custom components allow for flexibility, and you should only build these components if you find that the base components do not meet your needs, in terms of performance or UI.

In the next chapter, we will explore how we can use third-party JavaScript libraries inside Lightning components. We will also go over some of the factors that you should consider when integrating third-party libraries inside Lightning components.

7
Using External JavaScript Libraries in Lightning Components

Lightning Component framework has a rich set of JavaScript APIs that you can use to build client-side logic. However, there are a lot of open source libraries and frameworks that provide rich functionalities but can take a considerable amount of effort to rewrite using Lightning Component framework's native JavaScript APIs. One example of such a situation is if you are looking to build charts with Salesforce data, then building all the CSS and client-side JavaScript from scratch can consume a lot of time. Instead, you can import libraries such as **ChartJs** (`https://www.ChartJs.Org/`), **HighCharts** (`https://www.highcharts.com/`), or D3 (`https://github.com/d3/d3/wiki/Gallery`) to meet charting requirements with minimal code and without having to engineer everything from scratch.

Another example is using libraries such as jQuery to make client-side HTTP callouts. Similarly, if you already have a single-page application built using frameworks such as React or Angular, you can use the `Lightning:container` component to securely host your single-page application. Not all open source JavaScript libraries will be compatible with Lightning Components because of the Salesforce Locker Service that is in place for Lightning Components, to provide additional security. Therefore some libraries may require some manipulations before you can get them working under Locker Service.

The aim of this chapter is to show how to integrate external third-party libraries inside Lightning Components and test to make sure they work under Locker Service. We will be taking some well known third-party libraries such as jQuery, ChartJs, MomentJs, and many more to demonstrate the approach of using external libraries inside Lightning Components.

In this chapter, we will cover the following topics:

- Using third-party JavaScript libraries in Lightning Components
- Using the `ltng:require` tag
- Creating a Locker Service-compliant JavaScript bundle using webpack
- Examples of building custom components using ChartJs and MomentJs
- Rendering a React application in a Lightning Component using a Lightning:container

Third-party JavaScript libraries in Lightning Components

Salesforce Lightning Component framework provides the `ltng:require` tag, which allows you to add one or more JavaScript files referenced from Salesforce static resources to Lightning Components. When you use the `ltng:require` tag, the JavaScript loaded has the ability to manipulate the DOM within the component's boundaries.

In this section, we will take a third-party JavaScript library called `flipclock.js` to build a Lightning Component that displays a `flipclock`. Note that `flipclock.js` is completely compatible with locker and hence we do not need any modifications to the original library source code. Later, in the *Creating a Locker Service-compliant JavaScript bundle using webpack* section, we will take an example where libraries are not compatible with locker and understand the general process to make them compatible with locker.

Before we deep dive into its usage, let's look at some of the attributes and events provided by the `ltng:require` tag.

Attributes

The following table shows the definition of each of the attributes available on the `ltng:require` component:

Attribute name	Attribute type	Description
body	Component[]	The body of the component. In markup, this is everything in the body of the tag.
scripts	String[]	The set of scripts that will be loaded in dependency order.
styles	String[]	The set of style sheets that will be loaded in dependency order.

Events

The following table shows the definition of each of the events available on
the `ltng:require` component:

Event Name	Event Type	Description
afterScriptsLoaded	COMPONENT	Fired when `ltng:require` has loaded all scripts listed in `ltng:require.scripts`
beforeLoadingResources	COMPONENT	Fired before `ltng:require` starts loading resources

Integrating a third-party library into Lightning Components

In this section, we will take a third-party JavaScript library, `flipclock.js` (http://
FlipClock.js.com/), and build a Lightning Component that displays a clock and can be
used as a timer.

The example that we will be using to build a Lightning Component is shown in the
following code snippet:

```
<html>
  <head>
    <link rel="stylesheet" href="../compiled/flipclock.css">

    <script
src="http://ajax.googleapis.com/ajax/libs/jquery/1.10.2/jquery.min.js"></sc
ript>

    <script src="../compiled/flipclock.js"></script>
  </head>
  <body>
    <div class="clock" style="margin:2em;"></div>

    <script type="text/javascript">
      var clock;

      $(document).ready(function() {
        clock = $('.clock').FlipClock({
          clockFace: 'TwentyFourHourClock'
        });
      });
    </script>

  </body>
```

```
</html>
```

We are going to approach this step by step, and these steps apply to integrating any third-party libraries into a Lightning Component:

1. Create a static resource hosting a third-party library: The first step is to download the library to your local machine and upload it to static resource. Note that due to the Content Security Policy, you cannot use JavaScript hosted on CDN inside Lightning Components and *it is always recommended to upload to static resource*. Any dependent JavaScript should be referred to from the static resource and can be loaded in order. The `scripts` attribute allows us to load multiple JavaScript files in order. In our case, the `flipclock.js` requires the jQuery library to be loaded beforehand. Also, it is recommended to use a zipped folder that can hold JavaScript and CSS assets. For this project, download the ZIP file that needs to be uploaded from static resource available at `https://github.com/PacktPublishing/Learning-Salesforce- Lightning-Application-Development/blob/master/chapter7/libraries/flipclock.zip`.

2. Use the `ltng:require` tag and leverage the `afterScriptsLoaded` event to load the JavaScript files and styles. The following component code shows the use of the `ltng:require` component:

```
<aura:component
implements="force:appHostable,flexipage:availableForAllPageTypes"
access="global" >

    <ltng:require styles="{!$Resource.flipClock +
'/flipclock/flipclock.css'}" scripts="{!join(',',
$Resource.flipClock + '/flipclock/jquery-1.8.3.js',
$Resource.flipClock + '/flipclock/flipclock.js')}"
afterScriptsLoaded="{!c.afterScriptsLoaded}" />

    <div class="clock" style="margin:2em;">

    </div>
</aura:component>
```

3. Use third-party JavaScript functions and code in the `afterScriptsLoaded` attribute. Note that the `afterScriptsLoaded` function ensures that the DOM is loaded and ready. You can compare this to the `$document.ready(function(){})` call. The controller code is as follows:

```
({
    afterScriptsLoaded : function(component, event, helper) {
        var clock;
```

```
clock = $('.clock').FlipClock({
  clockFace: 'TwentyFourHourClock'
});
    }
})
```

4. You can test the clock by creating a test app with the following code snippet:

```
<aura:application >
    <c:flipClock/>
</aura:application>
```

5. If you got the clock working, the URL for the test application, once previewed, should be as shown in the following screenshot:

Note that since this is a Lightning Component, you can also drag this component onto any record view.

Integrating the Select2 JavaScript library into Lightning Components

Let's take another open source JavaScript library, Select2 (`https://select2.org/`), which provides functionality to autocomplete and allow the user to add multiple selections to an input.

The source code for this library can be downloaded from the Select2 Git repository (`https://github.com/select2/select2/releases`).

The example HTML code to integrate Select2, giving us the ability to add multiple choices to the input, is as follows:

```html
<html>
  <head>
    <link
href="https://cdnjs.cloudflare.com/ajax/libs/select2/4.0.6-rc.0/css/select2
.min.css" rel="stylesheet" type="text/css">
    <script type="text/javascript" src="jquery.js"></script>
    <script type="text/javascript"
src="https://cdnjs.cloudflare.com/ajax/libs/select2/4.0.6-rc.0/js/select2.m
in.js"></script>
  </head>
  <body>
    <select multiple="multiple" id="states" class="js-example-basic-
multiple">
      <option value="AL">Alabama</option>
      ...
      <option value="WY">Wyoming</option>
    </select>
    <input type="button" id="submit" value="Submit">click
    <script>
      $(document).ready(function() {
        $('.js-example-basic-multiple').select2();
      });
    </script>
  </body>
</html>
```

To integrate this library with Lightning Components, we will follow the same three steps listed in the previous section:

1. Create a static resource hosting third-party library: download the ZIP file used inside the Salesforce static resource from the git link provided at `https://` `github.com/PacktPublishing/Learning-Salesforce- Lightning-Application-Development/blob/master/chapter7/libraries/Select2.zip`.

2. Use the `ltng:require` tag and leverage the `afterScriptsLoaded` event to load the JavaScript files and styles. The component code is shown in the following code snippet. Let's name the component file `select2.cmp`:

   ```html
   <!--select2.cmp-->
   <aura:component
   implements="force:appHostable,flexipage:availableForAllPageType
   s,flexipage:availableForRecordHome,force:hasRecordId">
       <aura:attribute name="selectedStates" type="String[]"
   default="[]" />
   ```

```
<ltng:require styles="{!$Resource.Select2 +
'/Select2/select2.min.css'}" scripts="{!join(',',
$Resource.Select2 + '/Select2/jquery-1.8.3.js',
$Resource.Select2 + '/Select2/select2.min.js')}"
afterScriptsLoaded="{!c.afterScriptsLoaded}" />
    <select id="states" class="js-example-basic-multiple"
name="states[]" multiple="multiple" style="display:block;width:
100%">
        <option value="AL">Alabama</option>
        <option value="AK">Alaska</option>
        <option value="AZ">Arizona</option>
        <option value="AR">Arkansas</option>
        <option value="CA">California</option>
        <option value="CO">Colorado</option>
        <option value="CT">Connecticut</option>
        <option value="DE">Delaware</option>
        <option value="DC">District Of Columbia</option>
        <option value="FL">Florida</option>
        <option value="GA">GeOrgia</option>
        <option value="HI">Hawaii</option>
        <option value="ID">Idaho</option>
        <option value="IL">Illinois</option>
        <option value="IN">Indiana</option>
        <option value="IA">Iowa</option>
        <option value="KS">Kansas</option>
        <option value="KY">Kentucky</option>
        <option value="LA">Louisiana</option>
        <option value="ME">Maine</option>
        <option value="MD">Maryland</option>
        <option value="MA">Massachusetts</option>
        <option value="MI">Michigan</option>
        <option value="MN">Minnesota</option>
        <option value="MS">Mississippi</option>
        <option value="MO">Missouri</option>
        <option value="MT">Montana</option>
        <option value="NE">Nebraska</option>
        <option value="NV">Nevada</option>
        <option value="NH">New Hampshire</option>
        <option value="NJ">New Jersey</option>
        <option value="NM">New Mexico</option>
        <option value="NY">New York</option>
        <option value="NC">North Carolina</option>
        <option value="ND">North Dakota</option>
        <option value="OH">Ohio</option>
        <option value="OK">Oklahoma</option>
        <option value="OR">Oregon</option>
        <option value="PA">Pennsylvania</option>
        <option value="RI">Rhode Island</option>
```

```
                    <option value="SC">South Carolina</option>
                    <option value="SD">South Dakota</option>
                    <option value="TN">Tennessee</option>
                    <option value="TX">Texas</option>
                    <option value="UT">Utah</option>
                    <option value="VT">Vermont</option>
                    <option value="VA">Virginia</option>
                    <option value="WA">Washington</option>
                    <option value="WV">West Virginia</option>
                    <option value="WI">Wisconsin</option>
                    <option value="WY">Wyoming</option>
            </select>
            <div class="slds-align_absolute-center" style="height:
        5rem; ">
                    < Lightning:button variant="brand" label="Display
        Selected States" onclick="{!c.handleClick}" />
            </div>
            Selected States
            <ul class="slds-has-dividers_around-space">
                    <aura:iteration var="state"
        items="{!v.selectedStates}">
                        <li class="slds-item">{!state}</li>
                    </aura:iteration>
            </ul>
        </aura:component>
```

3. Use third-party JavaScript functions and code in the afterScriptsLoaded function. The controller code will be the code that's inside the <Script> tags:

```
({
    afterScriptsLoaded : function(component, event, helper) {
        $('.js-example-basic-multiple').select2();
    },

    handleClick : function(component, event, helper) {
        var selectedItems = $("#states").val();
        component.set("v.selectedStates",selectedItems);
        console.log(selectedItems);
    }
})
```

Note that the handleClick function is called from the button, retrieves the selected values from the input, and stores them in the Lightning attribute.

Create a small test app to test this component. The test app's code is as follows:

```
<aura:application extends="force:slds">
    <c:select2 />
</aura:application>
```

A functional component screen would look like the following screenshot:

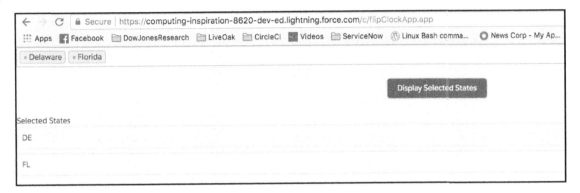

Integrating the MomentJs library into Lightning Components

MomentJs is an open source library that provides utility functions to handle date and time. The library works well with Salesforce Locker Service.

Here is an example component showing how to integrate MomentJs into Lightning Components. The steps to integrate the library are as follows:

1. Create a static resource hosting MomentJs: The source code for the library can be obtained from `https://MomentJs.com/downloads/Moment.Js`. Download and create a static resource file named MomentJs.

2. Use the `ltng:require` tag and leverage the `afterScriptsLoaded` event to load the JavaScript files and styles. The following is simple component code that demonstrates the use of the `ltng:require` tag:

```
<aura:component
implements="force:appHostable,flexipage:availableForAllPageTypes,fl
exipage:availableForRecordHome,force:hasRecordId" access="global" >
<ltng:require scripts="{!$Resource.MomentJs}"
afterScriptsLoaded="{!c.afterScriptsLoaded}" />
```

3. Use third-party JavaScript functions and code in the
   `afterScriptsLoaded` function. The controller file code to test the various
   functions provided by the library is as shown in the following code snippet:

```
({
afterScriptsLoaded : function(component, event, helper) {
    console.log(moment().format('MMMM Do YYYY, h:mm:ss a')); //
July 11th 2017, 11:23:19 am
    console.log(moment().format('dddd')); // Tuesday
    console.log(moment().format("MMM Do YY")); // Jul 11th 17
    console.log(moment().format('YYYY [escaped] YYYY')); // 2017
escaped 2017
    console.log(moment().format()); // 2017-07-11T11:23:19-04:00
    console.log(moment("20111031", "YYYYMMDD").fromNow()); // 6
years ago
    console.log(moment("20120620", "YYYYMMDD").fromNow()); // 5
years ago
    console.log(moment().startOf('day').fromNow()); // 11 hours ago
    console.log(moment().endOf('day').fromNow()); // in 13 hours
    console.log(moment().startOf('hour').fromNow()); // 27 minutes
ago
    console.log(moment().subtract(10, 'days').calendar()); //
07/01/2017
    console.log(moment().subtract(6, 'days').calendar()); // Last
Wednesday at 11:28 AM
    console.log(moment().subtract(3, 'days').calendar()); // Last
Saturday at 11:28 AM
    console.log(moment().subtract(1, 'days').calendar()); //
Yesterday at 11:28 AM
    console.log(moment().calendar()); // Today at 11:28 AM
    console.log(moment().add(1, 'days').calendar()); // Tomorrow at
11:28 AM
    console.log(moment().add(3, 'days').calendar()); // Friday at
11:28 AM
    console.log(moment().add(10, 'days').calendar()); // 07/21/2017
    console.log(moment.locale()); // en
    console.log(moment().format('LT')); // 11:29 AM
    console.log(moment().format('LTS')); // 11:29:23 AM
    console.log(moment().format('L')); // 07/11/2017
    console.log(moment().format('l')); // 7/11/2017
    console.log(moment().format('LL')); // July 11, 2017
    console.log(moment().format('ll')); // Jul 11, 2017
    console.log(moment().format('LLL')); // July 11, 2017 11:29 AM
    console.log(moment().format('lll')); // Jul 11, 2017 11:29 AM
    console.log(moment().format('LLLL')); // Tuesday, July 11, 2017
11:29 AM
    console.log(moment().format('llll'));
    var now = moment();
```

```
            console.log(now);
            var day = moment(1318781876406);
             console.log(day);
            }
        })
```

4. Monitor `console.log` from the Chrome developer **Console** to confirm the library is functioning inside Lightning Components. If the library is functioning, the output will resemble the following screenshot:

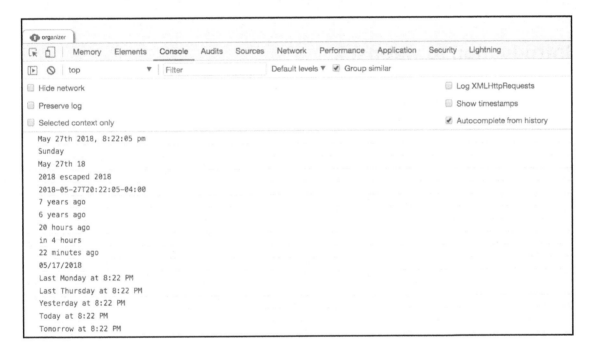

Creating a Locker Service-compliant JavaScript bundle using webpack

So far, we have been lucky that our JavaScript libraries have worked perfectly under Locker Service. There are libraries that may not work under Locker Service due to their use of unsupported elements. All the window, Document, and DOM APIs that are supported by locker are listed at `http://documentation.auraframework.Org/lockerApiTest/index. app?aura.mode=DEV`.

If you are using the `this` keyword in JavaScript for window reference, then note that the Lightning Component framework does not support it, and has to explicitly use window.

Webpack is a module bundler that allows us to transform the source code and bundle it. We can use the power of webpack to create a static resource file that is optimized and takes care of unsupported references in the library. Before we deep dive into how to use the webpack bundler, let's dive into the basics of webpack in the following section.

Introduction to webpack

Webpack is a static bundler for JavaScript-based applications.

Your JavaScript application may have multiple files, along with dependencies specified using ES2015 `import` statements (`https://developer.mozilla.Org/en-US/docs/Web/JavaScript/Reference/Statements/import`), using CommonJS modules that use `require` statements (`http://www.commonjs.Org/specs/modules/1.0/`), or using **Asynchronous Module Definition** (**AMD**) (`https://github.com/amdjs/amdjs-api/blob/master/AMD.md`). Webpack takes care of bundling multiple files with dependencies into one or more resource files.

Webpack consists of a config file that one can be configured to specify the entry point of the app and output directory. It uses loaders to pre-process files in different formats into a common bundle, and uses plugins to do asset management, environment variable injection, and optimization. In the next section, we will take a look into a sample config file and how each of these can be configured in the webpack config file.

Entry

The `webpack.config.js` file will have an `entry` object to provide an entry point to the app. The entry object configuration is as follows. The following code means our starting point for the dependency graph is the `index.js` file:

```
// source path for the code
const srcPath = path.join(__dirname, 'src')
..
...
// where our src file is present and sets context for entry
context: srcPath,
// single entry point
entry: {
    app: './index.js',
```

```
}
```

Output

The output object specifies where the resulting file, after processing and bundling, is stored:

```
const srcPath = path.join(__dirname, 'src'),
  distPath = path.join(__dirname, '../force-
app/main/default/staticresources'),
  extractCSS = new ExtractTextPlugin('styles.resource');

. . . . . . . . . . .

output: {
    // output file into SFDX staticresources location
    path: distPath,
    filename: 'app.resource',
    libraryTarget: 'window',
    library: 'StaticResource'
}
```

The preceding config means the output bundle will be stored in the SFDX static resource folder and the name of the file will be `app.resource`. When a module is generated, the entire source code is stored in the window object with a property named `"StaticResource"`, as shown in the following code snippet:

```
window["StaticResource"] =
/******/ (function(modules) { // webpackBootstrap
. . . . . .
/***/ })
```

Loaders

Loaders allow you to pre-process and transform files as you load them. An example would be converting TypeScript to JavaScript. Let's see an example snippet from the `webpack.config.js` file:

```
const path = require('path');

const config = {
  output: {
    filename: 'my-first-webpack.bundle.js'
  },
  module: {
    rules: [
```

```
            { test: /\.txt$/, use: 'raw-loader' }
        ]
    }
};

module.exports = config;
```

The preceding code snippet tells webpack to process all the text files using a loader named raw-loader, and loads raw UTF-8 content from the file.

Loaders are essentially node modules that is a function like the following one, and the source parameter consists of all the source code as a string:

```
const loaderUtils = require('loader-utils');

module.exports = function CustomLoader (source) {
    return source;
}
```

There are already predefined loaders that you can use in your projects. The list is located at https://webpack.js.Org/loaders/.

For Locker Service, you can write a custom loader to unpolyfill window properties or DOM properties that need to be protected. We will explore this when we see an example of fixing a broken Locker Service library in the *Integrating choices.js into Lightning Components* section.

Plugins

Plugins are the heart of webpack. Let's take an example of a simple webpack.config.js file to understand plugin use:

```
const HtmlWebpackPlugin = require('html-webpack-plugin'); //installed via
npm
const webpack = require('webpack'); //to access built-in plugins

const config = {
  module: {
    rules: [
      { test: /\.txt$/, use: 'raw-loader' }
    ]
  },
  plugins: [
    new HtmlWebpackPlugin({template: './src/index.html'})
  ]
};

module.exports = config;
```

In this example, we are using `HtmlWebpackPlugin`, which creates an HTML file to serve a webpack bundle. It uses an HTML template stored in the `src/index.html` path.

There are a lot of out-of-the-box plugins available for webpack. They are listed at `https://webpack.js.Org/plugins/`.

Now that we understand the basics of webpack, we are ready to explore a library that does not work under Locker Service, and we will use webpack to fix this. We will explore how to structure our JS-heavy project in SFDX and use bundlers such as webpack to generate an ES5 equivalent resource, using a transpiler such as the `babel-loader`.

 The Lightning Component framework does not support ES6 features completely, so if we are adopting a third-party library, we can use the babel transpiler to make it equivalent to ES5.

Integrating choices.js into Lightning Components

Choices.js serves as a great example to understand how a third-party library might not work under Locker Service, and how to make it compatible with Locker Service. To understand this, let's take the choices.js vanilla code and integrate it into Lightning Components.

The choices.js library can be downloaded from `https://github.com/jshjohnson/Choices/blob/master/assets/scripts/dist/choices.js`.

The Lightning Component code is as follows:

```
<aura:component >
    <ltng:require styles="{!join(',',$Resource.ChoicesJS +
'/choicesJS/base.min.css',$Resource.ChoicesJS +
'/choicesJS/choices.min.css')}" scripts="{!$Resource.ChoicesJS +
'/choicesJS/choices.min.js'}"
afterScriptsLoaded="{!c.afterScriptsLoaded}"/>
    <div id="divId">
        <input type="text" aura:id="choices" />
    </div>
</aura:component>
```

The controller code is as follows:

```
({
    afterScriptsLoaded : function(component, event, helper) {
        const choices = new Choices(component.find('choices').getElement(),
    {
```

```
        items: [ 'India', 'Australlia', 'China' ]
    })
  }
})
```

When this is tested, the component throws an error as follows:

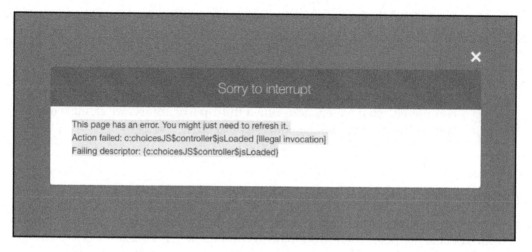

Inspecting the source code of choices.js, we see that the root causes of failure is because of the use of polyfill for custom events for the window variable. The following screenshot shows the code that breaks under Locker Service. The code can be looked at in detail at https://github.com/jshjohnson/Choices/blob/master/assets/scripts/src/lib/polyfills.js:

```
114
115    function CustomEvent (event, params) {
116      params = params || {
117          bubbles: false,
118          cancelable: false,
119          detail: undefined
120        };
121      var evt = document.createEvent('CustomEvent');
122      evt.initCustomEvent(event, params.bubbles, params.cancelable, params.detail);
123      return evt;
124    }
125
126    CustomEvent.prototype = window.Event.prototype;
127
128    window.CustomEvent = CustomEvent;
```

Structuring a JS-heavy project in Salesforce DX

For a JS-heavy project, it is recommended to keep a separate folder in the SFDX project. Let's call this folder `staticresources-src`. This folder holds all JS assets, including the `webpack.config.js` file, `package.json`, the `src` directory for `index.js`, and the `.eslintrc.yml` file. The following screenshot shows the folder structure with a `staticresources-src` folder for hosting all JavaScript and JavaScript build-related files:

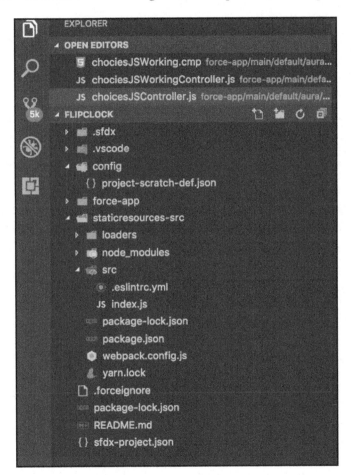

Creating a Locker Service-compatible bundle with webpack

Note that the tools we use here include webpack 3.0, npm, and Node.js. To run the project, it is assumed that your machine has the latest Version of Node.js, npm, and webpack 3.0 installed.

At the time of writing this book, my npm Version is 5.6.0, Node.js Version is 9.50, and webpack Version is 3.8.1.

If you do not have them, then install them using brew for macOS with the following commands.

For Node.js and npm, use the following:

```
brew install node
```

To install webpack, use the following. The following command installs it locally for a specific project and version:

```
npm install --save-dev webpack@3.8.1
```

Let's take a step-by-step look at how to use an ES6 JavaScript open source plugin, make it locker-compliant, and build it into a resource bundle that can be used inside Lightning Components:

1. Create an index.js file that imports the choices.js library: You will need a package.json file first that has all the node modules for dependencies and the dev dependencies for the project. The package.json is as follows:

```
{
    "name": "choicesJS",
    "version": "1.0.0",
    "main": "src/index.js",
    "author": "Mohith Shrivastava",
    "license": "BSD-3-Clause",
    "devDependencies": {
        "@Salesforce/eslint-plugin-aura": "^1.0.0",
        "babel-core": "^6.26.0",
        "babel-loader": "^7.1.2",
        "babel-preset-env": "^1.6.1",
        "css-loader": "^0.28.7",
        "eslint": "^4.10.0",
        "eslint-loader": "^1.9.0",
        "extract-text-webpack-plugin": "^3.0.2",
        "file-loader": "^1.1.5",
        "imports-loader": "^0.7.1",
        "loader-utils": "^1.1.0",
        "url-loader": "^0.6.2",
        "webpack": "^3.8.1"
    },
    "dependencies": {
```

```
      "choices.js": "^3.0.2"
    },
    "scripts": {
      "build": "webpack --config webpack.config.js"
    }
    "browserlist": "last 2 versions, ie 11"
}
```

Now, the `index.js` file will be in the `src` directory as following. We use TypeScript here, and later you will see our webpack is configured to transpile to ES5:

```
import 'choices.js/assets/styles/css/choices.css';
import Choices from 'choices.js';
export { Choices };
```

2. Create a webpack config file: The complete webpack config file is located at `https://github.com/PacktPublishing/Learning-Salesforce- Lightning-Application-Development/blob/master/chapter7/staticresources-src/webpack.config.js`. We will take a step-by-step look at it:

   1. The entry point in `webpack.config.js` will be `index.js`:

      ```
      // this is where our source code is stored
      context: srcPath,
      // single entry point
      entry: {
          app: './index.js',
      }
      ```

   2. Output: The output will be in the `staticresources` folder of the SFDX project, so the code snippet to configure it is as follows:

      ```
      output: {
          // output file into SFDX staticresources location
          path: distPath,
          filename: 'app.resource',
          libraryTarget: 'window',
          library: 'StaticResource'
      }
      ```

3. Loaders: We are using the following loaders that are pre-built:

Loaders	Description
babel-loader	Transpile ES2015 to ES5.
url-loader	Load all CSS files and compile them into a single artifact, styles.resource.
import-loader	To switch off AMD by using define as false. Locker does not support the AMD format.
css-loader	Load all pictures and fonts and embed them into styles.resource.

We also have a custom loader that's built to remove the polyfill on the window object so that the library works under Locker Service.

The code for the custom loader is as follows, and is placed in a folder named loader:

```
const loaderUtils = require('loader-utils');

const lockerObjects = [
    'CustomEvent',
    'Event',
    'Storage',
    'Object',
    'Node',
    'Notification',
    'RTCPeerConnection',
    'CanvasRenderingContext2D',
    'Navigator',
    'HTMLIFrameElement',
    'HTMLScriptElement',
];


module.exports = function UnpolyfillLoader (source) {
    const header = 'const _lockerObjects = { ' +
        lockerObjects.map(o => `'${o}':
window.${o}`).join(', ') +
        ' };\n';
    const footer = '\n' +
        lockerObjects.map(o => `window.${o} =
_lockerObjects.${o}`).join(';\n') +
        '\n';
    return header + source + footer;
}
```

The following code shows how webpack is configured to indicate the loaders:

```
const webpack = require('webpack'),
path = require('path'),
ExtractTextPlugin = require('extract-text-webpack-plugin');

const srcPath = path.join(__dirname, 'src'),
  distPath = path.join(__dirname, '../force-
app/main/default/staticresources'),
  extractCSS = new ExtractTextPlugin('styles.resource');

module.exports = {
module: {
    rules: [
        // Lint our ES6 code and transpile it into ES5 as a
part of app.resource
        {
            test: /\.js$/,
            exclude: /node_modules/,
            use: [{
                loader: 'babel-loader',
                options: {
                    presets: ['env'],
                }
            },
            { loader: "eslint-loader" },
            ]
        },
        // Load choices.js, remove polyfills' effects, and
include it into app.resource
        {
            test: /\/choices\.js\/assets\/scripts\/dist/,
            use: [ 'unpolyfill-loader', 'imports-
loader?define=>false' ],
        },
        // Load all CSS files and compile them in a single
artifact styles.resource
        {
            test: /\.css$/,
            use: ExtractTextPlugin.extract({
                use: 'css-loader',
            }),
        },
        // Load all pictures and fonts and embed them into
styles.resource
        {
            test: /\.(woff2?|ttf|eot|jpe?g|png|gif|svg)$/,
```

```
            use: 'url-loader',
        },
    ],
},
// resolve loaders from node_modules and our newly created
"loaders" folder
resolveLoader: {
    modules: [ 'node_modules', path.resolve(__dirname,
'loaders') ],
},
```

4. Plugins: All the plugins that are needed are shown in the following snippet:

```
resolve: {
    modules: ["node_modules"],
},
plugins: [
    new webpack.NoEmitOnErrorsPlugin(),
    extractCSS,
]
```

3. Use the `eslint` plugin `aura` for finding any linting and code issues. The `npm` module is located at `https://www.npmjs.com/package/@Salesforce/eslint-plugin-aura`. Create a `.eslintrc.yml` file for the project in the `src` folder with the following code snippet:

```
plugins:
  - "@Salesforce/eslint-plugin-aura"
extends:
  - "plugin:@Salesforce/eslint-plugin-aura/recommended"
parserOptions:
  ecmaVersion: 6
  sourceType: module
```

4. Build the bundle using the `npm build` command: Running `npm build` runs webpack and produces bundles named `app.resource` and `styles.resource`:

```
npm build
```

5. Include the library in Lightning Components using the `ltng:require` tag, and load `scripts` and `styles`. The working code is as follows:

```
<aura:component >
    <ltng:require styles="{!$Resource.styles}"
scripts="{!$Resource.app}" afterScriptsLoaded="{!c.jsLoaded}"
/>
```

```
        <div>
            <input type="text" aura:id="choices" />
        </div>
    </aura:component>
```

The controller code is as follows:

```
({
    jsLoaded : function(component, event, helper) {
        console.log(window);
        console.log(window.StaticResource);
        const choices = new
StaticResource.Choices(component.find('choices').getElement(),
{
                items: [ 'India', 'Australlia', 'China' ]
        })
    }
})
```

If your code is working, the component on the test app will look like the following screenshot:

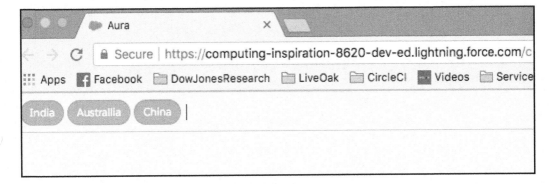

ChartJs in Lightning Components

ChartJs is an open source JavaScript library that allows us to create various types of charts, such as line, bar, pie, and stacked charts, and many more. The library can be explored at `https://www.ChartJs.Org/`.

In this section, we will see a simple example of how to include the ChartJs library in Lightning Components and build visualizations with a dataset.

The steps to integrate this library are the same as those in the preceding sections. The ChartJs library works well under Locker Service so there are no extra transformations required to integrate it.

The steps to create a Lightning Component with ChartJs are as follows:

1. Create a static resource hosting the ChartJs library; download the ChartJs library from this link: `https://cdnjs.cloudflare.com/ajax/libs/Chart.js/2.7.2/ Chart.bundle.min.js`.

2. Leverage the `ltng:require` tag and use the `afterScriptsLoaded` attribute to load the JavaScript files. The component code is as follows. Let's name the component file `ChartJsDemo`:

```
<aura:component>
    <ltng:require scripts="{!$Resource.ChartJs}"
afterScriptsLoaded="{!c.afterScriptsLoaded}"/>
    <div class="chart-container">
        <div class="pie-chart-container">
            <canvas aura:id="piechart" id="piechart"/>
        </div>
    </div>
</aura:component>
```

3. Use third-party JavaScript functions and code in the `afterScriptsLoaded` attribute:

```
({
    afterScriptsLoaded : function(component, event, helper) {
        var ctx =
document.getElementById("piechart").getContext('2d');
        var data = {
            datasets: [{
                data: [10, 20, 30],
                backgroundColor: [
                    "Red",
                    "Green",
                    "#E9967A"
                ]
            }],
            // These labels appear in the legend and in the
tooltips when hovering different arcs
            labels: [
                'Closed Cases',
                'In Progress Cases',
                'New Cases'
            ]
```

```
    };
    var myPieChart = new Chart(ctx,{
        type: 'pie',
        data: data
    });


    }
})
```

4. The component will render as shown in the following screenshot:

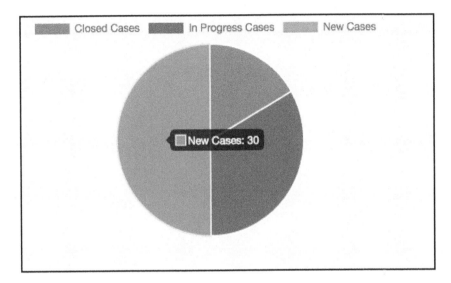

Making client-side calls to external sites using JavaScript

We can use JavaScript to make client-side calls to a third-party website, provided the site is listed as CSP. It's always recommended to use the server-side Apex to make HTTP calls; however, with CSP configured in Salesforce you can make client-side calls. CSP ensures security against various web vulnerabilities.

The following example shows how can we use the JavaScript XMLHttpRequest (`https://developer.mozilla.Org/en-US/docs/Web/API/XMLHttpRequest`) to make `GET` requests. Note you can use this approach to make `POST` as well as `PUT` requests to any API that's HTTPS and CSP-protected.

In this example, we are making an API call to a public API that gives us the latest currency rates against EUR. You can read about the API at `https://exchangeratesapi.io/`.

We will be working against a simple `GET` request, as shown in the following Postman screenshot:

The Lightning Component shows how to use the `XMLHttpRequest` object in the Lightning Component. Observe we use `$A.getCallback()` to asynchronously execute this.

The important step here is to understand that you will need to create a CSP setting in Salesforce.

To create a CSP setting, the navigation path in the setup menu is **Setup** | **Security** | **CSP Trusted Sites**. This is shown in the following screenshot:

The following screenshot shows the values you will need to enter into the **CSP Trusted Site** record to connect to `ExchangeRateAPI`:

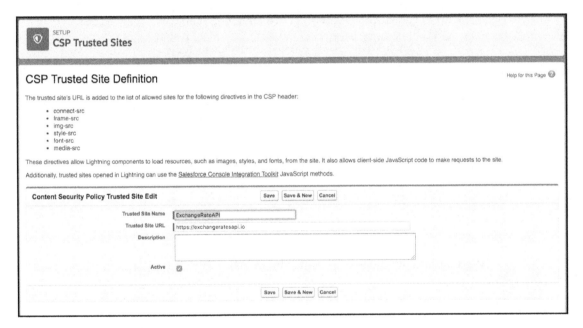

The `component` markup is as follows:

```
<aura:component>
    <aura:attribute name="exchangeRateData" type="List" default="[]"/>
    <aura:handler name="init" value="{!this}" action="{!c.doInit}"/>
    <div class="slds-box slds-align_absolute-center" style="height: 5rem;">
        Base Currency for Result is in <b> EUR </b>
    </div>
    <br/>
```

```
<div>
    <table class="slds-table slds-table_bordered slds-table_cell-buffer">
        <thead>
            <tr class="slds-text-title_caps">
                <th scope="col">
                    <div class="slds-truncate" title="Currency">
                        <b>Currency</b>
                    </div>
                </th>
                <th scope="col">
                    <div class="slds-truncate" title="Rate">
                        <b>Rate</b>
                    </div>
                </th>
            </tr>
        </thead>
        <tbody>
            <aura:iteration items="{!v.exchangeRateData}" var="item">
                <tr>
                    <th scope="row" data-label="Currency">
                        <div class="slds-truncate"
title="Currency">{!item.currency}</div>
                    </th>
                    <td data-label="Rate">
                        <div class="slds-truncate"
title="Rate">{!item.rate}</div>
                    </td>
                </tr>
            </aura:iteration>
        </tbody>
    </table>
</div>
</aura:component>
```

 We tabulate the data rows using the HTML table.

The controller code is as shown in the following code snippet:

```
({
    doInit : function(component, event, helper) {
        var xhttp = new XMLHttpRequest();
        xhttp.onreadystatechange = $A.getCallback(function() {
            if (this.readyState === 4) { // DONE
                if (xhttp.status === 200) {
                    var response = JSON.parse(xhttp.responseText);
```

```
                    var data = [];
                    for (var value in response.rates) {
                        var dataItem = {};
                        dataItem.currency = value;
                        dataItem.rate = response.rates[value];
                        data.push(dataItem);
                    }
                    component.set("v.exchangeRateData",data);
                }
                else {
                    console.log('Request failed. Returned status of ' +
xhttp.status);
                }
            }
        });
        xhttp.open("GET", "https://exchangeratesapi.io/api/latest");
        xhttp.send(null);
    }
})
```

The component will render the table with the results shown in the following screenshot:

Base Currency for Result is inEUR	
CURRENCY	RATE
AUD	1.5366
BGN	1.9558
BRL	4.3415
CAD	1.5058
CHF	1.1517
CNY	7.4174
CZK	25.907
DKK	7.4429
GBP	0.87143
HKD	9.0681
HRK	7.3903
HUF	320.05

Communication between the Lightning main frame and iframe

Your Lightning app may also include applications that are designed in Visualforce. Visualforce was used in the Salesforce classic experience before Lightning existed.

In this section, we will explore how can we communicate between a Visualforce iframe and a Lightning Component. Note that we have used Visualforce here, but technically one could use this approach to communicate between a Lightning window and any iframe loaded in the Lightning page. Use only unsecured data between frames, since the postMessages API that we use to communicate does not offer security.

This technique uses the postMessage API to do the communicating. You can read about postMessage at https://developer.mozilla.Org/en-US/docs/Web/API/Window/postMessage.

Communication from the Visualforce page to the Lightning Component

We will use the following code snippets to demonstrate this use case.

The Visualforce code is as follows. Observe the highlighted code where we post the message to the parent domain (in this case, the Lightning domain). We have obtained the domain dynamically using the Apex controller code that is linked to the Visualforce page. Let's name the Visualforce page testVF:

```
<apex:page controller="vfController">

    <apex:slds/>

    <input id="message" type="text"/>
    <button onclick="sendToLC()">Send to LC</button>

  <script>
     var lexOrigin = "https://{!JSENCODE(SalesforceDomain)}.
Lightning.force.com";

     console.log(lexOrigin);

     function sendToLC() {
         var message = document.getElementById("message").value;
         console.log('Message To Send..'+message);
         parent.postMessage(message, lexOrigin);
```

```
    }

  </script>

</apex:page>
```

The following code is for an Apex controller that gets the domain to the Visualforce code:

```
public with sharing class vfController {

    public String getSalesforceDomain(){
        return
System.Url.getSalesforceBaseURL().getHost().substringBefore('--');
    }

}
```

The Lightning Component uses a listener on the window object to listen for messages:

```
<aura:component implements="flexipage:availableForAllPageTypes"
                access="global">

    <aura:attribute name="message" type="String"/>
    <aura:attribute name="vfHost" type="String"
            default="computing-inspiration-8620-dev-ed--
c.cs62.visual.force.com"/>

    <aura:handler name="init" value="{!this}" action="{!c.doInit}"/>

    <div>
        <!-- The Visualforce page to send data to -->
        <iframe aura:id="vfFrame" src="{!'https://' + v.vfHost +
'/apex/testVF'}" />
    </div>
</aura:component>
```

The controller function is as follows. In the following code, the snippet that provides the ability to listen for messages is highlighted:

```
({

    doInit : function(component) {
        var vfOrigin = "https://" + component.get("v.vfHost");
        window.addEventListener("message", function(event) {
            if (event.origin !== vfOrigin) {
                // Not the expected origin: Reject the message!
                return;
            }
```

```
            // Handle the message
            console.log(event.data);
        }, false);
    }

})
```

Communication from the Lightning Component to the Visualforce page

In this example, we will take example code that sends a message from the Lightning Component to the Visualforce page. Note that we use the postMessage feature of JavaScript for this communication.

The code snippet for the Lightning Component is as follows:

```
<aura:component implements="flexipage:availableForAllPageTypes"
                access="global">

    <aura:attribute name="vfHost" type="String"
            default="computing-inspiration-8620-dev-ed--
c.cs62.visual.force.com"/>

    <!-- Input field for message "data" -->
    < Lightning:button label="Send to VF" onclick="{!c.sendToVF}"/>

    <div>
        <!-- The Visualforce page to send data to -->
        <iframe aura:id="vfFrame" src="{!'https://' + v.vfHost +
'/apex/testVF'}" />
    </div>
</aura:component>
```

The code for the controller is a follows:

```
({
    sendToVF : function(component, event, helper) {
        var message = component.get("v.message");
        var vfOrigin = "https://" + component.get("v.vfHost");
        var vfWindow =
component.find("vfFrame").getElement().contentWindow;
        vfWindow.postMessage(message, vfOrigin);
    }

})
```

The Visualforce page is named `testVF` and has a listener attached to its window to receive messages from the Lightning Component. The code for the page is as follows:

```
<apex:page controller="vfController">

    <apex:slds/>

<script>
    var lexOrigin = "https://{!JSENCODE(SalesforceDomain)}.
Lightning.force.com";

    console.log(lexOrigin);

    window.addEventListener("message", function(event) {
        if (event.origin !== lexOrigin) {
            // Not the expected origin: reject message!
            return;
        }
        // Handle message
        console.log(event.data);
    }, false);

</script>

</apex:page>
```

Rendering a React application in a Lightning Component using Lightning:container

The `Lightning:container` component allows us to load single-page JavaScript applications from static resources. If you have an application built using React, Angular, Vue.js, or any other framework, and want to load it inside a Salesforce Lightning Component, the quickest way would be to use the `Lightning:container` component and load the application into a static resource.

To understand how it works, let's create an HTML file with the following content and load it into a static resource named home:

```
<html>
    <head>

    </head>

    <body>
        Test Content
    </body>

</html>
```

Now, let's create a Lightning Component using the `Lightning:container`:

```
<aura:component
implements="force:appHostable,flexipage:availableForAllPageTypes,flexipage:
availableForRecordHome,force:hasRecordId,forceCommunity:availableForAllPage
Types,force: LightningQuickAction" access="global" >
    < Lightning:container src="{!$Resource.home}" />
</aura:component>
```

Once you load this component, you will see the HTML page content is displayed in an iframe in the Lightning Component.

Rendering reactApp using the LCC npm module in a Lightning Component

The previous section gave you an idea of how to use `Lightning:container`. In this section, we will explore how to build an ES6 React application, and host it inside a static resource and render it inside a Lightning Component. The app creates an account by calling an Apex class method that has all the logic to do DML on the account object.

We will be using the webpack bundler to bundle all the code and create a `bundle.js` file that is placed in the static resource.

The directory structure of your project with SFDX is shown in the following screenshot:

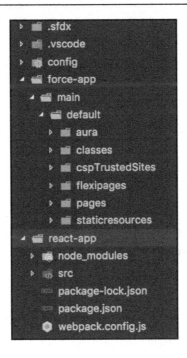

Note that all the JavaScript assets will be placed under `react-app/src`.

The static resource folder will have a `reactApp` folder that has `index.html`, slds, styles, and the `manifest.json` file. Note that all these are zipped. If you are using SFDX scratch Orgs, the static resource ZIP file is generated during execution of command:

```
sfdx force:source:push
```

Let's look into the `package.json` file in the following code snippet:

```
{
  "name": "react-app",
  "version": "1.0.0",
  "description": "",
  "main": "index.js",
  "scripts": {
    "build": "webpack"
  },
  "author": "",
  "license": "ISC",
  "devDependencies": {
    "babel-core": "^6.26.0",
    "babel-loader": "^7.1.4",
    "babel-preset-es2015": "^6.24.1",
```

```
      "babel-preset-react": "^6.24.1",
      "webpack": "^4.5.0",
      "webpack-cli": "^2.1.4"
    },
    "dependencies": {
      " Lightning-container": "^1.0.0",
      "react": "^16.3.1",
      "react-dom": "^16.3.1"
    }
  }
```

Note we are using webpack, babel for transpiling, and Lightning-container.

The Lightning-container npm module (https://www.npmjs.com/package/ Lightning-container) provides APIs to call Salesforce Apex remoting methods, and also provides the ability for Lightning Components to send messages from the iframe back to the app in the static resources.

Let's look into the webpack config file:

```
const webpack = require('webpack');
const path = require('path');

const config = {
    mode: 'development',
    entry: './src/index.js',
    output: {
        path: path.join(__dirname, '../force-
app/main/default/staticresources/reactApp'),
        filename: 'bundle.js'
    },
    module: {
        rules: [
            {
                test: /\.(js|jsx)$/,
                exclude: /node_modules/,
                loader: 'babel-loader',
                query: {
                    presets: ['es2015', 'react']
                }
            }
        ]
    }
};
module.exports = config;
```

The preceding code snippet takes all the sources from `index.js` as entries, creates a `bundle.js` in ES5 format using `babel-loader`, and places it in the `staticresource/reactApp` folder for the `reactApp`, where we have `index.html` and other assets for the application.

The code for the JavaScript is as follows. Note it uses ES6 classes and syntax, as well as JSX.

The `index.js` file is as follows:

```
import React from "react";
import ReactDOM from "react-dom";
import App from "./App";

ReactDOM.render(<App />, document.getElementById("app"));
```

The `App.js` file is as follows:

```
import React from "react";
import LCC from ' Lightning-container';

class App extends React.Component {

    constructor(props) {
        super(props);
        this.state = {
            account : {
                "Name" : "",
                "Phone" : "",
                "Website" : "",
                "Fax" : "",
            },
            accountId : ""
        }
        this.saveAccount = this.saveAccount.bind(this);
        this.onAccountNameChange = this.onAccountNameChange.bind(this);
        this.onAccountPhoneChange = this.onAccountPhoneChange.bind(this);
        this.onAccountFaxChange = this.onAccountFaxChange.bind(this);
        this.onAccountWebsiteChange =
this.onAccountWebsiteChange.bind(this);
    }

    saveAccount() {
        LCC.callApex("AccountController.saveAccount",
            this.state.account,
            (result, event) => {
                if (event.status) {
                    this.setState({accountId: result.Id });
```

```
                    var msg = {
                        action: 'openDetails',
                        id: result.Id
                    };
                    LCC.sendMessage(msg);
                    console.log(result);
                } else if (event.type === "exception") {
                    console.log(event.message + " : " + event.where);
                }
            },
            { escape: true });
    }

    onAccountNameChange(e) {
        var account = Object.assign({}, this.state.account);
        account.Name = e.target.value;
        this.setState({account});
    }

    onAccountPhoneChange(e) {
        var account = Object.assign({}, this.state.account);
        account.Phone = e.target.value;
        this.setState({account});
    }

    onAccountFaxChange(e) {
        var account = Object.assign({}, this.state.account);
        account.Fax = e.target.value;
        this.setState({account});
    }

    onAccountWebsiteChange(e) {
        var account = Object.assign({}, this.state.account);
        account.Website = e.target.value;
        this.setState({account});
    }

    render() {
        return (
        <div>
            <div class="slds-form-element__control">
                <input id="name" type="text" className="slds-input"
placeholder="Enter Account Name..." value={this.state.account.Name}
onChange={e => this.onAccountNameChange(e)}/>
            </div>
            <div class="slds-form-element__control">
                <input id="phone" type="text" className="slds-input"
placeholder="Enter Account Phone..." value={this.state.account.Phone}
```

```
onChange={e => this.onAccountPhoneChange(e)}/>
            </div>
            <div class="slds-form-element__control">
                <input id="fax" type="text" className="slds-input"
placeholder="Enter Account Fax..." value={this.state.account.Fax}
onChange={e => this.onAccountFaxChange(e)}/><br/>
            </div>
            <div class="slds-form-element__control">
                <input id="website" type="text" className="slds-input"
placeholder="Enter Account Website..." value={this.state.account.Website}
onChange={e => this.onAccountWebsiteChange(e)}/><br/>
            </div>
            <br/>
            <button className="slds-button slds-button_brand"
onClick={this.saveAccount}>Create Account</button>
        </div>
        );
    }

}

export default App;
```

Observe how we use the Lightning-container npm module's methods to call the Apex method and send messages to the component.

The Lightning Component markup and the JS controller code are as follows:

```
<aura:component access="global"
implements="flexipage:availableForAllPageTypes">
        <div class="slds-align_absolute-center">
            Create Account App
        </div>
        < Lightning:container aura:id="jsApp" src="{!$Resource.reactApp +
'/index.html'}" onerror="{!c.handleError}" onmessage="{!c.handleMessage}"/>
</aura:component>
```

The controller code is as follows:

```
({
    handleMessage: function (component, event, helper) {
        var message = event.getParams();
        var navigationEvent = $A.get("e.force:navigateToSObject");
    navigationEvent.setParams({
    "recordId": message.payload.id,
        "slideDevName": "details"
    });
    navigationEvent.fire();
```

```
        },

    handleError: function (component, event, helper) {
        var error = event.getParams();
        console.log(error);
    }
})
```

To build the bundle for the React application, use the following command:

npm build

To push the entire code to the scratch Org, run the following command. Note that this command automatically takes care of creating a static resource ZIP file from the static resource folder:

sfdx force:source:push

The preceding section assumes you are familiar with the React framework (https://reactjs.Org/).

Note that the principles discussed in this section apply to Angular, Vue.js, or any other framework.

The methods provided by the Lightning-container npm module are described in the following table:

Method	Description
LCC.sendMessage(message)	Sends a message to the hosting Lightning Component.
LCC.addMessageHandler(handler)	Registers a listener for messages sent by the hosting Lightning Component.
LCC.removeMessageHandler(handler)	Removes a listener for messages sent by the hosting Lightning Component.
LCC.callApex(method, params, callback, config)	Calls a method in an Apex controller.

Limitations of Lightning:container

Before using `Lightning:container`, know that there are the following limitations to consider before adopting this:

- It has performance and scrolling issues, since it essentially uses an iframe.
- It is not designed for a multi-page model, and hence does not store previous state or navigation history. Therefore, keep this method restricted to a single-page only.
- It does not implement the offline caching mechanism that is present in the Lightning experience.
- The static resource has a limit of 5 MB. So, if you have an application that's too large, `Lightning:container` might not fit your needs. For this scenario, we recommend hosting the application inside the Visualforce page and then iframing the Visualforce page to the Lightning Component.

Summary

This chapter provided examples and techniques to integrate third-party libraries and apps into the Lightning Component framework. In the next chapter, we will dive deeper into tools and techniques used to debug Lightning Components and Apex. We will cover tools such as the Lightning Inspector and use it to step through code and inspect the component hierarchy and DOM elements.

8
Debugging Lightning Components

On the client-side, Lightning Components consist of JavaScript, while on the server-side they are an Apex class that does all the server-side logic. Debugging Lightning Components involves an understanding of the debugging techniques used for JavaScript, as well as techniques used for debugging Apex classes.

In this chapter, we will explore the following topics:

- Chrome extensions that Salesforce offers to debug Lightning Components and analyze their performance
- Using Chrome developer tools for JavaScript debugging
- Leveraging the Salesforce Apex Replay Debugger for server-side Apex debugging

We will take the YouTube search component example we built in `Chapter 3`, *Lightning Component Building Blocks*, to understand debugging techniques.

Enabling Debug Mode

For production purposes, it is recommended to keep **Mode** off as it can impact performance. For development purposes, it is recommended to enable **Debug Mode** for the user. In the Salesforce **Setup** menu in **Quick find**, type `Debug` to find **Debug Mode** for **Lightning Component**.

The following screenshot shows how one can enable debugging for Lightning Components in the Salesforce Organization. Select the checkbox against each user from the list that requires debug logs enabled, and click on the **Enable** button:

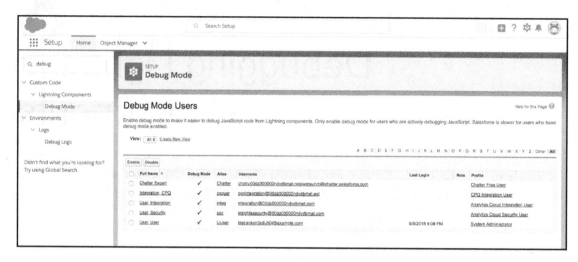

Observe that you can enable **Debug Mode** on a per-user basis. Enabling **Debug Mode** keeps the JavaScript of Lightning Components unminified, making it easier to debug.

Salesforce Lightning Inspector

Salesforce Lightning Inspector provides the excellent ability to inspect the **Component Tree**, component DOM markup, and events, as well as display actions, override actions, and profile performance. This tool can be great for inspecting issues, especially related to events firing and data coming from the Apex method.

You can add the *Salesforce Lightning Inspector* from the Chrome web store. Here is the link to add the inspector to the Chrome browser: `https://chrome.google.com/webstore/detail/Salesforce-Lightning-insp/pcpmcffcomlcjgpcheokdfcjipanjdpc?hl=en`

Once you add the Lightning inspector to Chrome, if a Salesforce page has Lightning Components, you will see a **Lightning** subtab in the developer **Console** of Chrome, as shown in the following screenshot:

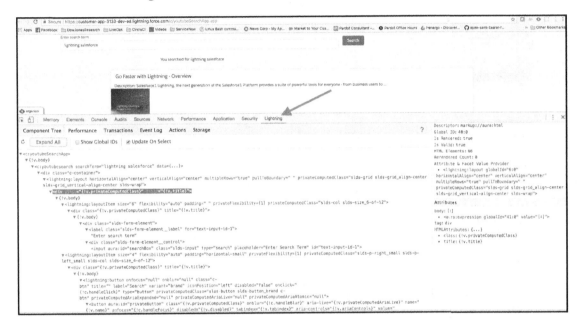

For this chapter, we will use the code from `Chapter 3`, *Lightning Component Building Blocks*. You can access the code from the Git repository here: `https://github.com/PacktPublishing/Learning-Salesforce-Lightning-Application-Development/tree/master/chapter3`.

Recall the YouTube search application searches videos from YouTube using search terms entered by users. Check out the following screenshot to recall how the application looks:

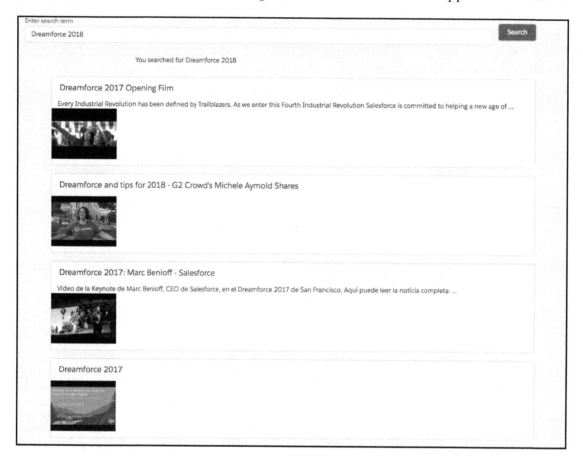

To create a scratch Org with all the components from the Chapter 3, *Lightning Component Building Blocks* repository, execute the following commands in your command line:

 This assumes you have the Salesforce DX CLI installed. To find instructions to download it, refer to the *Installing Salesforce DX CLI* section in Chapter 2, *Exploring Salesforce DX*. Also, you will need Salesforce Org with Developer Hub enabled. Refer to the *Enabling Developer Hub in your Salesforce Organization* section in Chapter 2, *Exploring Salesforce DX* to get instructions to start a Salesforce Trial Organization that has the option to enable DevHub.

1. Log in to DevHub using the CLI command:

   ```
   sfdx force:auth:web:login -d -a DevHub
   ```

2. Set your DevHub as the default hub using this command:

   ```
   sfdx force:config:set defaultdevhubusername=DevHub
   ```

3. cd into the chapter3 folder and create a scratch Org using this command:

   ```
   sfdx force:org:create -s -f config/project-scratch-def.json -a
   testorg
   ```

4. Set your scratch Org as the default Org using this command:

   ```
   sfdx force:config:set -u=testorg
   ```

5. Push the source code to the scratch Org using this command:

   ```
   sfdx force:source:push
   ```

6. Optionally, you can open the Org directly from the CLI using this:

   ```
   sfdx force:org:open
   ```

In the YouTube search Apex class, you will need the API key for the component to work. Refer to the *Wiring the client-side to the server using Apex controllers* section in `Chapter 3`, *Lightning Component Building Blocks* for instructions on how to obtain the key.

Lightning Salesforce Inspector tabs

This section assumes you have the YouTube search Lightning app opened in your browser using this URL

format: `https://<myDomain>.Lightning.force.com/c/youtubeSearchApp.app`.
Note that `<myDomain>` should be replaced with your Salesforce domain.

Component Tree

This tab shows the **Component Tree** of the Lightning Component application. In our case, it should resemble the following screenshot:

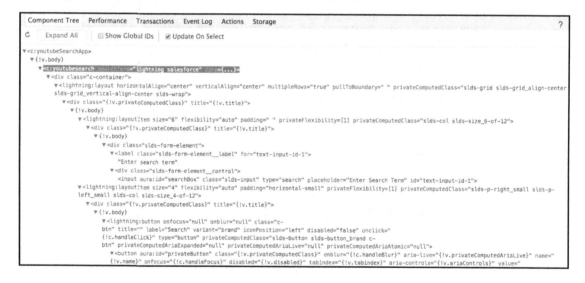

You can click on each of the components to select them. The commands we discuss in the next subsection apply after selecting one of the components from the **Component Tree**.

$auraTemp

This section describes a few commands that you can run in the browser console to inspect the DOM and get its attribute values. Let's take a look at them with the help of an example:

- Clicking on the component and executing `$auraTemp+""` in the Chrome developer **Console** shows the component.
- `$auraTemp.getElement()` shows the actual DOM elements of the components.
- To inspect the component by opening the console, use `inspect($auraTemp.getElement())`. This will navigate you to the Chrome console directly and select the DOM element for inspection.
- To get the attribute values that are on the component, run the following command in the **Developer Console**:

  ```
  $auraTemp.get("v.attributeName");//Note that here attributeName is
  the name of the attribute that is declared in the component markup
  ```

- The following screenshot shows the display in the **Developer Console** if we select the `youtubesearch` component and execute the `$auraTemp` commands we discussed already:

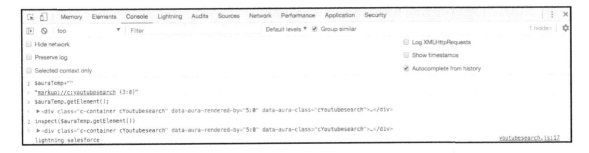

Transactions tab

The **Transactions** tab allows the logging of all the HTTP requests and the total time taken for the response. This will be pretty useful to analyze the time taken by responses to every server request from the client. This screenshot shows the transaction metrics collected once we click the **Search** button to call the Apex method that invokes the search action:

Performance tab

The **Performance** tab shows a **flame graph** of the creation time for your components.

Use the Record ⬤, Clear ◯, and show currently collected ▊▎▊▎ buttons to gather performance data about specific user actions or collections of user actions:

1. To start gathering performance data, press ⬤
2. Take one or more actions in the application
3. To stop gathering performance data, press ⬤

You can switch between graph mode and tree mode or heavy top-down mode as shown in the following screenshots.

The following screenshot shows the chart mode. Look at the longer and deeper portions of the graph for potential performance bottlenecks:

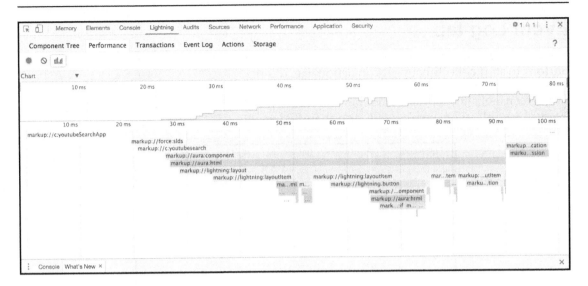

The following screenshot shows Heavy (bottom-up) mode, which shows self-time, indicating a percentage of time from the aggregate taken by component for creation:

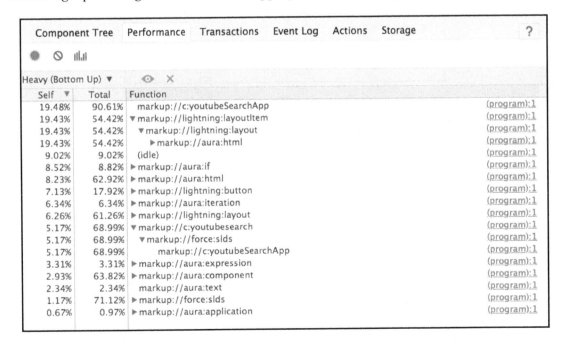

Event Log tab

The **Event Log** tab takes care of logging all the application and component events. Use the buttons to start collecting events on action execution.

The screenshot shows events fired once the **Search** button was clicked on. You can filter the events by application, component, or unhandled events:

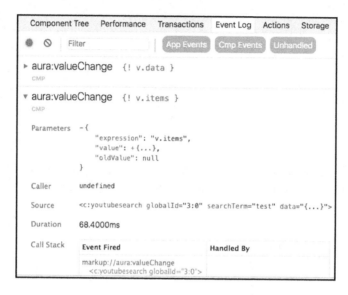

Notice we can also use the toggle Grid to display the event chain. The screenshot shows changes in events that are triggered by clicking the **Search** button for a value change in the attribute that holds the data:

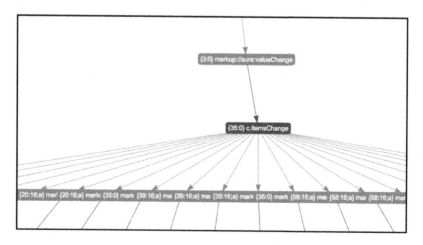

Actions tab

The **Actions** tab logs any action that the user executes in the application. In our scenario, once we click on the **Search** button, notice that the search action is logged. This allows us to inspect the parameters sent to the Apex method, and also the response structure and data from the server.

Also, you can drop any action to the override section and change the result set to see how the UI performs with different datasets. You can also trigger the error for any action and see the application state.

The following screenshot shows how you can override the result set from the **Actions** tab:

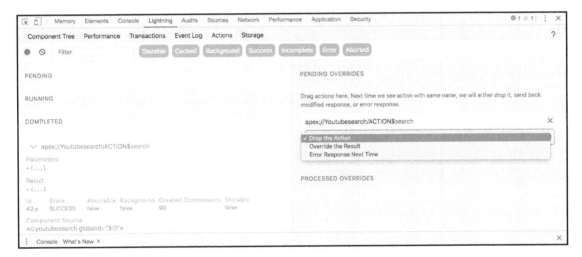

Storage tab

Actions marked as storable can be seen in the **Storage** tab. Storable actions are automatically configured in **Lightning Experience** and the Salesforce mobile application. To use storable actions in a standalone app (the .app resource), you must configure client-side storage for cached action responses.

Read more about client-side storage here: https://developer. Salesforce.com/docs/atlas.en-us.Lightning.meta/Lightning/ controllers_server_storable_enable.htm.

Salesforce community page optimizer

This Chrome extension allows us to figure out the performance bottlenecks in your components. You can install the Chrome extension from `https://chrome.google.com/webstore/detail/Salesforce-community-page/alkcnclapbnefkodhbkpifdkceldogka`, which takes you to the Chrome store.

Let's run the performance optimizer on our YouTube search application to gather some performance metrics. To run the tool, click on the extension icon found in the extreme top-right section of Chrome, as shown in the following screenshot:

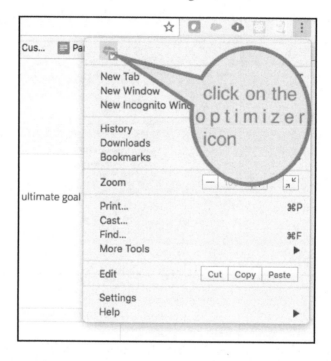

The following screenshot shows the optimizer score after running the performance optimizer on our application:

Results from the optimizer chrome extension plugin that is used to analyze performance of the Lightning Page

It can be inferred that the time taken by the server can be optimized further. The following screenshot shows the time taken by each of the components to create and render:

Rendering time for components on the page

The following screenshot shows the time taken by the search action:

Actions Details of components displayed by performance optimizer plugin

 Chapter 9, *Debugging Lightning Components*, discusses how to resolve some of the performance issues in Lightning applications.

Using the Chrome developer Console

Lightning Components can benefit from the Chrome console to a greater extent for JavaScript debugging. You can use `console.log()` to debug the variable value.

Observe how, in the following code snippet, we `console.log` the request parameters and also the response values from the backend Apex method:

```
setSearchTerm : function(component, event) {
        var searchTerm = component.find('searchBox').getElement().value;
        console.log(searchTerm);
        component.set("v.searchTerm",searchTerm);
        // create a one-time use instance of the search action
        // in the server-side controller
```

```
var action = component.get("c.search");
action.setStorable();
action.setParams({ searchstr : searchTerm});
action.setCallback(this, function(response) {
    var state = response.getState();
    if (state === "SUCCESS") {
        var responseData = JSON.parse(response.getReturnValue());
        console.log(responseData);
        console.log(responseData.kind);
        component.set("v.data",responseData);
    }
}
```

The following screenshot shows the **Console** values:

Setting breakpoints in the Chrome developer Console

If you want your code to stop during runtime, you can add the debugger keyword in the code. Open the **Console** and execute the action, and you will notice that the code stops at the breakpoint. Now, hover over the variables to inspect them.

> You don't even need a debugger keyword, as you can find the source file in Chrome now and add breakpoints.

The following screenshot shows how to use the **Sources** tab to find the source code. Click on the line number to automatically inject breakpoints and execute actions:

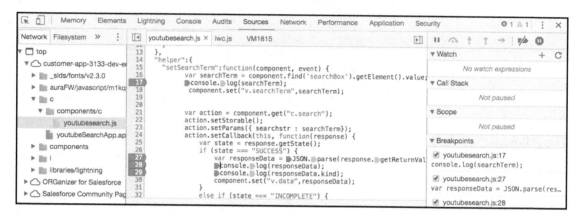

Once you execute an action, you can step through each line of code using the step over next function call, as shown in the following screenshot, to inspect the variables:

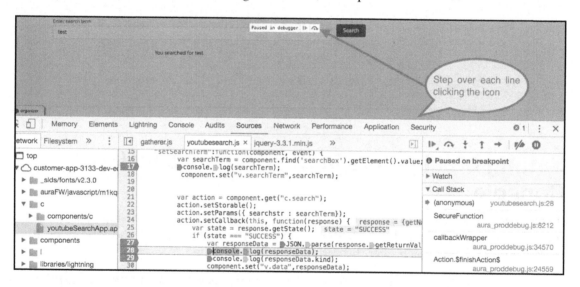

Also note that Call Stack allows us to display the function calls that got you to the line you are debugging.

Pause on caught exceptions

Use the **Pause on caught exceptions** option if you are getting an internal error. Using this exception, you can step through each line of code to find the cause of the failing script. Note there is a pretty point at the bottom of the source file, where you can use this to unminify to simplify debugging.

The following screenshot shows how to turn **Pause on caught exceptions** on. Find all the scripts that are breaking but getting handled by catch blocks to figure out what's breaking:

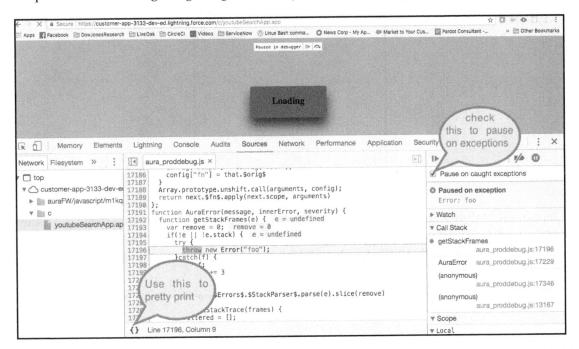

Apex debugging

In this section, we will describe how you can debug Apex classes. The traditional way to debug Apex has been to add `system.debug()` statements and trace variable values in debug logs. `System.debug()` prints the variable value in the logs.

You can set the logs in Salesforce by using the setup menu and following the **Environments | Logs | Debug logs** path. The following screenshot shows how to find the **Debug Logs** menu from **Setup**:

Once in the **Debug Logs** menu, you can set the trace flags to start capturing the logs for the user. Check out the following screenshot for how to set up logs. Once logs are set up, any Apex executed is logged. There is a maximum size limit for the logs and it is currently 5 MB:

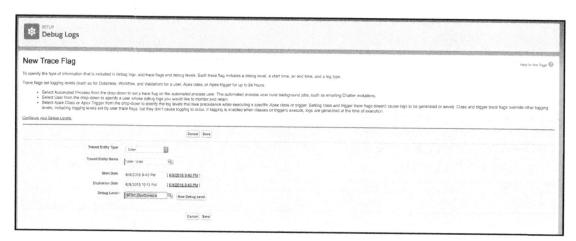

Read more about debug logs here: `https://developer.Salesforce.com/docs/atlas.en-us.Apexcode.meta/Apexcode/Apex_debugging_debug_log.htm`.

Using the Salesforce CLI to stream logs

The Salesforce CLI provides the option to stream logs directly from the command line. To tail the logs, you can execute the following command in the command-line window:

```
sfdx force:apex:log:tail -c
```

You can also filter the result set from the logs using the GREP Unix command. Let's say you want to only see the USER_DEBUG results, then the command to the filter will be as follows:

```
sfdx force:apex:log:tail --color | grep USER_DEBUG
```

In our case, we can add `system.debug` to the response from the HTTP call and execute the application to stream logs on the CLI. The following screenshot shows the logs captured from the `tail` command:

```
20:48:52.0 (395151472)|HEAP_ALLOCATE|[18]|Bytes:5574
20:48:52.0 (395252662)|VARIABLE_SCOPE_BEGIN|[18]|res|System.HttpResponse|true|false
20:48:52.0 (395538460)|VARIABLE_ASSIGNMENT|[18]|res|"System.HttpResponse[Status=OK, StatusCode=200]"|0x53dcb269
20:48:52.0 (395577196)|STATEMENT_EXECUTE|[19]
20:48:52.0 (395594629)|HEAP_ALLOCATE|[19]|Bytes:12
20:48:52.0 (396347315)|HEAP_ALLOCATE|[19]|Bytes:5566
20:48:52.0 (396419795)|HEAP_ALLOCATE|[19]|Bytes:5578
20:48:52.0 (396531130)|USER_DEBUG|[19]|DEBUG|RESULTS..>>>{
 "kind": "youtube#searchListResponse",
 "etag": "\"DuHzAJ-eQIiCIp7p4ldoVcVAOeY/iqZHzAEgo9IpA9kjtGyPbdp73HI\"",
 "nextPageToken": "CAUQAA",
 "regionCode": "US",
 "pageInfo": {
  "totalResults": 1000000,
  "resultsPerPage": 5
 },
 "items": [
  {
```

Also, note the Visual Studio code editor extension for `sfdx` can capture these logs, and you can open them in your IDE. The following screenshot shows how you can retrieve the logs:

You will see the logs in the `sfdx/tools/debug/logs/` folder.

 One common misconception is that you need scratch Orgs to work with the Salesforce CLI. However, this is not true and you can use the Salesforce DX CLI to authorize with any Org and some of these functionalities such as tailing logs are available.

Advanced debugging with the Replay Debugger

Salesforce scratch Orgs also offer Apex Replay Debugger for free to do some advanced debugging by setting breakpoints and inspecting variables from the captured logs.

The latest Salesforce extensions for the Visual Studio Code plugin (v 43.0 onward) have the ability to use this feature. The following are the steps to enable this feature:

1. Turn the debugger on by selecting the Visual Studio command **SFDX: Turn On Apex Debug Log for Replay Debugger** from the command palette shown in the following screenshot:

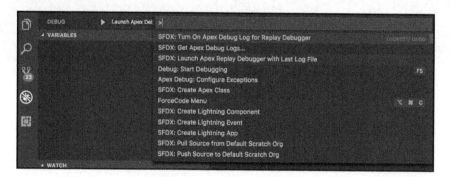

2. The next step is to set breakpoints in the Apex code by clicking on the line number where you want to inspect the values:

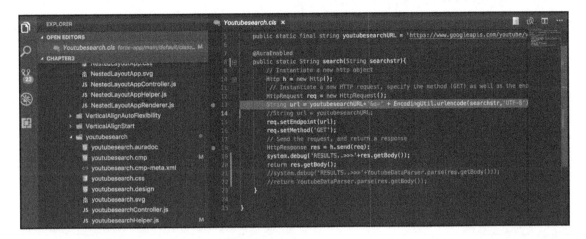

3. Start tailing the logs via the command line by executing the following command:

```
sfdx force:apex:log:tail -c
```

4. Execute the action that triggers the Apex method. In our case, we will click the **Search** button of the YouTube application.

5. Retrieve the logs tailed using **SFDX: Get Apex Debug Logs...** from the Visual Studio code editor command palette:

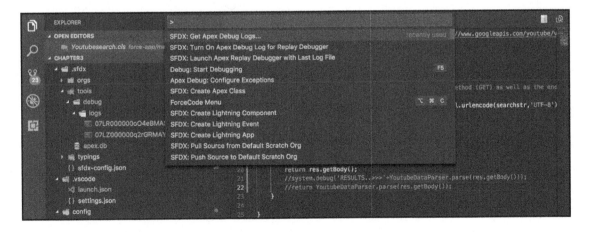

6. Left-click on the latest logs collected in the `logs` folder and click on **Launch** to replay the Apex debugger. The following screenshot shows how to launch the replay of the debugger with the logs:

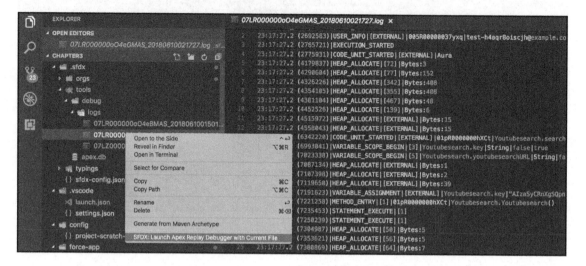

7. Step through using the pane on the top of each line to see the values of the variable. The following screenshot shows how the debug pane on the left parses all the values:

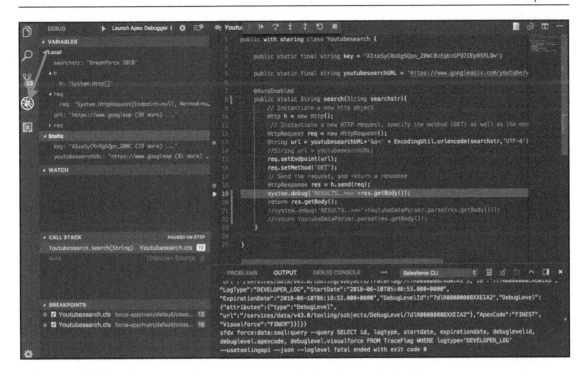

Apex Replay Debugger is a very useful utility for debugging Apex code. Sometimes, downloading logs manually from the Orgs can be time-consuming, so using the Replay Debugger with the IDE helps to download and debug without manually logging to a Salesforce instance.

Summary

In this chapter, we covered in greater depth how to debug Salesforce Lightning Component code on the frontend and Salesforce Apex on the backend. In Chapter 9, *Performance Tuning Your Lightning Component*, we will focus on how we can resolve performance bottlenecks in Lightning Components, and discuss best practices to improve rendering and Apex performance.

9
Performance Tuning Your Lightning Component

In this chapter, we will dig deeper into performance considerations when you are building Lightning Components. We will explore the concept of **stored actions**, which are caching mechanisms available to cache a dataset to improve its performance. We will also learn how to design your backend Apex code to improve performance.

We will explore how tags such as `aura:if` used inside `aura:iteration` within a large dataset can cause rendering issues. We will look into strategies to keep the number of components to a minimum to improve load and rendering time. We will also look into some Lightning base components that can reduce work and code complexity and can add significant performance improvements.

In this chapter, we will explore the following topics:

- Storable actions
- Lightning Component tags that can cause performance issues
- The benefits of lazy loading using `$A.createComponent()`
- Events architecture for improving performance
- Server-side Apex optimization for performance improvements

Storable actions

In Chapter 3, *Lightning Component Building Blocks*, you learned that, to make a call to a server (using the Apex method) from the Lightning Component client-side controller/helper function, we can enqueue an action, using the following code snippet:

```
var action = component.get("c.getResults");
action.setCallback(this, function(response) {
  // handle response
};
$A.enqueueAction(action);
```

In the code snippet, whenever an action is invoked via events (onInit, click, or custom events), the client makes a call to get the latest data or performs **data manipulation (DML)**, such as the creating, deleting, or editing of records.

This framework provides the ability to mark an action as storable. To mark an action as storable, the code snippet is as follows (pay special attention to the highlighted line):

```
var action = component.get("c.getResults");
action.setStorable();
action.setCallback(this, function(response) {
  // handle response
};
$A.enqueueAction(action);
```

When an action is marked storable, the results are cached locally for an expiration time (this is not configurable at this point and is fixed at 900 seconds in the framework). Every 30 seconds, a background action is triggered to get the latest data.

> To learn more about how Lightning Component caching works on storable actions, refer to the blog by Salesforce at https://developer.salesforce.com/blogs/developer-relations/2017/03/Lightning-components-best-practices-caching-data-storable-actions.html.

When to use storable actions?

Storable actions are helpful if you have two or more components that you navigate back-and-forth and they call the same Apex method. Marking them as storable allows you to retrieve the values from the cache, instead of making server trips every time.

If you are performing filtering and pagination of data, then marking an action as storable makes a lot of sense, because you know that user interactions can be in bursts of short spans, and performance can be improved by caching the data, instead of retrieving it from the server each time.

Also remember that actions involving DML (create, edit, or delete) do not mark the action as storable, since you want a fresh set of data entered by the user to save the database, and not the cached results.

Avoiding nested aura:if in aura:iteration

To understand this scenario, let's take an example component code. Let's name the component `ifElseLadder`. The component displays numbers in a nested manner.

The component code is as follows:

```
<aura:component >

    <aura:attribute name="truthy" type="Boolean" default="false"/>
    <aura:attribute name="innerCmpDisplay" type="Boolean" default="true"/>
    <aura:attribute name="arraySize" type="List" default="[]"/>

    <aura:handler name="init" value="{!this}" action="{!c.doInit}"/>

    <aura:iteration items="1,2,3,4,5" var="item">
    <aura:if isTrue="{!v.truthy}">
        True
        <aura:set attribute="else">
          <aura:iteration items="{!v.arraySize}" var="i">
            <aura:if isTrue="{!v.innerCmpDisplay}">
                <div>
                    {!i}
                </div>
                <aura:iteration items="{!v.arraySize}" var="j">
                    <aura:if isTrue="{!v.innerCmpDisplay}">
                        <div>
                            {!j}
                        </div>
                    </aura:if>
                </aura:iteration>
            </aura:if>
          </aura:iteration>
        </aura:set>
    </aura:if>
```

```
        </aura:iteration>
    </aura:component>
```

The controller code is as follows:

```
({
    doInit : function(component, event, helper) {
        console.time("renderladder");
        var arrayList = [];
        for(var i=0 ; i<=100 ; i++){
            arrayList.push(i);
        }
        component.set("v.arraySize",arrayList);
        console.timeEnd("renderladder");
    }
})
```

Try to test this by creating a test app such as the following one:

```
<aura:application extends="force:slds">
    <c:ifElseLadder />
</aura:application>
```

If you preview this application, you will notice that each application takes an enormous amount of time to render the component.

If you run the following snippet in the browser's console, you can keep track of a number of components created:

```
$A.componentService.countComponents();
```

If you inspect the Lightning Application, using the performance tool discussed in the previous chapter, the results are as follows (notice a large cycle for the component):

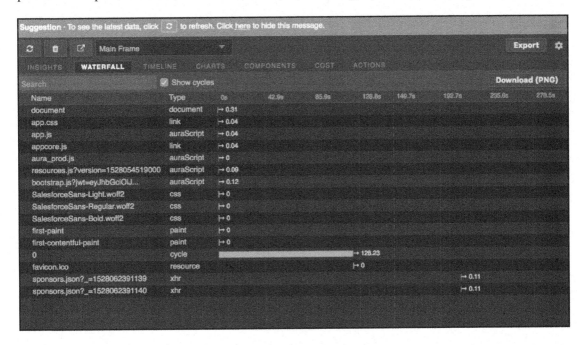

Screenshot shows the performance cost for a component with nested else if a ladder

The following screenshot is from the performance optimization tool, and you can clearly see that the count of the number of components is huge:

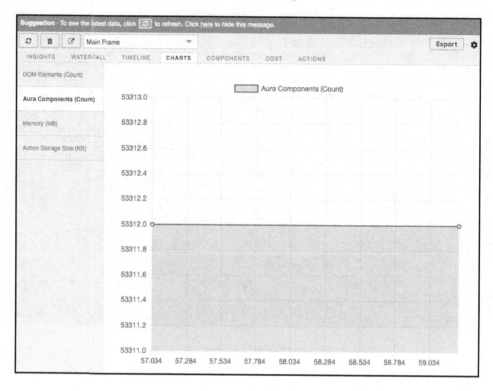

The screenshot shows the number of the aura components used in the page

For our current code, you can see that the number of components created is greater than 20K. This causes rendering issues. Hence, it is recommended to examine the size of the list carefully when you have a complex frontend branch using `aura:if`. Do not use a lot of rows of data, and use techniques such as filtering and paginate to keep the number of rows to a minimum.

If you have backend Apex code fetching rows of data, then it is recommended to use the SOQL offset to implement server-side pagination.

Similarly, if you are connecting to a third-party API to get some data recommended, that API is designed to not return more than 100 rows in one call. The API should implement filtering and searching capabilities and restrict the number of results to hundreds, and not thousands, to keep things performant.

$A.createComponent() for lazy loading

If you have too many `aura:if` statements inside `aura:iteration`, you can transfer some logic to the controller to create markups conditionally using the `$A.createComponents()` API. The code snippet for this technique is shown, and, depending on the conditions, you can build the final component markup. Let's take a look at the code:

```
$A.createComponent(componentName, options, function(comp) {
    var body = component.get("v.body");
    body.push(comp);
    component.set("v.body",cmp);
});
```

This method reduces the number of components and improves performance. However, you are still using the framework, and there is some rendering cost consumed from the framework.

Using plain old JavaScript to gain maximum performance

If you want to display a large number of read-only rows, then prefer plain old JavaScript over framework code. This will improve the rendering performance. The code for this would look like the following snippet, which produces the same result as the logic covered in the earlier section. Let's take a look at the code:

```
<aura:component>
    <aura:handler name="render" value="{!this}" action="{!c.onRender}"/>
    <div aura:id="main">
    </div>
</aura:component>
```

The controller code uses JavaScript ECMA5 script to draw the DOM via JavaScript:

```
({
    onRender : function(component, event, helper) {
        var mainBody = component.find("main").getElement();
        for(var i=0 ; i<=100 ; i++){
            var parentDiv = document.createElement("div");
            parentDiv.innerHTML = i;
            mainBody.appendChild(parentDiv);
            for(var j=0 ; j<=100 ; j++){
                var childDiv = document.createElement("div");
                childDiv.innerHTML = j;
```

```
                  parentDiv.appendChild(childDiv);
              }
          }
      }
})
```

You should have noticed a couple of things from the preceding code:

- We have used the render event to make sure the DOM is completely loaded before we further manipulate the DOM.
- We use plain old JavaScript to build the DOM elements.

If you test the preceding code, you will see a drastic change in the rendering time of the result set. The following is a screenshot, using the Lightning **Inspector** plugin (notice that the rendering time, the time taken for the component to render on a browser, is less than in the previous scenario):

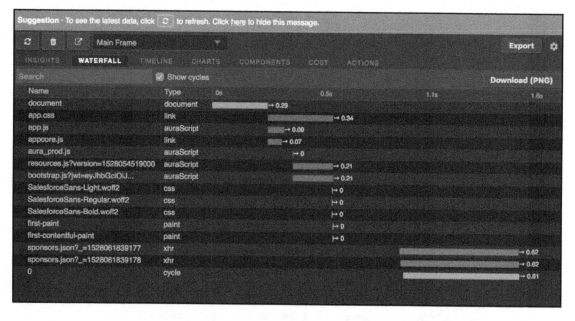

Screenshot confirms performance gains when using native javascript to form the DOM elements

Events strategy for performance and ease of code maintenance

Application events can take significant performance. Hence, it is recommended that if you need to communicate between two components that follow a hierarchy and there is no business need to couple the components loosely, use a component event instead of an application event.

Also, as a rule of best practice, *use only one component event throughout the application.* For additional details, refer to the *Advanced Event Architecture* section in `Chapter 5`, *Events in the Lightning Component Framework.*

Event anti-patters that can cause a performance bottleneck

Do not fire an event in the renderer. This can cause an infinite loop. The following code shows the anti-pattern that should be avoided:

```
afterRender: function(cmp, helper) {
    this.superAfterRender();
    $A.get("e.myns:mycmp").fire();//This is an Anti pattern
}
```

> You can't use different actions for `onclick` and `ontouchend` events in a component. The framework translates touch-tap events into clicks and activates any `onclick` handlers that are present.

\<aura:iteration\> – multiple items set

If you see the following warning message in the browser console, this occurs if your component sets the items attribute of an `<aura:iteration>` tag multiple times in the same rendering cycle:

"WARNING: [Performance degradation] markup://aura:iteration [id:5:0] in c:iterationMultipleItemsSet ["3:0"]
had multiple items set in the same Aura cycle"

The following code shows how <indexentry content="events strategy: tag"> you can generate performance degradation when using aura:iteration.

```
<!--c:iterationMultipleItemsSet-->
<aura:component>
    <aura:attribute name="sports" type="List"
                    default="[ 'Cricket', 'Tennis', 'Football' ]"/>
    <aura:handler name="init" value="{!this}" action="{!c.init}"/>

    <aura:iteration items="{!v.sports}" var="item">
        <p>{!item}</p>
    </aura:iteration>
</aura:component>
```

When the component is created, the items attribute of the <aura:iteration> tag is set to the default value of the sports attribute. After the component is created, but before rendering, the init event is triggered.

The init() function in the client-side controller sets the sports attribute, which resets the items attribute of the <aura:iteration> tag.

The controller code with the init event is shown here:

```
/* c:iterationMultipleItemsSetController.js */
({
    init: function(cmp) {
        var list = cmp.get('v.sports');
        // Some logic
        cmp.set('v.sports', list); // Performance warning trigger
    }
})
```

Performance degradation in the aura:iteration tag encountered in the previous code snippet can be fixed by removing the default from the list. The following code changes, highlighted in bold, show changes made to the previous code to fix degradation issues:

```
<!--c:iterationMultipleItemsSetFixed-->
<aura:component>
    <!-- FIX: Remove the default from the attribute -->
    <aura:attribute name="sports" type="List" />
    <aura:handler name="init" value="{!this}" action="{!c.init}"/>

    <aura:iteration items="{!v.sports}" var="item">
        <p>{!item}</p>
    </aura:iteration>
</aura:component>
```

The controller code is as follows:

```
/* c:iterationMultipleItemsSetFixedController.js */
({
    init: function(cmp) {
        var sportslist = ['Cricket', 'Football', 'Tennis'];
        // Some logic
        cmp.set('v.sports', sportslist);
    }
})
```

Optimizing JavaScript in Lightning Components

The Lightning Component framework uses JavaScript on the frontend. Hence, anything that improves JavaScript performance should be considered.

Some of these techniques include the following:

- Image optimization, by using `Lightning:icon` and `Lightning:buttonIcon`.
- Using minified JavaScript bundle if you are using any third-party JavaScript library for production releases. It is recommended not to use any third-party libraries if the framework can do the work for you.
- Using a bundler, such as Webpack Bundler with CSS Purify to minify JavaScript and remove unnecessary selectors.
- Using `console.time()`, `console.timeEnd`, and performance (https://developer.mozilla.Org/en-US/docs/Web/API/Performance) APIs to gather metrics to uncover performance issues.

Unbound expression bindings

Two-way data-binding, using `{!v.expression}` is expensive on performance. If you do not need to keep your UI in sync with model changes, then prefer one-way data bindings. This can improve the rendering time of the application, since the framework need not maintain event listeners.

The syntax for the unbound expression is as follows:

```
{#!v.expression}
```

Let's consider the following example code snippet, where you will need to pass an attribute value from parent to child, using an unbound expression. With one-way binding, notice that any changes to the child attribute are not propagated to the parent. Let's take a look:

```
<!--c:childExpr-->
<aura:component>
    <aura:attribute name="childAttr" type="String" />

    <p>childExpr childAttr: {!v.childAttr}</p>
    <p><Lightning:button label="Update childAttr"
        onclick="{!c.updateChildAttr}"/></p>
</aura:component>
```

The controller code to update a child is as follows:

```
/* childExprController.js */
({
    updateChildAttr: function(cmp) {
        cmp.set("v.childAttr", "updated child attribute");
    }
})
```

The parent component is as follows:

```
<!--c:parentExpr-->
<aura:component>
    <aura:attribute name="parentAttr" type="String" default="parent
attribute"/>

    <!-- Instantiate the child component -->
    <c:childExpr childAttr="{#v.parentAttr}" />
    <p>parentExpr parentAttr: {!v.parentAttr}</p>
    <p><Lightning:button label="Update parentAttr"
        onclick="{!c.updateParentAttr}"/></p>
</aura:component>
```

The controller code is as follows:

```
/* parentExprController.js */
({
    updateParentAttr: function(cmp) {
        cmp.set("v.parentAttr", "updated parent attribute");
    }
})
```

Testing this with a sample application is as follows:

```
<!--c:exprApp-->
<aura:application >
    <c:parentExpr />
</aura:application>
```

Notice that any change to the parent is not being synced to the child, and vice versa. However, the performance is improved significantly. Using aura:method as an alternative, we can pass values from the parent to the child, and improve performance.

> To pass values from the parent to the child, you can use aura:method. aura:method allows for communication from parent to child components, without much performance impact, other than two-way binding.

Using the Lightning data service

Using the Lightning data service significantly improves performance. The Lightning data service provides access to the single record data and performs DML on the data. The service also has a baked-in security configured by the Salesforce administrators of the platform. Consider leveraging this for a single record. Obviously, for the list of data, you will need to use the custom Apex class with an SOQL to fetch data.

Note that you can lazy load the forceRecord component, using the $A.createComponent(). A good example would be when a user sees a list of records and clicks a single record. You can use $A.createComponent() to inject the Lightning data service component force:recordData dynamically and then, once the modal is closed, destroy the component.

Leveraging Lightning base components

Lightning base components have a baked-in functionality to handle the formatting of data, validating data , connecting with the Salesforce object, using SLDS, and many more. They are optimized for performance, and hence wherever applicable developers should leverage them. An example use case would be, instead of using custom SVG components, use Lightning:icon and Lightning:buttonIcons.

Creating a record form, using Lightning:recordForm

The `Lightning:recordForm` component is one of the most powerful components that Salesforce offers that allows the user to edit and insert data into a Salesforce object, with minimal code. It can be used to present record form in `edit` mode, `detail` view, and `readOnly` view.

To create a simple contact form, you will need a code snippet that contains the `recordForm` component. Notice this code example does not include any Apex logic:

```
<aura:component>
    <aura:attribute name="newContact" type="String[]"
default="['LastName','Email','Phone']" />
    <Lightning:recordForm
        objectApiName="Contact"
        layoutType="COMPACT"
        fields="{!v.newContact}"
        columns="2"
        mode="edit"
        onsubmit="{!c.handleSubmit}" />
</aura:component/>
```

Optimizing Apex code

In this section, we will discuss improvements that you can make to your server-side Apex controllers, to reduce database time and provide Lightning Components with data in an optimized format so that the framework renders the components faster.

Limiting data rows for lists

If your Salesforce SOQL query is fetching large amount of results, consider limiting the number of data rows by using a LIMIT clause and using server-side pagination.

Look for opportunities where data from the server can be lazy loaded. For example, if you have three tabs, load data only for the first tab that will be rendered on the screen. Render the data for the second tab only when a user clicks the second tab.

Reducing server response time, using the platform cache

Redundant SOQL can be expensive, and you can significantly improve performance by using the platform cache feature of the Salesforce Lightning platform. Salesforce offers two types of caching mechanisms namely Org cache and session cache:

- Session cache: This caches data for a user session, and the cache expires once the user session expires.
- Org cache: This is accessible across sessions, requests, and Org users and profiles. You can set an expiration time for this type of cache.

The document here (`https://developer.Salesforce.com/docs/atlas.en-us.Apexcode.meta/Apexcode/Apex_platform_cache_limits.htm`) shows the size of the cache that's available for each Salesforce edition Org. You can purchase additional caching if needed.

The following is a simple code example of how you can leverage the `CacheBuilder` interface to cache API calls in Org cache:

```
public class APIResultCache implements Cache.CacheBuilder {
    public Object doLoad(String parameters) {
        Http http = new Http();
    HttpRequest request = new HttpRequest();
request.setEndpoint('https://th-Apex-http-callout.herokuapp.com/animals');
    request.setMethod('GET');
    HttpResponse response = http.send(request);
    // If the request is successful, parse the JSON response.
      if (response.getStatusCode() == 200) {
          return response.getBody();
      }else{
          return 'call Failed';
      }
    }
}
```

Now you can retrieve the cached results, using the following code snippets for session and Org caches, respectively:

```
String animals = (String) Cache.Org.get(UserInfoCache.APIResultCache,
'key');//From Org cache

User animals = (String) Cache.Session.get(UserInfoCache.APIResultCache,
'key');//From Org cache
```

```
//Use following for retrieval from partition cache

User animals = (String) Cache.Partition.get(UserInfoCache.APIResultCache,
'key');//From Org cache
```

We won't be digging much into the platform cache in Apex, as this is beyond the scope of this book. However, there are great resources provided in the Apex implementation guide (`https://developer. Salesforce.com/docs/atlas.en-us.Apexcode.meta/Apexcode/Apex_ cache_namespace_overview.htm`).

Avoiding sending responses from Apex as wrapper objects

To understand how you should structure response data from the Apex controller, let's take an example of Apex code that is needed to display a list of accounts for a Lightning Component:

```
public class AccountController{

    @AuraEnabled

    public Static List<AccountWrapper> queryAllAccounts(){
        List<AccountWrapper> accountWrapperList = New
List<AccountWrapper>();
        List<Account> myAccounts = [Select id, Name, BillingState.
                                        (Select id
                                            From Contacts)
                                    From Account];
        if(!myAccounts.isEmpty()){
            for(Account currentAccount : myAccounts){
                accountWrapperList.add(new AccountWrapper (..) );
            }
        }

        return accountWrapperList;
    }

}
```

This is the message/wrapper class code:

```
public class AccountWrapper{
        @AuraEnabled
```

```
Account currentAccount;

@AuraEnabled
Integer noOfContacts;

@AuraEnabled
Boolean isPartnerAccount;

@AuraEnabled
//Few more variables

    public AccountWrapper(Account currentAccount, Integer noOfContacts,
Boolean isPartnerAccount,..){
        this.currentAccount = currentAccount;
      ....
    }
  }
```

Note that in this scenario the service is returning responses as a custom Apex type. It has been observed that using a JSON string as the response type improves the performance, compared to the return type of Apex that is custom-defined. The platform under the hood suffers from some performance issues, and this is more noticeable with large datasets.

Instead, we can return as the JSON, using the following code snippet:

```
public class AccountQueryController{

    @AuraEnabled

    public static String queryAllAccounts(){

        List<AccountWrapper> accountWrapperList = New
List<AccountWrapper>();

        List<Account> myAccounts = [Select id, Name, BillingState.
                                      (Select id
                                          From Contacts)
                                    From Account];

        return JSON.serialize(myAccounts);

    }
```

You can then parse the string response into a valid JavaScript object, using JSON.parse() on the JavaScript. It has been observed that the performance is significantly improved via this method.

Disabling Debug Mode for production

For production purposes, ensure that the Debug Mode is disabled. Note that you can enable and disable the Debug Mode for the Lightning Component on a per-user basis.

The following screenshot shows the screen for enabling and disabling Debug Mode:

Debug Mode Users	Help for this Page
Enable debug mode to make it easier to debug JavaScript code from Lightning components. Only enable debug mode for users who are actively debugging JavaScript. Salesforce is slower for users who have debug mode enabled.	
View: All ☑ Create New View	<Previous Page	Next Page>
	A B C D E F G H I J K L M N O P Q R S T U V W X Y Z Other |All
Enable Disable	

Screenshot shows how you can enable debug mode for lightning components per user

Summary

In this chapter, we explored techniques to improve the performance of Lightning Components, both on the client-side and on the server-side. The Salesforce community page optimizer Chrome plugin (download the plugin from `https://chrome.google.com/webstore/detail/Salesforce-community-page/alkcnclapbnefkodhbkpifdkceldogka`) can help a great deal in identifying the performance bottlenecks of your components.

In the next chapter, we will explore how you can take Lightning Components outside the Salesforce platform, using Lightning Out technology. We will use the YouTube search component that we built in `Chapter 3`, *Lightning Component Building Blocks,* and render it inside a Heroku Node.js application, using Lightning Out technology.

10
Taking Lightning Components out of Salesforce Using Lightning Out

Using **Lightning Out**, you can take custom-built Lightning Components out of the Salesforce platform. Out of the Salesforce platform here refers to any application on the web that supports JavaScript, HTML, and CSS. Common examples would be a web application built using Node.js on Heroku, a SharePoint site, WordPress, an Electron desktop application, a Ruby web application, and so on. In this chapter, our aim is to show the steps that you will need to follow to use Lightning Out technology in your web application.

This chapter will cover the following topics:

- Leveraging Lightning Out in Visualforce pages to render Lightning Components
- Lightning Out in Node.Js applications
- Lightning Out for unauthenticated users (public websites)
- Lightning Out considerations and limitations

Lightning Out in Visualforce

Visualforce has been in Salesforce for some years and prior to the Lightning Component framework, all custom user interfaces were built using Visualforce. Currently, there are a lot of applications on the Salesforce platform built using Visualforce, and a lot of users still use these applications with a Visualforce page. Lightning Out allows developers to use Lightning Components, developed for Lightning Experience work, in Visualforce pages.

Salesforce also makes it easy to style Visualforce pages for a new SLDS look. An attribute named `LightningStylesheets` can be set to `true` to style Visualforce pages to look better. The code snippet for changing the stylesheet of a classic Salesforce VF is as follows:

```
<apex:page LightningStylesheets="true">
```

In this section, we will discover how to use the YouTube search component we built in Chapter 3, *Lightning Component Building Blocks*, to render inside a Visualforce page leveraging Lightning Out.

Creating a Lightning dependency application

The first step for using Lightning Out is creating a dependency application. A dependent Lightning Application extends from `ltng:outApp`. Note that extending from `ltng:outApp` also involves incorporating Salesforce Lightning design systems. If you want your Lightning Components not to have design systems imported in Lightning Out, then you can use `ltng:outAppUnstyled`.

The following is a code snippet for the dependency application that exposes the `youtubesearch` component:

```
<aura:application access="GLOBAL" extends="ltng:outApp">
    <aura:dependency resource="youtubesearch"/>
</aura:application>
```

The `<aura:dependency>` tag enables you to declare dependencies. If you are using any event, such as `force:navigateToURL`, it needs to be declared in the dependent application as well, as shown in the following code snippet. Let's name the application `youtubesearchOutApp`:

```
<aura:application access="GLOBAL" extends="ltng:outApp">
    <aura:dependency resource="youtubesearch"/>
    <aura:dependency resource="markup://force:navigateToURL" type="EVENT"/>
</aura:application>
```

 By default, the type is component in `aura:dependency` and for events or interfaces, use `EVENT` and `INTERFACE`, respectively. Using an asterisk (*) for wildcard matching is deprecated.

Adding Lightning Components for the Visualforce JavaScript library

To add the JavaScript library for the Visualforce Salesforce, the Visualforce component library provides a standard markup tag, `<apex:includeLightning>`. Let's create a Visualforce page named `"youtubeSearch"`, as shown in the following code:

```
<apex:page>
    <apex:includeLightning />

    <div id="Lightning" />

</apex:page>
```

Adding JavaScript to create a component on a Visualforce page

The JavaScript code to create a Lightning Component on a Visualforce page is as follows:

```
<apex:page>
    <apex:includeLightning />

    <div id="Lightning" />

    <script>
        $Lightning.use("c:youtubesearchOutApp", function() {
            $Lightning.createComponent("c:youtubesearch",
            { },
            "Lightning",
            function(cmp) {
                // do some stuff
            });
        });
    </script>
</apex:page>
```

Notice that `$Lightning.use()` accepts two parameters:

- The name of the Lightning Out dependency application, along with its namespace.

- A `callback` function. The `callback` function receives no arguments. This `callback` is usually where you call `$Lightning.createComponent()` to add your app to the page (see the next section, *Lightning Out in a Node.js application*).

Also, note that `$Lightning.createComponent` takes four parameters, described as follows:

- The name of the Lightning Component that you want to render, along with its namespace.
- Attributes that you want to pass as an object. Attributes declared in components can be passed from JavaScript as an object.
- The DOM element ID where the component needs to render. In our case, we have a `div` with the ID Lightning.
- A `callback` function called once the component is rendered.

Once you preview the page in the classic UI using `/apex/youtubesearch`, you can see that the component is rendered and works as is. The following screenshot shows the working application in classic Visualforce:

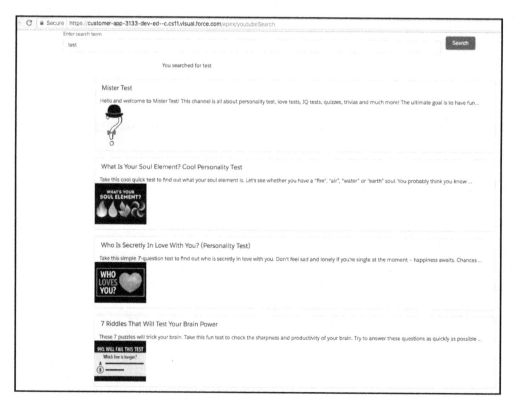

Lightning Out in a Node.js application

In this section, we will build a Node.js web application that will be hosted on Heroku and renders the YouTube search component we have built using Lightning Out.

This section assumes you are familiar with webpack fundamentals, ES6 syntax for JavaScript, and Node.js fundamentals. This section also assumes you have the Heroku CLI installed from `https://devcenter.heroku.com/articles/heroku-cli`.

The application consists of the Lightning Out application, which we covered in the previous section. You can use SFDX to deploy the application to the scratch Org from the repository at `https://github.com/PacktPublishing/Learning-Salesforce-Lightning-Application-Development/tree/master/chapter10/force-app/main/default`.

You can create a scratch Org and push the code using the following commands. This assumes you have authenticated to the `DevHub` using the Salesforce DX CLI:

```
$sfdx force:org:create -s -f config/project-scratch-def.json -a testOrg
//This creates scratch Org

$sfdx force:config:set defaultusername=<username|alias> // Sets the scratch
Org as default

$sfdx force:source:push // Push code in the repository to the scratch Org

$sfdx force:org:open // To open the scratch Org
```

Creating a connected application

The first step is to make sure the Node.js app can authenticate with Salesforce and obtain the access token that the Lightning Out application will need. In order to do this, we will create a connected application in Salesforce that will allow the Node.js application to go through the OAuth flow.

Prior to creating a connected application, we will need to create a Heroku application. Use the following commands to create a new Heroku app. Let's make a local directory for this application and name it `ltngOutApp`:

```
$ mkdir ltngOutApp  // Make a directory named ltngOutApp
$ cd ltngOutApp // cd into the directory
$ git init // Initialize the Git repository
$ heroku apps:create ltngOutApp  // Create a Heroku application named
ltngOutApp
```

To create a connected application in Salesforce, navigate to **Setup** | **Apps** | **Connected Apps** | **New**. This is shown in the next screenshot.

You will need a `callback` URL for the connected app. To set the callback URL, you can provide a localhost URL like `http:localhost:8200/oauthcallback.html` and a Heroku app URL obtained from the Heroku application creation commands listed earlier. There can be many callback URLs in connected apps and they are separated by line breaks, as shown in the following screenshot:

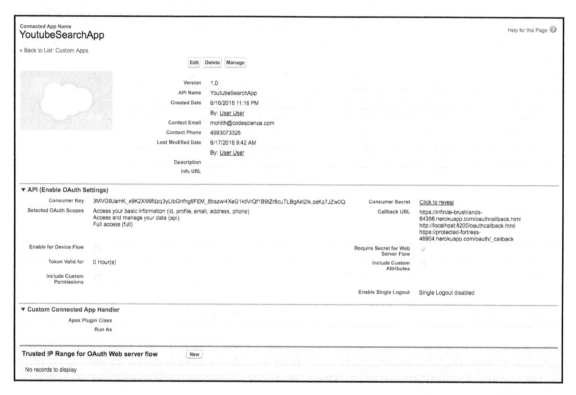

 The consumer key is created from the connected application.

Setting up a Node.js application

In this section, we will be building a Node.js application that renders the YouTube search component. We will be leveraging Lightning Out and some open source npm libraries, such as forcejs (`https://github.com/ccoenraets/forcejs`) and webpack, to build this application. The application will be hosted on the Heroku platform.

The following are the steps to build a working Node.js application:

1. Assuming we have Node.js and npm installed, let's initialize a Node.js app using the following command, in the same directory where we created a Heroku application, and accept the default prompts. This will create a `package.json` file in your current project folder:

   ```
   npm init
   ```

2. We will be using a forcejs library from the `https://github.com/ccoenraets/forcejs` repository, which helps to achieve OAuth. To install this as a dependency, run the following command:

   ```
   npm install forcejs --save-dev
   ```

3. There is a lightweight development server that can be optionally installed if you want to use the local dev server for development. Note that you will need to implement SSL and make it HTTPS if you are using this for Lightning Out. To install the dev dependency, use the following command:

   ```
   npm install force-server --save-dev
   ```

4. Babel transpiles all the ES6 into its ES5 equivalent using the transpiler and webpack. The following code installs webpack, babel-loader, babel-core, and other dependencies needed to transpile ES6 to ES5 code:

   ```
   npm install babel-core babel-loader babel-preset-es2015 webpack --
   save-dev
   ```

5. The `package.json` file will add scripts to start the webpack build and local server. The complete `package.json` should resemble the following code snippet. Edit `package.json` using the editor to use the following code:

```
{
  "name": "ltngoutapp",
  "version": "1.0.0",
  "description": "A sample node app for Lightning Out
demonstration",
  "main": "index.js",
  "author": "",
  "license": "ISC",
  "devDependencies": {
    "babel-core": "^6.26.3",
    "babel-loader": "^7.1.4",
    "babel-preset-es2015": "^6.24.1",
    "force-server": "0.0.8",
    "forcejs": "^2.2.1",
    "webpack": "^4.12.0",
    "webpack-cli": "^2.1.4"
  },
  "scripts": {
    "webpack": "webpack",
    "start": "force-server"
  },
  "engines": {
    "node": "9.5.0",
    "npm": "5.6.0"
  }
}
```

We also added engines so that when this is pushed to the Heroku build, Heroku recognizes it's a Node.js application and applies the Node.js build pack to build the application with the necessary dependencies.

6. Create a webpack config file (`webpack.config.js`) that takes the entry from the `app.js` file and creates a bundle named `app.bundle.js`. The webpack config file code is as follows:

```
var path = require('path');
var webpack = require('webpack');

const config = {
    mode: 'development',
    entry: './app.js',
```

```
output: {
    path: path.join(__dirname, '/app.bundle.js'),
    filename: 'app.bundle.js'
},
module: {
    rules: [
        {
            test: /\.js$/,
            exclude: /node_modules/,
            loader: 'babel-loader',
            query: {
                presets: ['es2015']
            }
        }
    ]
}
};
module.exports = config;
```

Note it uses the `babel-loader` to transpile the ES6 code to ES5, which all browsers can support.

 We are using ES6 because it encourages code to be modular and allows us to use fat arrow functions that are easy to type. Also, ES6 supports promises and so we can avoid callbacks and nested callbacks.

Creating a Lightning Out application

To create a Lightning Out application, the page will need a little JavaScript code, as shown here:

```
<script>
    $Lightning.use("c:youtubesearchOutApp", // name of the Lightning Out app
        function() { // Callback once framework and app loaded
            $Lightning.createComponent(
                "c:youtubesearch", // top-level component of your app
                { }, // attributes to set on the component when created
                "LightningLocator", // the DOM location to insert the component
                function(cmp) {
                    // callback when component is created and active on the page
                }
            );
```

```
    },
    'https://<myDomain>.Lightning.force.com/' ,// endpoint
    accessToken // access Token by authenticating to Salesforce
    );
</script>
```

The HTML page will need the following JavaScript script tag to load the Lightning Out library from the Salesforce domain, as shown here:

```
<script
src="https://<myDomain>.my.salesforce.com/Lightning/Lightning.out.js"></scr
ipt>
```

The code for the HTML page will be as follows:

```
<!DOCTYPE html>
<html>
<body>
    <h1>Lightning Out Youtube Search Component Demo</h1>
    <script
src="https://ability-page-3410-dev-ed.my.salesforce.com/Lightning/Lightning
.out.js"></script>
    <script src="app.bundle.js/app.bundle.js"></script>
    <div id="youtubeApp" />
</body>
</html>
```

Let's create the app.js entry file, which will primarily undergo the following steps:

1. OAuth with Salesforce to obtain the token
2. Execute the Lightning Out scripts to render the Lightning Out component

The app.js code is as follows:

```
import {OAuth} from 'forcejs';


let oauth = OAuth.createInstance("<clientId>"
                                ,"<sandbox/login url>",
                                "<redirectURL>"
                                );
oauth.login()
  .then(oauthResult => {
        //console.log(oauthResult);
        renderLightningOutComponent(oauthResult);
    });
```

```
let renderLightningOutComponent = (oauthResult) => {
    const token = oauthResult.accessToken;
    const LightningEndPointURI =
"https://ability-page-3410-dev-ed.Lightning.force.com";
    $Lightning.use("c:youtubesearchOutApp", () => {
        $Lightning.createComponent("c:youtubesearch", {},
            "youtubeApp",
            (cmp) => {
                //Component COde
            });
    },LightningEndPointURI,token );


}
```

Note that with `forcejs`, the OAuth process can be done with this:

```
oauth.createInstance("<clientId>","<sandbox/login url>","<redirectURL>")
```

`clientId` is the consumer key obtained from the connected app. `login url` will be `login.salesforce.com` for the developer Org and PROD, and for the `sandbox` and scratch Org it is `test.salesforce.com`. The `redirect url` is the Heroku callback URL.

Notice that once we perform OAuth, we use the following code to create the Lightning Out component on the `div` with the ID `youtubeApp`:

```
let renderLightningOutComponent = (oauthResult) => {
    const token = oauthResult.accessToken;
    const LightningEndPointURI =
"https://ability-page-3410-dev-ed.Lightning.force.com";
    $Lightning.use("c:youtubesearchOutApp", () => {
        $Lightning.createComponent("c:youtubesearch", {},
            "youtubeApp",
            (cmp) => {
                //Component
            });
    },LightningEndPointURI,token );
```

To create a bundle using webpack, run the following command. This generates a bundle that is imported in the HTML file:

```
npm run webpack
```

On successful build, the Terminal screen will resemble the following screenshot:

```
Mohiths-MacBook-Air:ltngOutApp mohith$ npm run webpack

> ltngoutapp@1.0.0 webpack /Users/mohith/Desktop/ForceProjects/Learning-Salesfor
ce-Lightning-Application-Development/chapter10/ltngOutApp
> webpack

Hash: 072352646ad326181e4e
Version: webpack 4.12.0
Time: 1189ms
Built at: 06/17/2018 4:33:38 PM
        Asset      Size  Chunks             Chunk Names
app.bundle.js  21.1 KiB    main  [emitted]  main
[./app.js] 852 bytes {main} [built]
    + 1 hidden module
Mohiths-MacBook-Air:ltngOutApp mohith$
```

Deploying Node.js application on Heroku

Deploying the Node.js application to Heroku would involve the following command:

```
//assumes you have ran $ heroku apps:create ltngOutApp
git add

git commit -m "Lightning Out App"
git push heroku master
```

On successful build, you can open the Heroku app from a Terminal using the `heroku open` command.

Configure `CORS` for the Heroku URL, as shown in the following screenshot in your Salesforce instance. `CORS` can be found by navigating to **Set up** | **Security Controls** | **CORS**.

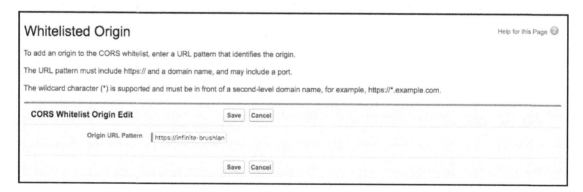

The application will ask for credentials and, once logged in, you will see the YouTube search component functional on the Heroku instance, as shown in the following screenshot:

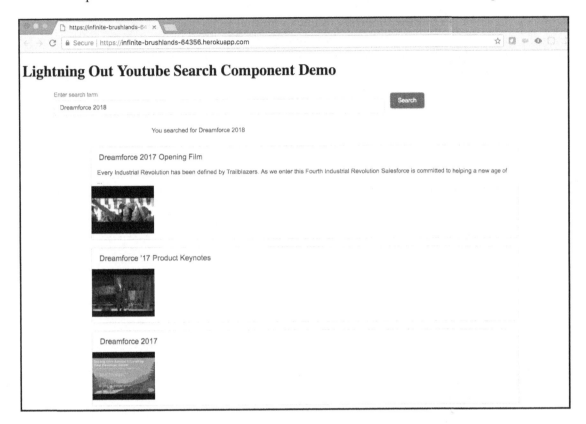

Lightning Out for unauthenticated users

In the last section, we required a connected app and authentication from Salesforce to render the Lightning Component. Authentication is needed if you want the application to securely fetch data from Salesforce using the user credentials.

However, let's say you want a non-secure component to be hosted on your site. An example could be a simple web to read from or a contact information collection form, and you do not want your users to log in.

For this scenario, the Lightning Out application will implement a special interface named `ltng:allowGuestAccess` and you will also need to create a Salesforce community that is published for the public.

Let's take a step-by-step walkthrough of how to take components outside Salesforce for unauthenticated users:

1. Create a Lightning Out dependency app that implements `ltng:allowGuestAccess`. The simple code modification to our YouTube Lightning Out application will be as follows. The name of the app is `youtubesearchOutApp`:

```
<aura:application access="GLOBAL" extends="ltng:outApp"
implements="ltng:allowGuestAccess">
    <aura:dependency resource="youtubesearch"/>
</aura:application>
```

2. Create a Salesforce community, as shown, by going to **Setup** | **Communities** | **All Communities** | **New Community**. Choose the **Customer Service** template, as shown here:

3. Make the community accessible by the public, as shown in the following screenshot, using the **General** settings. Notice the **Public Access** checkbox:

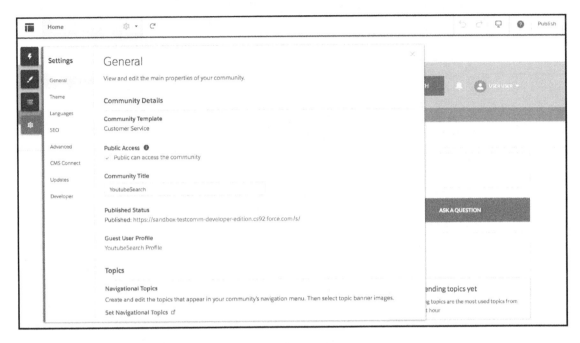

4. Publish the community using the **Publish** button on the extreme right. Note down the community domain and the URL from the **Setup** menu, as shown in the following screenshot. For example, in our case, the community URL is `https://sandbox-testcomm-developer-edition.cs92.force.com`:

5. Modify the previous Node application `index.html` to use the new community URL, as shown in the following code. Notice that we don't need all the webpack setup and JS bundler anymore as we no longer need to do OAuth and the application will render without asking for the credentials:

```html
<!DOCTYPE html>
<html>
<body>
    <h1>Lightning Out Youtube Search Component Demo</h1>
    <script
src="https://<yourCommunityDomain/communityURL>/Lightning/Lightning.out.js"></script>
    <!--<script src="app.bundle.js/app.bundle.js"></script>-->
    <div id="youtubeApp" />
</body>
<script >
    $Lightning.use("c:youtubesearchOutApp", function() {
        $Lightning.createComponent("c:youtubesearch", {},
            "youtubeApp",
            function(cmp) {
                // do some stuff
            });
    },"<communityURL>/");
</script>
</html>
```

6. Note that you will need a CORS for the Heroku URL, as shown in the following screenshot:

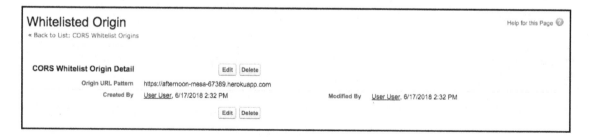

I have created a public website with the YouTube search component, which will allow you to play with the application without authentication at `https://afternoon-mesa-67389.herokuapp.com/`.

 It's a free Heroku application and, currently, free Heroku apps live on a single dyno, and hence may take some time to render.

Lightning Out limitations and considerations

Lightning Out has some limitations, as highlighted here:

- Not all the events provided by the component framework are supported. Some events work only inside Salesforce Lightning Experience, as they leverage `one.app` container. `one.app` container is comprised of a set of JavaScript events and functions that are only available in Salesforce Lightning Experience and the Salesforce 1 mobile application.
- Not all standard components are supported in Lightning Out. Specifically, ones that are dependent on the `one.app` container library are not supported.
- Lightning Out requires customers to allow third-party cookies in their browser settings.

Summary

In this chapter, we explored the basic concepts of Lightning Out and the JavaScript code to render the Lightning Component outside the Salesforce platform. We leveraged OAuth and connected our app to provide an authenticated experience for the Lightning Out application. For unauthenticated and public-facing site use cases, we explored the Lightning Out interface for guest users.

In the next chapter, we will focus on how we can make these components available for Salesforce Lightning flows.

11
Lightning Flows

The Flow builder in Salesforce allows Salesforce system administrators to build forms, add business logic, and perform data queries and data manipulation using the drag and drop widget.

Flow can also help build a multi-step wizard experience, where users can navigate back and forth between multiple views. Lightning Flows provide the ability to integrate Lightning Components with the Flow builder. You can pass data back and forth between custom-built Lightning Components and Salesforce Flows.

In this chapter, we will explore the following topics:

- Introducing Flows
- Running Flows in Lightning Experience
- Adding customized Lightning Components to the Flow builder
- Debugging Flows
- Flow's local actions

Introducing Flows

In this section, we will explore the basic Flow elements that the Flow builder provides. To create a Flow in Salesforce, navigate to **Setup** | **Process Automation** | **Flows**.

A Flow can be composed of one or more of the following elements:

- Screen elements allow you to use input and output fields and Lightning Components. The following screenshot shows the input screen and the output display elements:

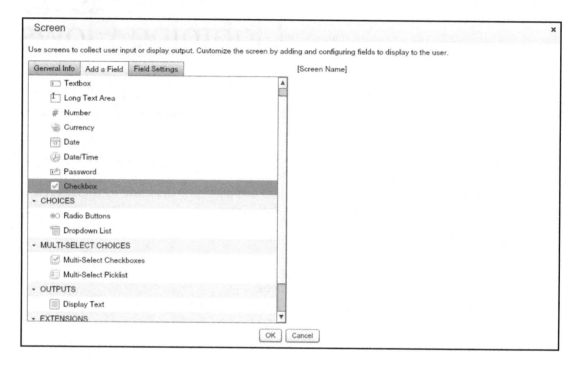

- Logical elements include **Decision**, **Loop**, **Wait**, and **Assignment**. This is shown in the following screenshot:

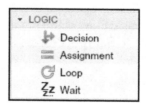

- Data elements include the ability to query a single record (**Record Lookup**), query multiple records (**Fast Lookup**), insert a record (**Record Create**), and to create multiple records (**Fast Create**). Note that elements with a name starting with *Fast* allow you to work with rows of data. The following screenshot shows the data elements:

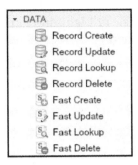

- The resource palette allows the adding of variables to hold a single row of data, the collection of data, single variable, write formulas, and many more. The following screenshot shows the resource palette:

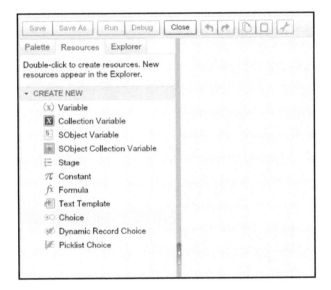

Creating the Lead Finder app using the Flow builder

In this section, we will follow step-by-step instructions to create a page that can help find leads from Salesforce using the email of the lead, and if the lead is not found, it takes the user to a screen where they can create a lead. The aim of this section is to learn how to use the Flow builder to build forms and to add logic.

You can search for Flows in the Classic or Lightning Experience setup: **Setup | Process Automation | Flows**. The final finished version of the Flow should resemble what is shown in the following screenshot:

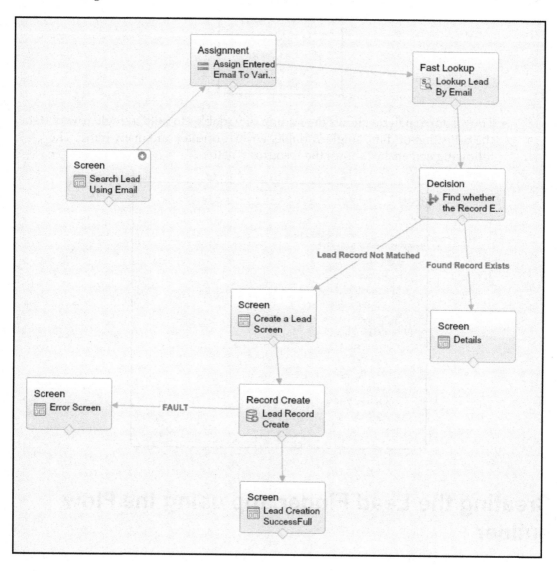

1. Create a **Screen** element with an input field to allow users to input their email. The screen element can be dragged from the palette to the canvas, as shown in the following screenshot. Add the input form field of thee text type. Let's take a look:

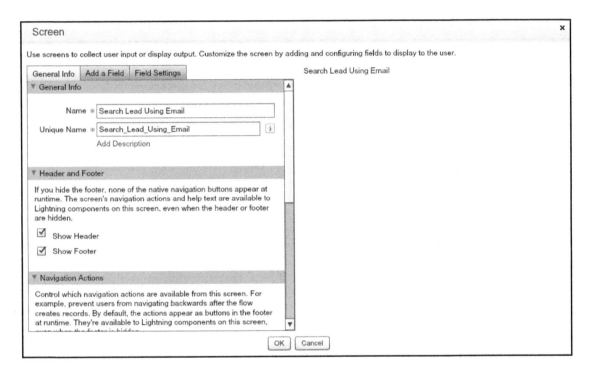

2. Assign the input element bounded to the textbox to a private variable (this can be avoided; however, for demonstration purposes, we are showing you how you can store the values in the private variables). Notice that an input variable is automatically created once you add an input field. Refer to the following screenshot:

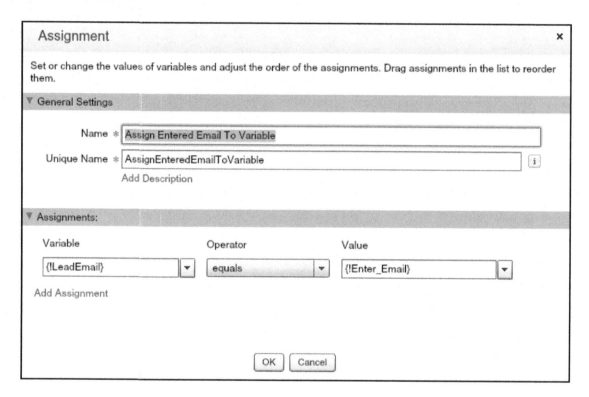

3. Add a **Fast Lookup** element to search for the record from the database, and assign the result to an object private variable that we created. This is shown in the following screenshot:

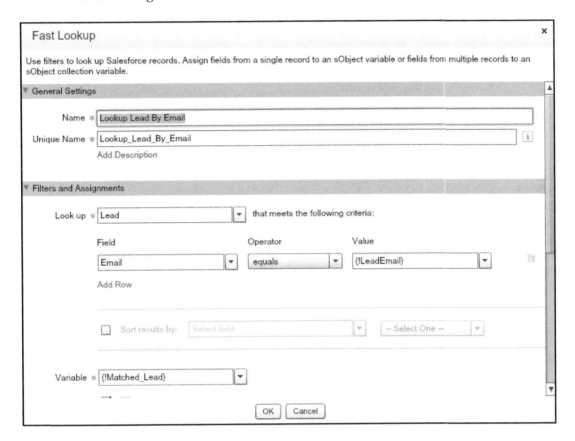

4. Add a decision element to branch into one when the lookup returns a record and another when the lookup has no result. Notice in the condition section that we used **Resource** as the **FAST LOOKUP** to see whether it evaluates to true:

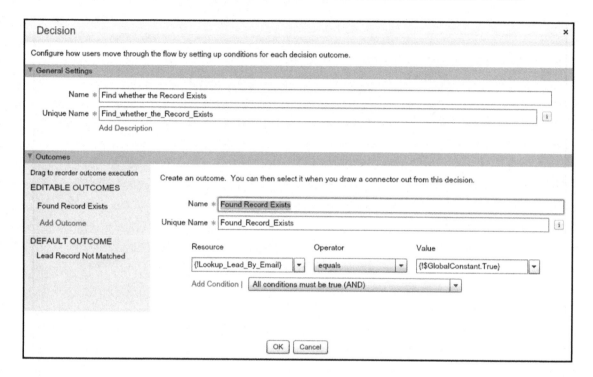

5. The display screen for the successful outcome is as follows:

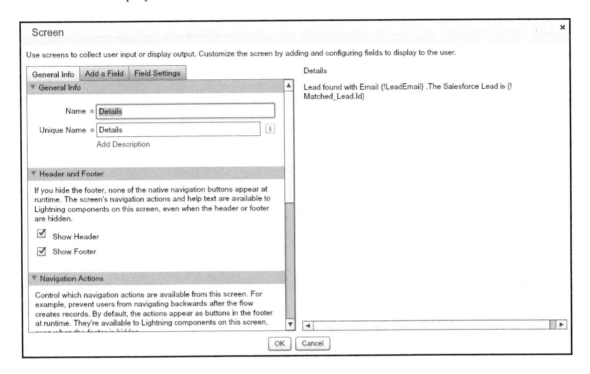

6. If no records are found, we display a new screen with the necessary fields. Create some new screen elements with fields, as follows:

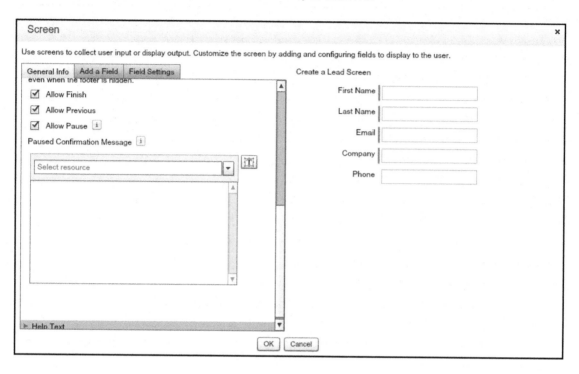

7. On record creation, we display the ID of the lead record. Also, note that we can handle faults when we run a **Fast Lookup** or **Record Create**, or any of the DML elements to show an exception or to handle exceptions:

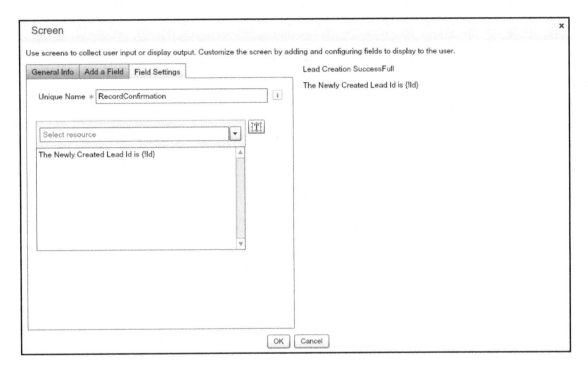

Once you have completed the Flow, you can run the Flow in both Salesforce Classic and Lightning Experience.

Running Flows in Lightning Experience

In Lightning Experience, you can drag and drop the Flow on the home page, record page, or custom-built pages using the **App Builder** standard Flow components. This is shown as follows:

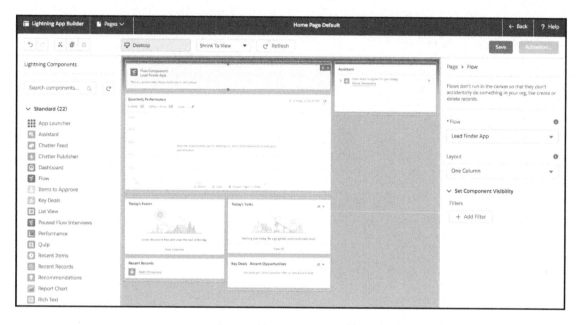

This is how you can drag a flow component and associate a visual flow

The component on the home page could co-exist with other components, as shown in the following screenshot:

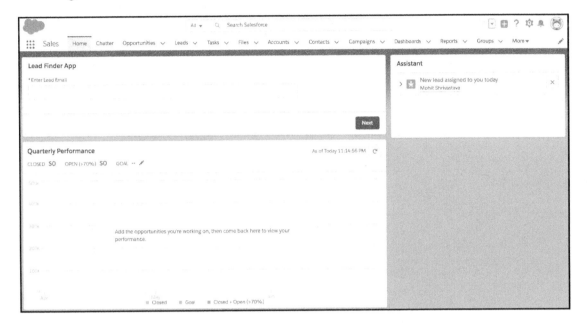

Debugging Flows

You can debug Flows using the **Debug** button on the Flow designer. The following screenshot shows how the Flow debugging details are logged when the debugger is run:

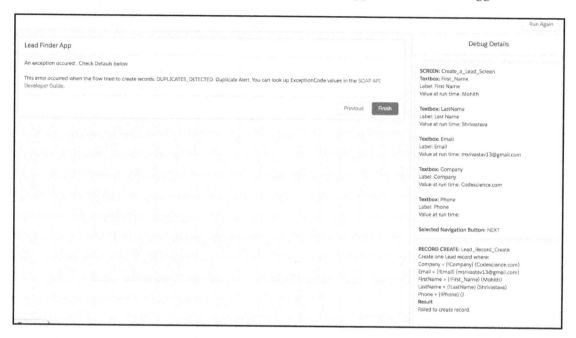

Adding custom components in Flow builder

In this section, we will give an example of how you can add a custom Lightning Component in Flows and pass data between the Flow input and the Lightning Component, and vice versa.

he following screenshot shows how you could pass parameters and values from Flow to a Lightning Component:

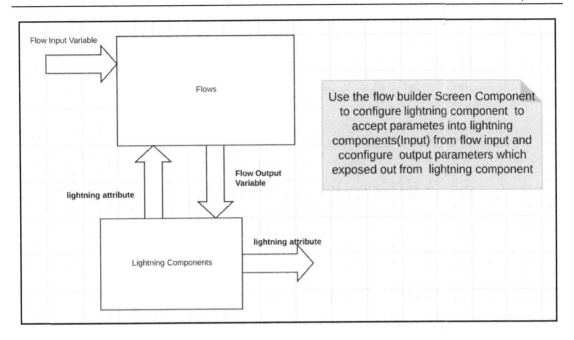

The last example covered in the previous section, *Creating the lead finder app using Flow builder*, had the last step for just displaying the ID of the record. How about using a lightning screen at the end of the Flow, where the user can edit more fields, based on the page layout set by the system administrator?

To achieve this, let's build a custom Lightning Component that us comprised of `recordForm` to add editing capabilities. For more information on `recordForm`, go to `https://developer.Salesforce.com/docs/component-library/bundle/lightning:recordForm/documentation`.

To make your component available for the Flow screen, the component needs to implement , `lightning:availableForFlowscreens` interface, and any input that will be exposed in the Flow builder needs an *attribute and a design file*.

For example, in our use case, we can pass the `leadId` to the custom component that displays the Lead Edit form. The code for the Lightning Component is as follows:

```
<--LeadEditForm-->
<aura:component implements="lightning:availableForFlowscreens"
access="global">
    <aura:attribute name="leadId" type="String" access="global" />
    <lightning:recordForm
    recordId="{!v.leadId}"
    objectApiName="Lead"
```

```
        layoutType="Full"
        mode="view" />
</aura:component>
```

To pass the attribute from the Flow to the component, we need to define a design file, as shown in the following screenshot:

```
<design:component >
    <design:attribute name="leadId" label="leadId" />
</design:component>
```

Note that the design file is a required step if we want these to be available in Flows. Check the following screenshot that shows the attribute that's available as the input parameter in the Flow component:

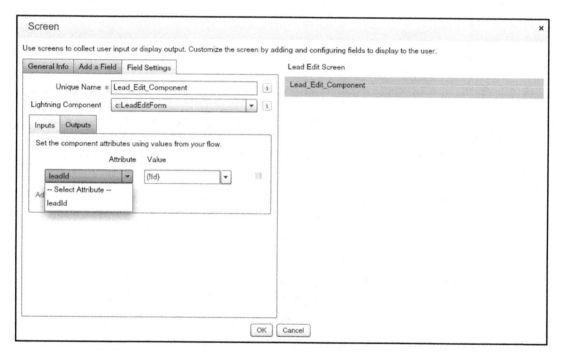

 The Lightning Component implementing `lightning:availableForFlowscreens` is available as part of the **Screen** element in Flows. When we drag the screen component, we can pick one from the available Lightning Component list.

Also note that when we add a Lightning Component to Flow, the Flow can run only in Lightning Experience. Check the following screenshot, which warns that this Flow won't work in Classic:

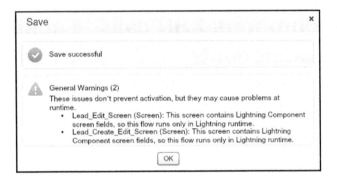

Once you have the Flow screens with the Lightning Components, the Flow builder components should resemble something such as the following:

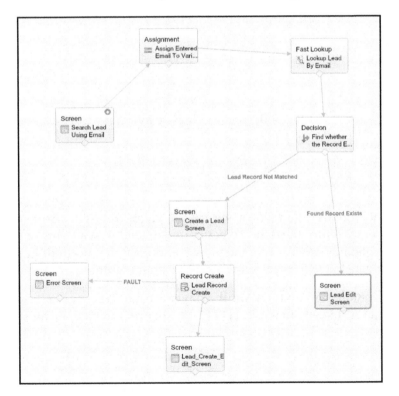

Screenshot shows the Lead Finder Flow With Custom Lightning Component as Screen element

On a successful run, you should see a form with a pencil icon to inline edit all fields on the layout.

Using asynchronous XHR calls in customized Lightning Components

Custom Lightning Components can make asynchronous calls, which can include calling a third-party API client using an XHR request. Also, you can read the navigation options configured by the admins, and navigate the Flow to the next screen.

The boilerplate code is as follows, and is used to detect all the available actions:

```
var availableActions = component.get('v.availableActions);
for (var i = 0; i < availableActions.length; i++) {
    if (availableActions[i] == "PAUSE") {
    } else if (availableActions[i] == "BACK") {

    } else if (availableActions[i] == "NEXT") {

    } else if (availableActions[i] == "FINISH") {

    }
}
```

To navigate back-and-forth, the boilerplate code is as follows:

```
var actionClicked = "NEXT";
var navigate = component.get('v.navigateFlow');
navigate(actionClicked);//actionClicked can be one from PAUSE, BACK, NEXT,
and FINISH
```

To make an asynchronous call in Flows, we can use JavaScript XHR client-side calls from the `init` handler and return the data. To better understand this, let's make a third-party call to an email validator service from the Flow component that we built in the previous section, and navigate to the next screen from the custom Lightning Component.

For this demonstration, sign up for a **Mailboxlayer** account (https://mailboxlayer.com), which provides an API key to make an HTTPS GET in order to validate an email.

The request payload is as follows, along with an API key. In the payload, replace the API key with the one obtained when you signed up for a mailbox layer account. Refer to the following code:

```
http://apilayer.net/api/check

    ? access_key = <accessKey>
    & email = msrivastav13@gmail.com
    & smtp = 1
    & format = 1
```

A valid response returns Boolean flags for a format check, SMTP check, and a score percentage. The response will be similar to the following JSON object:

```
{
  "email":"msrivastav13@gmail.com",
  "did_you_mean":"",
  "user":"msrivastav13",
  "domain":"gmail.com",
  "format_valid":true,
  "mx_found":true,
  "smtp_check":true,
  "catch_all":null,
  "role":false,
  "disposable":false,
  "free":true,
  "score":0.8
}
```

Let's build a Lightning Component that accepts the input from Flow as email and shows the validity score from the API, and then allows users to navigate for further actions.

The Flow will require a custom Lightning Component that makes a third-party callout. The code for the Lightning Component is as follows:

```
<aura:component implements="lightning:availableForFlowscreens"
access="global">

    <aura:attribute type="String" name="email" />
    <aura:attribute type="Boolean" name="validEmail"/>
    <aura:attribute type="Object" name="serviceResponse" default="{}"/>
    <aura:handler name="init" value="{!this}" action="{!c.init}"/>

    <!--Markup for the checks-->
    <div>
        <b>Valid Format</b>
        <aura:if isTrue="{!v.serviceResponse.format_valid}">
                <lightning:icon iconName="action:update_status"
```

```
            alternativeText="Approved" />
                <aura:set attribute="else">
                    <lightning:icon iconName="action:close"
alternativeText="Rejected" />
                </aura:set>
            </aura:if>
        </div>

        <br/>
        <br/>

        <div>
            <b>SMTP Check</b>
            <aura:if isTrue="{!v.serviceResponse.smtp_check}">
                    <lightning:icon iconName="action:update_status"
alternativeText="Approved" />
                <aura:set attribute="else">
                    <lightning:icon iconName="action:close"
alternativeText="Rejected" />
                </aura:set>
            </aura:if>
        </div>

        <br/>
        <br/>
        <div>
            <b>Score</b>
            <lightning:progressBar value="{!mult(v.serviceResponse.score,100)}"
size="large" variant="circular"/>
        </div>

</aura:component>
```

The client-side controller file is as follows:

```
({
    init : function(component, event, helper) {
        helper.validateEmailService(component, event);
    }
})
```

The code to perform an HTTP call using ES6 promises is shown in the following code snippet. Notice that we use the native browser's XMLHttpRequest API to make XHR calls from the client-side:

```
({
    validateEmailService : function(component, event) {
        this.mailBoxLayerValidateEmail(component, event).then(
            function(response) {
                console.log("Success!", response);
                component.set("v.serviceResponse",response);
            },function(error) {
                console.error("Failed!", error);
            }
        )
    },

    mailBoxLayerValidateEmail : function(component, event){
        return new Promise($A.getCallback(function(resolve, reject) {
            var xhttp = new XMLHttpRequest();
            xhttp.onreadystatechange = $A.getCallback(function() {
                if (this.readyState === 4) { // DONE
                    if (xhttp.status === 200) {
                        var response = JSON.parse(xhttp.responseText);
                        console.log(response);
                        resolve(response);
                    }
                    else {
                        reject();
                    }
                }
            });
            var requestUrl =
"http://apilayer.net/api/check?access_key=<accessKeyHere>&email=";
            requestUrl = requestUrl + component.get("v.email") + '&smtp=1'
+ '&format=1';
            xhttp.open("GET", requestUrl);
            xhttp.send(null);
        }));
    }

})
```

We can wire the API response lightning to the Flows to make sure that the screen, after the email ID is entered by the user, is a Lightning Component screen that makes a third-party API call.

The following screenshot shows the `Screen` input to the Lightning Component:

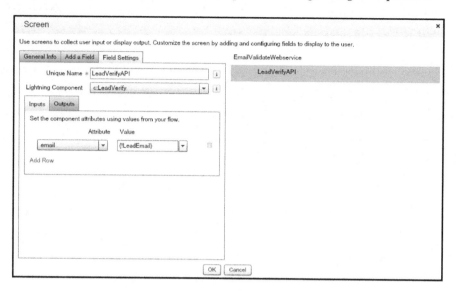

The Flow builder should resemble the following screenshot, once we have the Lightning Component screen:

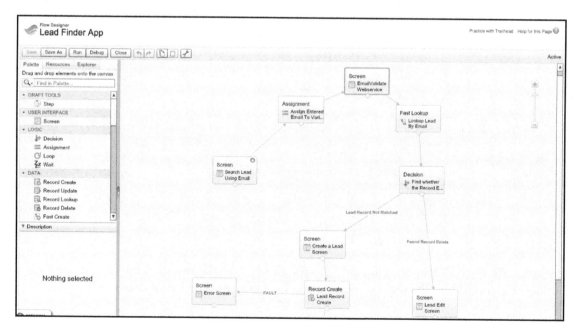

The component screen is as follows, which shows the score and checks:

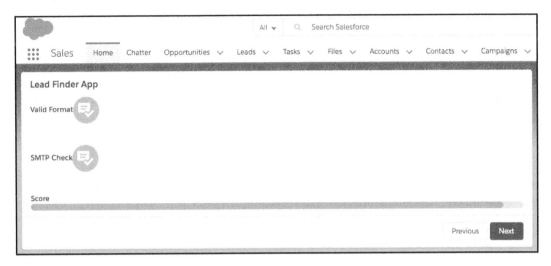

Now, let's customize the footer by making our own footer and hiding the default ones that the Flow provides. To hide the footer in the Lightning Component screen, in the Flow builder, click on the Lightning Component Flow element and disable the footer, as shown in the following screenshot:

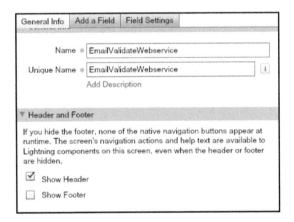

Let's modify our Lightning Component so that we can add our own implementation for the footer buttons. Add the following code to the Lightning Component markup in order to create our own navigation button:

```
<div class="slds-clearfix">
```

```
            <div class="slds-clearfix">
                <div class="slds-float_left">
                    <lightning:button label="Previous" aura:id="BACK"
onclick="{!c.handleClick}"/>
                </div>
                <div class="slds-float_right">
                    <lightning:button label="Next" aura:id="NEXT"
onclick="{!c.handleClick}"
disabled="{!not(and(v.serviceResponse.format_valid,v.serviceResponse.smtp_c
heck,(v.serviceResponse.score > 0.4)))}" variant="brand"/>
                </div>
            </div>
        </div>
```

Notice that we disable the *Next* button if the email is invalid as per the information retrieved from the API, using an expression syntax.

The controller code to invoke the navigation is as follows:

```
handleClick : function(component, event, helper) {
        // Figure out which action was called
        var actionClicked = event.getSource().getLocalId();
        // Fire that action
        var navigate = component.get('v.navigateFlow');
        navigate(actionClicked);
    }
```

The following screenshot shows the use case when the email format is invalid and the button is disabled:

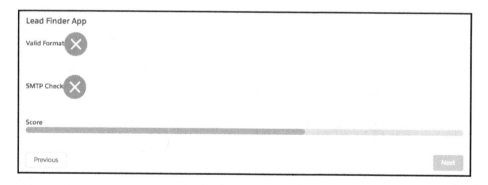

 The header of the Flow can also be hidden and customized with the custom implementation using the same approach: by using a customized Lightning Component that acts as a header.

Using Lightning Components as local Flow actions

Local Flow actions in the Flow are comprised of quick actions and other utility actions, such as posting to chatter, sending emails, submitting for approvals, adding tasks, adding call records, and many more. The following screenshot shows some of the quick actions that are available in the Flow builder out of the box:

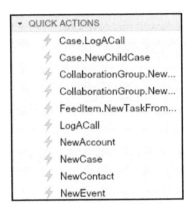

A Lightning Component can also be used as a Flow action. This allows you to execute client-side third-party API calls (using an XHR request to the server), tap into browser-related APIs to access the camera, and capture photos, videos, record audios, and many more utilities.

A Lightning Component requires an interface called `lightning:availableForFlowActions` to allow the components to be available as a local Flow action.

Also, you would need to define a design file and attributes, similar to the one we covered in the *Adding Custom Components in the Flow builder* section, to allow parameters to be available as input and output variables in the Flow builder.

Finally, you would need an `invoke` method. Note that when Flow executes as a local action, it looks for the method named `invoke` in the controller file, as shown in the following code snippet:

```
({
    // When a Flow executes this component, it calls the invoke method
    invoke : function(component, event, helper) {
    }
})
```

To understand this further, let's build a simple Lightning Component that implements `lightning:availableForFlowActions` and fetches the location of the user, using the browser's location API described here: `https://whatwebcando.today/geolocation.html`.

If you want to execute an asynchronous code that includes callbacks, then prefer promises to avoid callback hell. We will use the following boilerplate code to perform asynchronous requests in Flow's local actions:

```
({
    invoke : function(component, event, helper) {
        return new Promise(function(resolve, reject) {
            // Do something asynchronously, like get data from
            // an on-premise database

            // Complete the call and return to the Flow
            if (/* request was successful */) {
                // Set output values for the appropriate attributes
                resolve();
            } else {
                reject(new Error("My error message")); }
        });
    }
})
```

The Lightning Component code for the `LocationFinder` component is as follows:

```
<aura:component implements="lightning:availableForFlowActions"
access="global">
    <aura:attribute name="latitude" type="String" access="global" />
    <aura:attribute name="longitude" type="String" access="global" />
</aura:component>
```

Notice that to expose latitude and longitude as the variable from the Flow designer, we need to create a design file, as follows:

```
<design:component >
    <design:attribute name="latitude" label="Latitude" />
    <design:attribute name="longitude" label="Longitude" />
</design:component>
```

The `invoke` method gets executed when the Flow's local action executes; here is the `invoke` method that calls the navigator API:

```
({
    invoke : function(component, event, helper) {
        return new Promise(function(resolve, reject) {
            // Do something asynchronously, like get data from
```

```
                    // an on-premise database
                    // Complete the call and return to the Flow
                    if ('geolocation' in navigator) {
                        // Set output values for the appropriate attributes
                        navigator.geolocation.getCurrentPosition(function (location)
    {
    component.set("v.latitude",location.coords.latitude.toString());
    component.set("v.longitude",location.coords.longitude.toString());
                            resolve();
                        });
                    } else {
                        reject(new Error("My error message"));
                    }
                });
        }
    })
```

Once we have the component, let's use the Flow builder and configure a Flow with a welcome and a finish screen, as shown in the following screenshot. Create two variables of the string type to hold the latitude and longitude returned from the Flow's local action. The following screenshot shows the Flow named LocationFinder and its components:

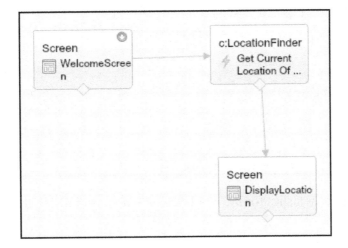

The following screenshot shows the configuration required to output values:

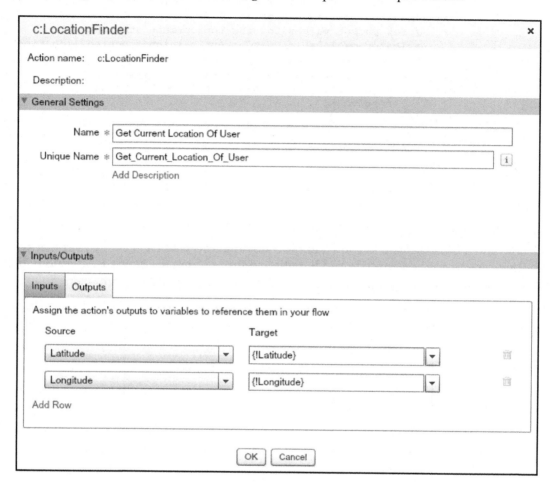

The following is the screenshot for the result screen when used inside the Lightning Application builder:

Embedding Flows into a Lightning Component

So far, in the previous subsections, we explored how a Lightning Component can be part of the Flow builder. In this section, we will explore how you can embed the Flow inside a custom Lightning Component and pass variables in and out from the Flows to the custom Lightning Components.

To embed the Flow inside the Lightning Component, use the `lightning:Flow` tag and assign an `aura:id`. The following code snippet shows how to declare a markup that can render Flow inside the Lightning Component:

```
<aura:component>
    <aura:handler name="init" value="{!this}" action="{!c.init}"/>
    <lightning:Flow aura:id="myFlow"
onstatuschange="{!c.handleStatusChange}" />
</aura:component>
```

The JavaScript code to render the Flow and then handle the status change is as follows:

```
({
    init : function (component) {
        // Find the component whose aura:id is "myFlow"
        var Flow = component.find("myFlow");
        // In that component, start your Flow. Reference the Flow's Unique
Name.
        Flow.startFlow("myFlow");//Assumes Flow unique name is myFlow
    },
    handleStatusChange : function (component, event) {
        if(event.getParam("status") === "FINISHED") {
            // Get the output variables and iterate over them
            var outputVariables = event.getParam("outputVariables");
            var outputVar;
            for(var i = 0; i < outputVariables.length; i++) {
                outputVar = outputVariables[i];
                // Pass the values to the component's attributes
                if(outputVar.name === "x") {
                } else {
                }
            }
        }
    },
})
```

Notice that the `handleStatusChange` event is fired every time the Flow navigates, and `event.getParam("status")` and `event.getParam("outputVariables")` provide status and the output variables from the Flow.

To pass variables when a Flow is started, use input variables as parameters. Check the following syntax and the expected format:

```
var inputvariables = [

    {
       name : "var1", //This assumes var1 is a Flow builder generated
variable
       type : "FlowDataType", // Data type can be String, number, Array,
Sobject, Boolean
       value : valueToSet
    },
    {
       name : "var2",//This assumes var1 is a Flow builder generated variable
       type : "FlowDataType",
       value : [ value1, value2] //Not value can be an Array and an Sobject
Array as well
    }

]

  var Flow = component.find("myFlow");
       // In that component, start your Flow. Reference the Flow's Unique
Name.
       Flow.startFlow("myFlow",inputVariables);
```

The following is a diagrammatic representation of the preceding concepts:

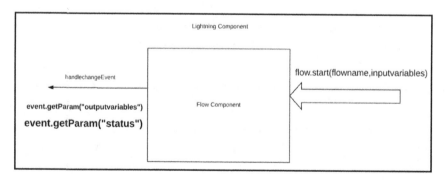

Let's apply the preceding concept and extend the `LocationFinder` Flow. We have to customize the finish action to open a window with the latitude and longitude populated on Google Maps. The URL to open a Google Map is as follows:

```
https://maps.google.com/maps?&z=15&q=latitude + '+' + longitude + '&ll=' +
latitude + '+' + longitude
```

Since we have the Flow already working, let's just wrap the Flow inside the Lightning Component and handle the event to detect the FINISHED status and open another window with Google Maps with latitude and longitude.

The component markup is as follows. Notice that we need the unique ID of the Flow:

```
<aura:component implements="flexipage:availableForAllPageTypes">
    <aura:handler name="init" value="{!this}" action="{!c.init}"/>
    <lightning:Flow aura:id="myFlow"
onstatuschange="{!c.handleStatusChange}" />
</aura:component>
```

The controller code to handle the override finish behavior is as follows:

```
({
    init : function(component, event, helper) {
        // Find the component whose aura:id is "myFlow"
        var Flow = component.find("myFlow");
        // In that component, start your Flow. Reference the Flow's Unique
Name.
        Flow.startFlow("LocationFinder");//Assumes Flow unique name is
myFlow
    },

    handleStatusChange : function (component, event) {
        if(event.getParam("status") === "FINISHED") {
            // Get the output variables and iterate over them
            var outputVariables = event.getParam("outputVariables");
            var outputVar;
            var latitude;
            var longitude;
            for(var i = 0; i < outputVariables.length; i++) {
                outputVar = outputVariables[i];
                // Pass the values to the component's attributes
                if(outputVar.name === "latitude") {
                    latitude = outputVar.value;
                } else if (outputVar.name === "longitude"){
                    longitude = outputVar.value;
                }
            }
            var mapURL = 'https://maps.google.com/maps?&z=15&q=' + latitude
+ '+' + longitude + '&ll=' + latitude + '+' + longitude;
            window.open(mapURL, "_target");
        }
    },
})
```

Summary

In this chapter, we explored how Lightning Components can be used in the Flow builder and can pass data between Flow elements and components. This chapter also covered code samples for embedding Flows into Lightning Components and configuring Lightning Components as screen elements or using them to act as local actions in Flow builder.

In the next chapter, we will explore how we can use Lightning Components with the Salesforce 1 mobile application, Salesforce Communities, and Salesforce Console apps.

12
Making Components Available for Salesforce Mobile and Communities

Salesforce offers a mobile application on the Apple App Store for iOS and Google Play for Android devices that provides most of the functionality that a web application provides. Lightning Components can be used in the Salesforce mobile application in various places, such as **Global Actions**, **Object-Specific Actions**, and navigation. In this chapter, we will explore how you can use Lightning Components to customize the Salesforce mobile application.

Salesforce communities provide the ability to create customer-facing portals and online discussion forums. Salesforce communities leverage Community Builder and Lightning Components, and they theme layouts to provide a customized experience. We will uncover some of these in this chapter.

In this chapter, we will cover the following topics:

- Using Lightning Components in a Salesforce mobile application
- Using Lightning Components in Salesforce Community Cloud

Using Lightning Components in a Salesforce mobile application

The Salesforce mobile application for iOS can be downloaded from the Apple store (`https://itunes.apple.com/us/app/true/id404249815?mt=8`), and for Android, the app can be downloaded from the Google Play store (`https://play.google.com/store/apps/details?id=com.Salesforce.chatter`). In this section, we will dig into how to add our YouTube search component as a quick action and a global action and to the left navigation of the Salesforce mobile application.

> The Salesforce mobile application is also commonly referred to as Salesforce1.

The setup home page for the lightning experience provides a **Go Mobile** button. The following is a screenshot of the wizard that you need to navigate through in order to get to Go Mobile, with the Salesforce mobile app:

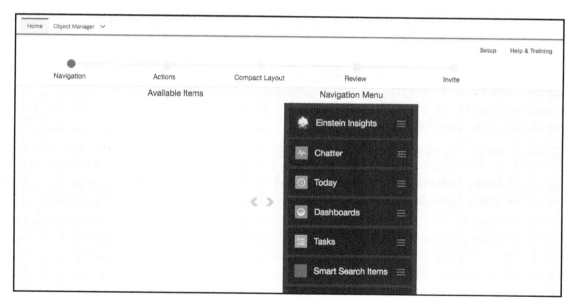

Setting up the Chrome browser to simulate the Salesforce mobile app experience

For this section, we will use the Chrome browser to simulate the mobile-device experience. Use your Chrome browser to log into the Salesforce Instance, right-click to open the console, and click on the device menu, as shown in the following screenshot.

Select the **iPhone X** model, and set the device width to **50% – 100%**. The following screenshot shows the configuration needed in the Chrome console:

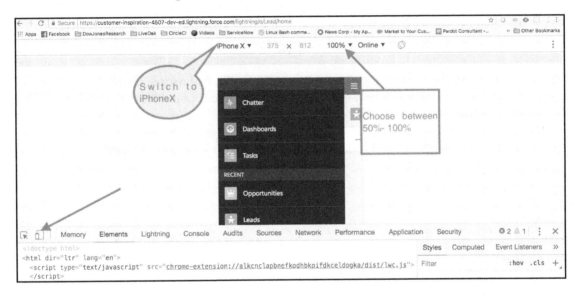

To navigate to the Salesforce1 experience in your browser type, strip everything after the domain name and add `one/one.app`.

For example, if your URL
is `https://customer-inspiration-4507-dev-ed.lightning.force.com/xx/xxx/x`
`x`, to simulate a mobile app, experience the URL
would be `https://customer-inspiration-4507-dev-ed.lightning.force.com/on`
`e/one.app`.

Salesforce recommends doing actual device testing if you are building Lightning Components for Salesforce mobile.

Adding a Lightning Component to the Salesforce mobile navigation

To add Lightning Components to the Salesforce mobile application navigation, you need to make sure that Lightning Component implements the `force:appHostable` interface:

```
<aura:component implements="force:appHostable">
```

Let's add the YouTube search component we created to the Salesforce mobile application navigation menu. To do this, let's deploy the Lightning Component by using SFDX commands to push source code from the git repository at `https://github.com/PacktPublishing/Learning-Salesforce-Lightning-Application-Development/tree/master/chapter12` to the scratch Org, as shown in the following code snippet:

```
# Authenticate to Dev Hub
sfdx force:auth:web:login -d -a DevHub

# Set as Default Devhub
sfdx force:config:set defaultdevhubusername=DevHub

# Create a scratch Org with alias testOrg
sfdx force:org:create -s -f config/project-scratch-def.json -a testOrg

# Set an existing scratch Org as default
sfdx force:config:set defaultusername=<username|alias>
```

```
# push code
sfdx force:source:push

# Open the scratch Org with alias 'testOrg' in browser
sfdx force:org:open -u testOrg
```

The next step is to create an *app page using the lightning app builder* and make sure that we have the YouTube search component added in, as shown in the following screenshot. The app builder can be found using the setup menu:

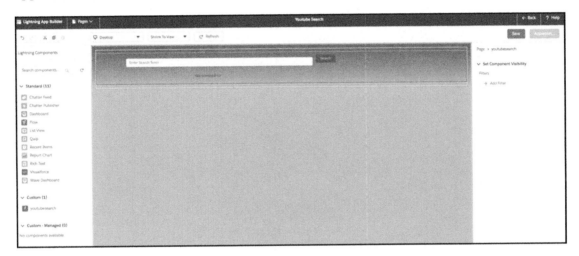

Screenshot shows how you can drop youtube search component on a Lightning App Builder Page

Once you activate the Lightning Application page (the activation button is located in the top right of the builder page), navigate to **Mobile Subsection,** and make sure to add the app page to the navigation, as follows:

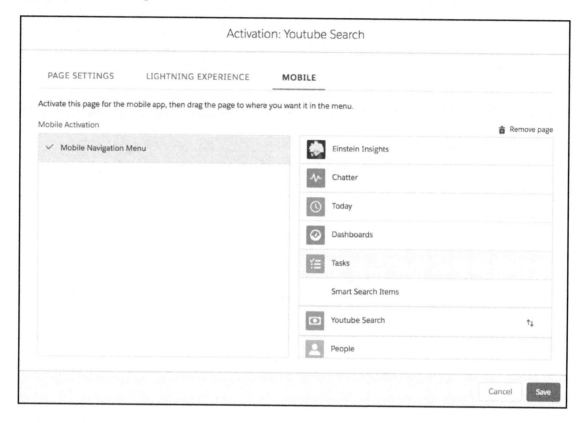

Alternatively, navigate to **Setup** | **Mobile Apps** | **Salesforce** | **Navigation** from the setup menu and add the YouTube search app page, as shown in the following screenshot:

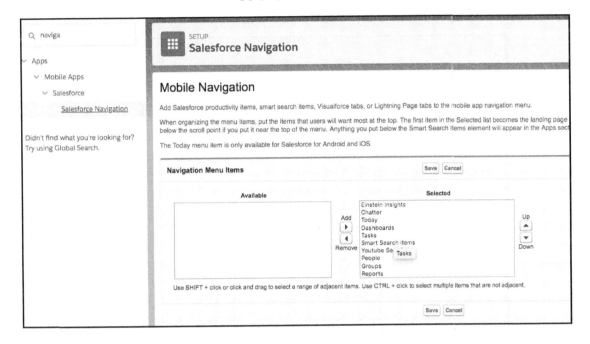

To test the application, set your Chrome browser settings to view in device mode, as covered in the previous section, and you will see the component working in the Salesforce mobile application:

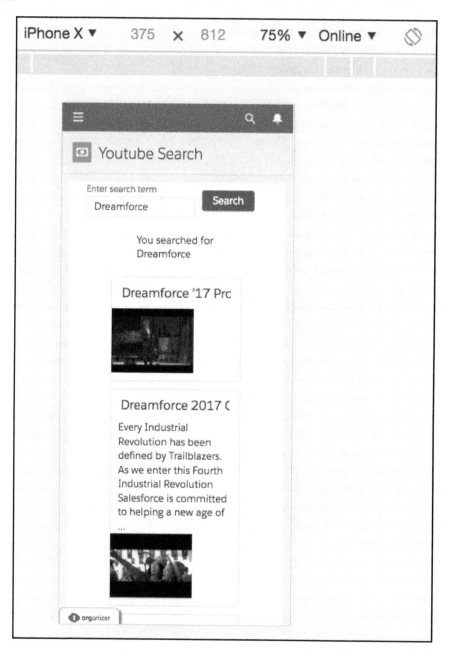

Adding Lightning Components as global and object-specific actions

The other way you can incorporate Lightning Components in the Salesforce mobile application is via the **Lightning-Quick** action or **Global** actions.

The difference between a global action and a lightning-quick action is that global actions are available from the **Chatter** tab (they appear in the top right in Lightning Experience) and are available across, while an object-specific action only appears in the record detail view of the object (provided they are part of the page's layout).

 Note that in Lightning Experience, these actions open within a modal.

To make a Lightning Component available for a global action, use the `force:lightningQuickAction` interface on the Lightning Component. Take a look at this code line:

```
<aura:component implements="force:lightningQuickAction">
```

Let's create a global action for a YouTube search that uses the YouTube search component. To create it in Salesforce, navigate to **Setup** | **Global Actions**.

The following screenshot shows how to create a global action:

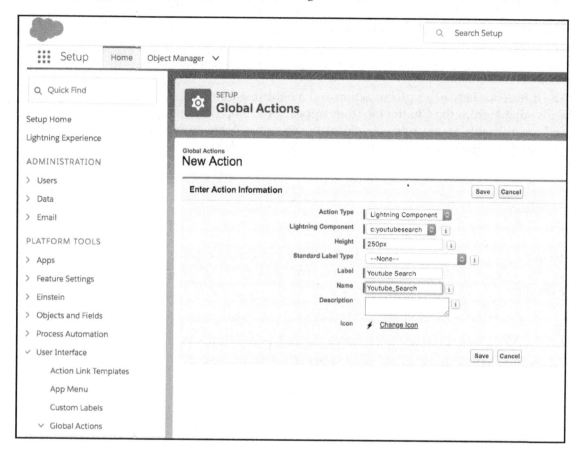

For the global action to appear, you need to add the Lightning Component to the publisher layout, as shown in the following screenshot:

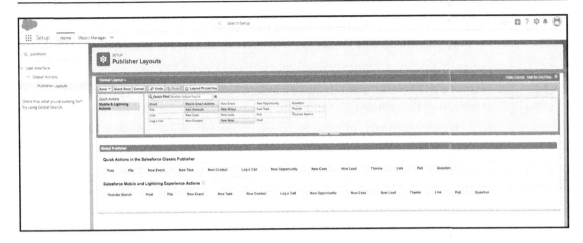

Screenshot shows the Publisher Layout configuration to add Custom Lightning Component as Quick Action

Once you have added the global action, if you are on the **Chatter** tab, you can see the global action, as shown in following screenshots:

Similarly, you can also use a Lightning Component on object-specific actions. You can include it in the page layout, and this appears when a record detail is viewed.

Use `force:lightningQuickActionWithoutHeader` if you want to remove the header from the quick action and add your own headers to the customized Lightning Component.

Lightning Components in Community Cloud

Salesforce Community Cloud provides the ability to quickly build a portal and communities for employees, partners, and customers. The Community Cloud provides the ability for Salesforce contacts to log into communities as an authenticated user. The chatter components and the chatter experience is baked into the communities. Chatter allows you to collaborate using `@mentions`, providing the ability to create groups and private messages and to share content and files. The Community Cloud platform comes with a Community Builder that allows you to create a page that can be comprised of one or more standard and custom components.

When you create communities, you can choose from predefined templates and customize the layout, theme, and branding, or you can even build your own template, using custom components and some defined interfaces. In this section, we will briefly cover how you can build your own templates, themes, navigation, and add custom components to your template.

Creating communities in Salesforce

Before you create a community, ensure you have the necessary license (either customer community, partner community, community plus, or community login licenses) purchased from Salesforce. For training and learning purposes, these licenses are available in the Salesforce developer and scratch Orgs.

Follow these steps to create a community in Salesforce:

1. In your Salesforce Organization, navigate to the feature settings from the **Setup** screen and search for communities, as shown in the following screenshot, and click on **Enable Communities**. Specify a domain name that is unique:

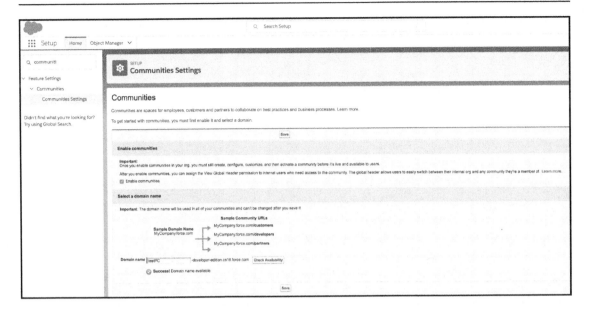

2. Click On **New Community**, and choose **Build Your Own** from the templates:

3. Name the community and click on **Create**, as shown in the following screenshot:

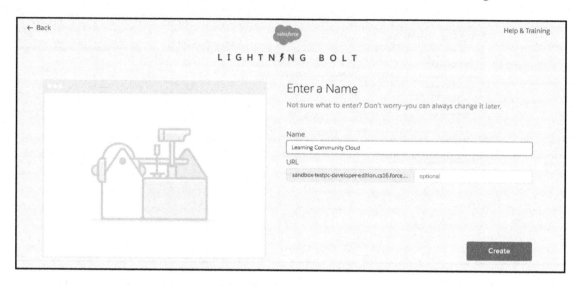

4. Navigate to the builder to customize the community pages, and view and publish the communities, as shown in the following screenshot:

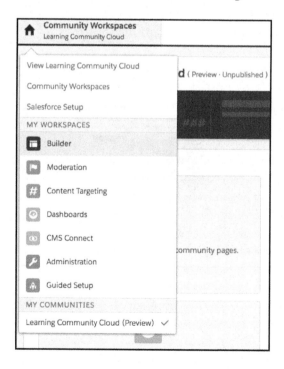

5. The Community Builder interface provides the ability to add components, control layouts, and fonts, add CMS content, and other functionalities. The following screenshot shows various configuration capabilities of the Community Builder:

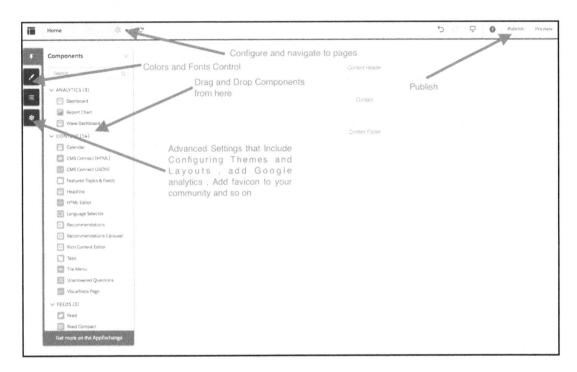

Once you publish the community, to begin with, it will be blank. However, if you begin with templates such as customer community, partner central, or any other pre-defined templates, you will have a set of predefined layouts, components, and page structures. However, note that you can still override some CSS and layouts, themes, and branding.

For a more extensive documentation, it is recommended that you follow the Salesforce Communities Developer Guide (`https://developer. Salesforce.com/docs/atlas.en-us.communities_dev.meta/ communities_dev/communities_dev_intro.htm`) and the communities' help article (`https://help.Salesforce.com/articleView?id=networks_ overview.htmtype=5`) for help and training.

Creating a theme layout

A theme layout provides the ability to create a common header, common footer, search box, navigation menu, profile interface, and content layout. The content layout can vary from one page to another and can be changed. Salesforce out of the box also provides a header, footer, search box, navigation menu, and profile menu. However, you can customize and override them further by implementing various interfaces.

In this section, we will create a theme layout, as shown in the following diagram:

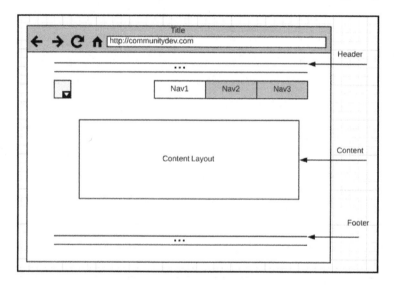

To build a theme layout, we can leverage SLDS Grid (`https://www.lightningdesignsystem.com/utilities/grid/`) as the starting point. Also note that you will need an interface called `forceCommunity:themeLayout` for your Lightning Component, to customize the theme layout.

We also want to expose a logo as a component so that admins can drag and drop a logo component on the theme. For navigation, let's assume we use standard navigation that Salesforce provides out of the box.

Out of the box, the components provided by Salesforce with a default theme layout have aura components such as `navBar`, `profileMenu`, and `search`, and you can simply use them by declaring an attribute with the exact same name. For example, if we want to use the out-of-the-box navBar in our custom theme layout, the attribute can be declared as shown follow:

```
<aura:attribute name="navBar" type="Aura.Component[]"/>
```

It can be referenced in the theme layout component as the value provider `{!v.navBar}`.

The Lightning Component code for the custom theme component for the interface we have in the preceding code snippet is as follows. The component is named `customThemeLayout`, and this appears in the builder. Take a look at this code block:

```
<aura:component implements="forceCommunity:themeLayout">
    <aura:attribute name="logo" type="Aura.Component[]"/>
    <aura:attribute name="navBar" type="Aura.Component[]"/>

    <div>
        <div class="slds-text-heading_large slds-align_absolute-center
slds-m-top_large">
            Header
        </div>
        <div class="slds-text-heading_Medium slds-align_absolute-center
slds-m-top_large">
            Neque porro quisquam est qui dolorem ipsum quia dolor sit amet,
consectetur, adipisci velit..."
        </div>
    </div>

    <div class="slds-grid slds-gutters slds-align_absolute-center slds-m-
top_large">
        <div class="slds-col slds-size_6-of-12">
          {!v.logo}
        </div>
        <div class="slds-col slds-size_6-of-12 navBar">
            {!v.navBar}
        </div>
    </div>

    <div>
        {!v.body}
    </div>

    <div class="slds-grid footer slds-align_absolute-center slds-m-top_x-
large">
        Footer
    </div>
</aura:component>
```

Note that if we need to add a custom component, we declare a component of type `Aura:Component[]`, and this allows the admin to drag the components.

Also notice that we have used the SLDS grid system to design the layout. We can add some customized CSS as well to make the layout cleaner. The CSS file is as follows:

```
.THIS {
    position: relative;
    z-index: 1;
}

.THIS.header {
   height : 100px;
   max-height: 100px;
}

.THIS.footer {
    height : 100px;
    max-height: 100px;
 }

.THIS.navBar {
    background-color: white;
 }

.THIS.forceCommunityGlobalNavigation {
    background-color: white;
    color: black;
}
```

Notice that we have overridden the CSS for the global navigation (it is highlighted in bold). We can, sparingly, if needed, overwrite the styles of some of the standard components. However, be sure to test them with every release. These documents (`https://developer.Salesforce.com/docs/atlas.en-us.communities_dev.meta/communities_dev/communities_dev_migrate_css.htm`) show how you can override the standard component CSS.

To override the themes, you have to use settings in the builder to select the custom component as the theme as shown in the following screenshot:

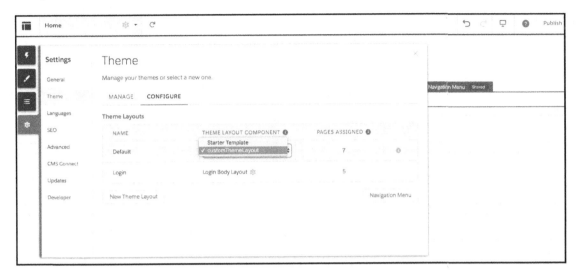

To add any custom component to the Community Builder, the Lightning Component must implement the `forceCommunity:availableForAllPageTypes` interface. The following is the code for the Lightning Component's logo component:

```
<aura:component implements="forceCommunity:availableForAllPageTypes">
    <img src="{!$Resource.logo}" style="margin-left: 500px;"/>
</aura:component>
```

This component implements the `forceCommunity:availableForAllPageTypes` interface, and hence appears in the builder. Let's also add this interface to the YouTube component so that it appears for us to drag onto the builder.

Let's customize the home page with these components. The Community Builder page is shown in the following screenshot; we have added the custom component and the logo component:

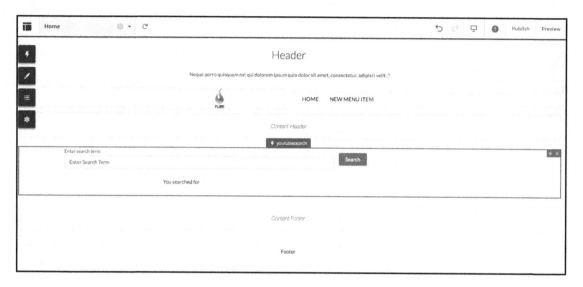

Screenshot shows Community Builder Screen with Custom Lightning Component

Also notice that we can add the navigation items to the community using the native navigations, as shown in the following screenshot, which can be used to link to a custom community page, a record detail page, or other external links:

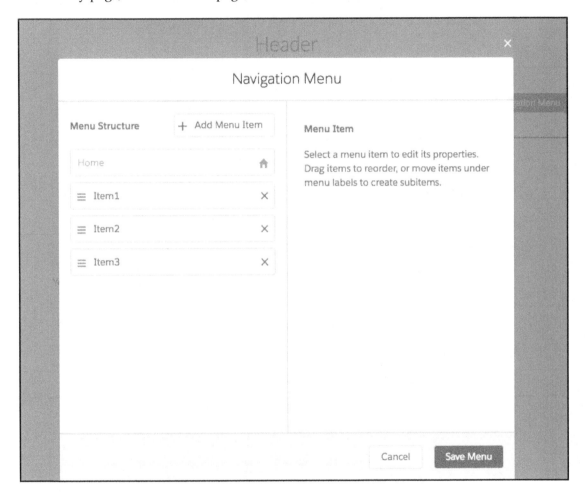

Publish the community and preview it to make sure that it works and looks as follows:

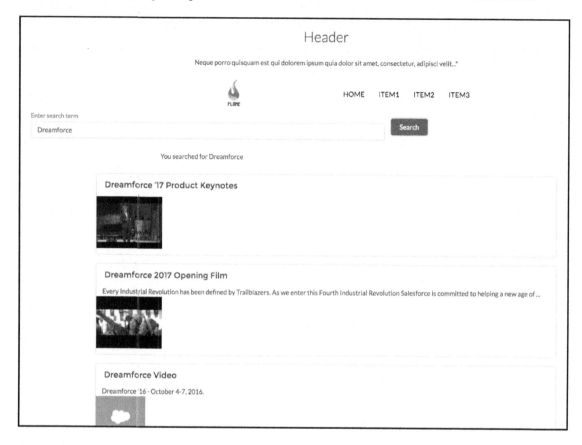

Creating custom content layouts

You can create a new community page using the **New Page** menu obtained from the gear icon that we can see next to the home page. This is shown in the following screenshot:

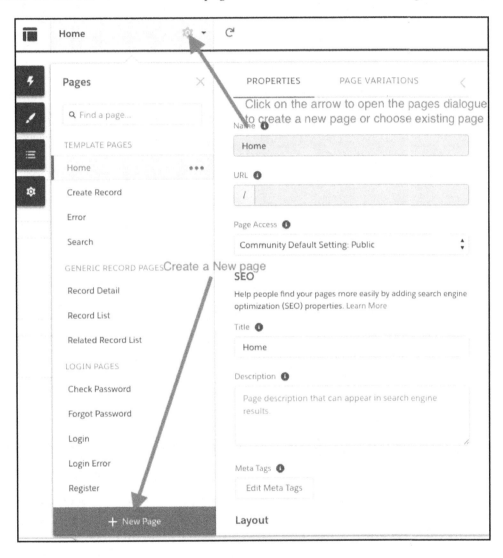

When you click on **New Page,** you will see that you can choose from a standard page, create a blank page, or choose a custom object and override its layout. The standard layout options available are as follows:

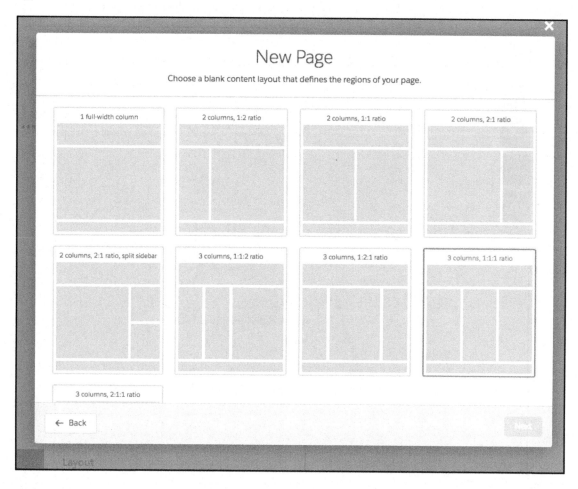

But what if you want to add your own layout? An example use case for this would be for a home page. We need to make sure that the YouTube search component is center aligned. We can create a one-column layout that is center aligned, with padding on the right and the left.

To write your own layout, the component will need to implement the `forceCommunity:layout` interface. Let's create a custom layout that is one column but aligns in the center, with sufficient padding. We can use the Salesforce lightning design system grids.

The following is a simple component code that creates a custom layout:

```
<aura:component implements="forceCommunity:layout" description="Custom
Content Layout" access="global">
    <!---->
    <aura:attribute name="column1" type="Aura.Component[]"
required="false"/>
    <div class="container">
        <div class="slds-grid contentPanel">
            <div class="slds-col slds-size_4-of-12">
            </div>
            <div class="slds-col slds-size_8-of-12">
                {!v.column1}
            </div>
        </div>
    </div>
</aura:component>
```

Now, to use this layout, let's use a page variation for the home page. Page variation allows you to create a different view for the same page and assign it to an audience. An audience can be a combination of profiles, locations, and record types.

The following screenshot shows how different page variations exists for the page. Notice that we have the home page and a YouTube search page that is a variation of the **Home** page:

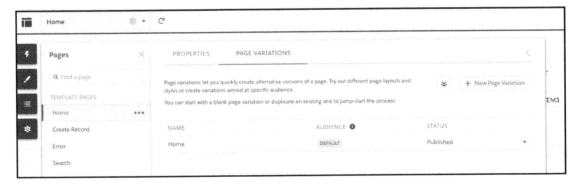

The following shows the custom layout that we created. It appears when we create a new page:

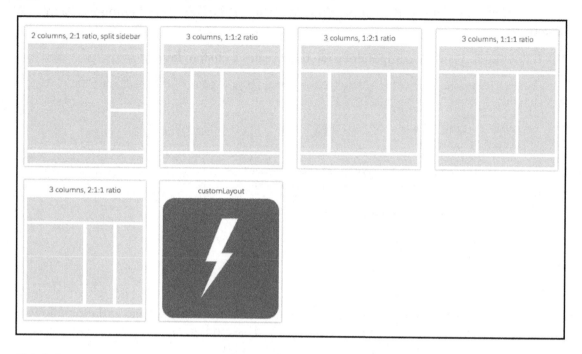

The following is a screenshot of the builder with this new layout. Notice that we can tweak things such as the text color and the home logo from the builder:

Community builder page with custom layout

Overriding search, profile menu, and navigation in communities using customized Lightning Components

In this section, we will see how we can override some standard components that come out of the box for a community, with a customized experience.

Overriding a standard search interface

To override a search component and add your own search experience, you will have to implement `forceCommunity:searchInterface`. The sample code snippet is as follows:

```
<aura:component implements="forceCommunity:searchInterface"
access="global">
    <div class="search">
        <div class="search">
            <form class="search-form">
                <div class="search-input">
                    <input class="search-input-field" type="text"
placeholder="My Search"/>
                </div>
                <input type="hidden" name="language" value="en" />
            </form>
        </div>
    </div>
</aura:component>
```

Overriding a profile menu

To override a profile menu, you will have to implement an interface called `forceCommunity:profileMenuInterface`. The following code snippet shows how to create a custom component to override a profile menu:

```
<aura:component implements="forceCommunity:profileMenuInterface"
access="global">
    <lightning:buttonMenu alternativeText="Toggle menu">
        <lightning:menuItem label="My Account" value="account"
iconName="utility:table" />
        <lightning:menuItem label="Add Credit Card" value="addCard"
iconName="utility:table" />
    </lightning:buttonMenu>
</aura:component>
```

Adding custom navigation

To add your own navigation capability, create a Lightning Component that extends `forceCommunity:navigationMenuBase`. The code snippet to get started is given in the following code. Note that `{!v.menuItems}` automatically adds the `menuItems`, which was configured in the navigation menu by the community admin. Take a look at this code block:

```
<aura:component extends="forceCommunity:navigationMenuBase">
    <div class="slds-grid slds-grid--vertical slds-navigation-list--
vertical">
        <ul onclick="{!c.onClick}">
            <aura:iteration items="{!v.menuItems}" var="item">
                <li class="{!item.active ? 'slds-is-active' : ''}">
                    <a href="javascript:void(0);" data-menu-item-
id="{!item.id}" class="slds-navigation-list--vertical__action slds-text-
link--reset">
                        {!item.label}
                    </a>
                </li>
            </aura:iteration>
        </ul>
    </div>
</aura:component>
```

The controller code is as follows:

```
({
    onClick : function(component, event, helper) {
        var id = event.target.dataset.menuItemId;
        if (id) {
            component.getSuper().navigate(id);
        }
    }
})
```

If you are in communities built from one of the Salesforce provided templates, you can override the search and the profile menu using the theme settings of the builder, as shown in the following screenshot:

The possibilities with the Community Cloud are huge, and knowing how to leverage custom Lightning Components in the builder to customize the user experience can make your communities user-friendly and easy to use. To get more insight into the events and components available, refer to the documentation at `https://developer.Salesforce.com/docs/atlas.en-us.communities_dev.meta/communities_dev/communities_dev_basics_supported.htm`.

Finally, note that you can use Salesforce Dx to create scratch Orgs with communities enabled and communities deployed.

The `config` folder needs a file called `project-def.json`, as shown in the following code:

```
{
    "OrgName": "mohith Company",
    "edition": "Developer",
    "OrgPreferences" : {
        "enabled": ["S1DesktopEnabled","NetworksEnabled"]
    },
    "features": ["Communities"]
}
```

You can run the following commands if you have a Salesforce DX set up to create a scratch Org with communities enabled, as shown in the following code:

```
//Clone the source from the git repo

git clone
https://github.com/PacktPublishing/Learning-Salesforce-Lightning-Applicatio
n-Development.git

//CD into chapter 12
cd chapter12

//Create a scratch Org
sfdx force:org:create -s -f config/project-scratch-def.json -a testOrg

//Set as the Default for push and pull
sfdx force:config:set defaultusername=testOrg

//Push the source code to the scratch Org
sfdx force:source:push
```

Note that you may get some errors regarding guest users that can't be found. This is expected. After creating a community, navigate to scratch Org and Community Builder, and publish the community.

Summary

In this chapter, we covered various code snippets in order to use custom Lightning Components for Salesforce Mobile and Salesforce communities. Salesforce community templates are a great fit for building online communities, help, and the training portal. They can also be used to provide customers with an online self-service portal to track their case status or order status. In the upcoming chapter, we will explore lightning navigation, the Console API for Lightning Console Apps, and the Utility Bar API.

13
Lightning Navigation and Lightning Console APIs

The Lightning navigation service provides the ability to navigate from one Lightning Component to another and helps users to navigate to standard object pages in Lightning Experience. In this chapter, we will familiarize ourselves with the Lightning Navigation Component and its usage.

Lightning Console apps provide the ability to open multiple subtabs from the main tab to enhance the productivity of the user. They do this by allowing us to view or compare data from multiple records. The console APIs provide a rich set of JavaScript components for developers to control navigation. In this chapter, we will see how to work with the console APIs using relevant code snippets.

We will also explore some standard Lightning events that are baked into the Salesforce Lightning container in order to navigate to create records and edit forms.

In this chapter, we will explore the following topics:

- Adding navigation support using Lightning :navigation
- Lightning Component support in the Lightning Console
- The workspace API
- The **Utility Bar**

Adding navigation support using Lightning :navigation

The Lightning :navigation component uses a special type of JavaScript object named pageReference to navigate to other Lightning Components or standard views and standard object pages. The Lightning Component must implement a special interface named Lightning :isUrlAddressable to allow itself to be navigated from other components.

A pageReference object structure is shown in the following code snippet. (Note that it is comprised of a type (string type), attributes (object), and state (object). Let's take a look at it:

```
var pageReference = {
        type: 'standard__objectPage', //standard__component
,standard__knowledgeArticlePage,standard__namedPage,standard__navItemPage,s
tandard__objectPage,standard__recordPage,standard__recordRelationshipPage
        attributes: {
            objectApiName: 'Account',
            actionName: 'list'
        },
        state: {
            filterName: "MyAccounts"
        }
    };
```

The type is one from the predefined list shown in the doccumentation: https://developer.Salesforce.com/docs/atlas.en-us.Lightning .meta/Lightning /components_navigation_page_definitions.htm. The attributes and state object differ, based on the type. The state object allows the passing of query parameters.

The code snippet to navigate to various components using Lightning :navigation is as follows:

```
<aura:component
implements="force:appHostable,flexipage:availableForAllPageTypes">
    <Lightning :navigation aura:id="navService"/>
    <Lightning :button label="Navigate" onclick="{!c.handleClick}"/>
</aura:component>
```

The controller code showing how to redirect to the `Account` home page is as follows:

```
({
    handleClick: function(component, event, helper) {
        var navService = component.find("navService");
        // Uses the pageReference definition in the init handler
        var pageReference = {
            type: 'standard__objectPage',
            attributes: {
                objectApiName: 'Account',
                actionName: 'home'
            }
        };
        //Generate URL from the pageReference object use the generateUrl
promise as shown as follows
        navService.generateUrl(pageReference)
            .then($A.getCallback(function(url) {
                console.log('url from service',url);
            }), $A.getCallback(function(error) {
            }));
        navService.navigate(pageReference);
        //navService.navigate(pageReference,true);//Override Browser
History if additional attribute is true
    }

})
```

Notice that `navService` provides two methods: `navigate()` for navigation and `generateUrl()`, which returns a promise object to obtain the actual URL.

To demonstrate an example with different `pageReference` types, let's create a component that covers various types and attributes.

The component screen is as shown in the following screenshot. Clicking on each of these links takes us to a different path, depending on the controller method:

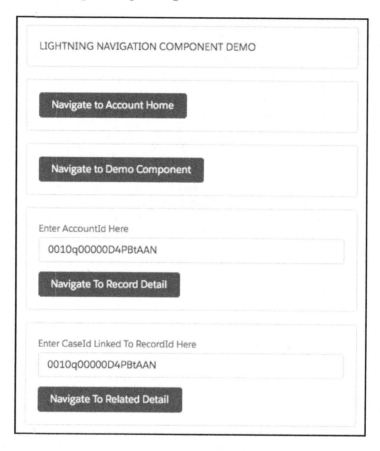

The following code for the component comprises buttons to show how you can navigate to objects, Home, Record Detail, other components, and Record Detail:

```
<!--navigationComponentDemo.cmp -->
<aura:component implements="flexipage:availableForAllPageTypes">

    <aura:attribute name="accountId" type="String"/>

    <Lightning :navigation aura:id="navService"/>

    <div>

        <div class="slds-m-around_medium slds-box">
            Lightning  Navigation Component DEMO
```

```
            </div>


        <div class="slds-m-around_medium slds-box">
            <Lightning :button variant="brand" label="Navigate to Account
Home" title="Go to Account Home" onclick="{! c.navigateToAccountHome }" />
        </div>


        <div class="slds-m-around_medium slds-box">
            <Lightning :button variant="brand" label="Navigate to Demo
Component" title="Navigate to Demo Component" onclick="{!
c.navigateToDemoComponet }" />
        </div>


        <div class="slds-m-around_medium slds-box">
            <div>
                <Lightning :input name="recordId" label="Enter AccountId
Here" value="{!v.accountId}"/>
            </div>
            <div class="slds-m-top_small">
                <Lightning :button variant="brand" label="Navigate To
Record Detail" title="Navigate To Record Detail" value="{!v.accountId}"
onclick="{! c.navigateToRecordDetail }" />
            </div>
        </div>


        <div class="slds-m-around_medium slds-box">
            <div>
                <Lightning :input name="relatedId" label="Enter CaseId
Linked To RecordId Here" value="{!v.accountId}"/>
            </div>
            <div class="slds-m-top_small">
                <Lightning :button variant="brand" label="Navigate To
Related Detail" title="Navigate To Related Detail" onclick="{!
c.navigateToRecordRelated }" />
            </div>
        </div>

    </div>

</aura:component>
```

The controller code is as follows:

```
//navigationComponentDemoController.js
({
    navigateToAccountHome : function(component, event, helper) {
        var navService = component.find("navService");
```

```
            // Sets the route to /Lightning /o/Account/home
        var pageReference = {
            type: 'standard__objectPage',
            attributes: {
                objectApiName: 'Account',
                actionName: 'home'
            }
        };
        navService.navigate(pageReference);
    },

    navigateToDemoComponet : function(component, event, helper) {
        var navService = component.find("navService");
        var pageReference = {
            type: 'standard__component',
            attributes: {
                "componentName": "c__demoComponent"
            },
            state: {
                "simpleMsg": 'Hello Demo Component'
            }
        };
        navService.navigate(pageReference);
    },

    navigateToRecordDetail : function(component, event, helper) {
        var navService = component.find("navService");
        var pageReference = {
            "type": "standard__recordPage",
            "attributes": {
                "recordId": component.get("v.accountId"),
                "objectApiName": "Account",
                "actionName": "view"
            }
        }
        navService.navigate(pageReference);
    },

    navigateToRecordRelated : function(component, event, helper) {
        var navService = component.find("navService");
        var pageReference = {
            "type": "standard__recordRelationshipPage",
            "attributes": {
                "recordId": component.get("v.accountId"),
                "objectApiName": "Account",
                "relationshipApiName": "Cases",
                "actionName": "view"
            }
```

```
        }
        navService.generateUrl(pageReference)
        .then($A.getCallback(function(url) {
            console.log('url from service',url);
        }), $A.getCallback(function(error) {
            console.log(error);
        }));
        navService.navigate(pageReference);
    }
})
```

Notice that we use a component named `c_demoComponent` to navigate from the `navigationComponentDemo` component. The code for the demo component is as follows:

```
<!-- demoComponent.cmp-->
<aura:component implements="flexipage:availableForAllPageTypes,Lightning
:isUrlAddressable">
    <aura:attribute name="simpleMsg" type="String"/>

    <aura:handler name="init" value="{!this}" action="{!c.init}" />

    <div class="slds-m-around_medium slds-box">
        DEMO COMPONENT
    </div>

    <div class="slds-m-around_medium slds-box">
            CONTENT FROM MAIN PAGE {!v.simpleMsg}
        </div>

</aura:component>
```

The `demoComponentController.js` code for the `demoComponent` is as follows:

```
({
    init : function(component, event, helper) {
        var pageReference = component.get("v.pageReference");
        component.set("v.simpleMsg", pageReference.state.c__simpleMsg);
    }
})
```

Introducing the Lightning Console

Lightning Console apps provide split views, workspaces, **Tabs**, and a **Utility Bar**, which enhance productivity. To create a console app, make sure to select that the application be of console type.

To create an app, go to **Setup** | **App Manager** | **New Lightning App**.

The following screenshot shows the radio button that you need to select to in order to create a Salesforce console application:

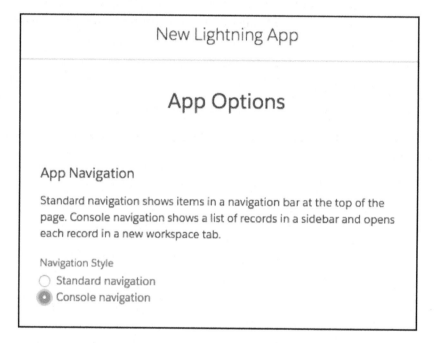

The console app screen resembles something such as the following, with the ability to open **Parent Records** as subtabs, and further related records can subtab themselves from the **Parent** tab:

Utility Bar component

The **Utility Bar** sits in the footer of the screen and provides an extensive set of APIs. To use the **Utility Bar**, the Lightning Component needs to use a special component named `Lightning :utilityBarAPI`. The following code shows a sample component code snippet that uses this API component:

```
<aura:component implements="flexipage:availableForAllPageTypes"
access="global" >
    <Lightning :utilityBarAPI aura:id="utilitybar" />
    <Lightning :button label="Get All Utility Info" onclick="{!
c.getAllUtilityInfo }" />
</aura:component>
```

The controller code that can call all the functions is as follows:

```
({
    getAllUtilityInfo : function(component, event, helper) {
        var utilityAPI = component.find("utilitybar");
        utilityAPI.getAllUtilityInfo().then(function(response) {
            var myUtilityInfo = response[0];
            utilityAPI.openUtility({
                utilityId: myUtilityInfo.id
```

```
            });
        })
          .catch(function(error) {
            console.log(error);
          });
      }
    })
```

The full documentation is provided in the documentation here: `https://developer.` `Salesforce.com/docs/atlas.en-us.api_console.meta/api_console/sforce_api_` `console_methods_Lightning _utility.htm`.

The following code is an example of how to work with `utilityAPI` objects:

```
<aura:component implements="flexipage:availableForAllPageTypes">

    <Lightning :utilityBarAPI aura:id="utilitybar" />
    <div class="slds-m-around_medium">
        <Lightning :button label="Get All Utility Info" onclick="{!
c.getAllUtilityInfo }" />
    </div>

    <div class="slds-m-around_medium">
        <Lightning :button label="Get Enclosing Utility ID" onclick="{!
c.getEnclosingUtilityId }" />
    </div>

    <div class="slds-m-around_medium">
        <Lightning :button label="Open Utility" onclick="{! c.openUtility
}" />
    </div>

    <div class="slds-m-around_medium">
        <Lightning :button label="Set Utility Highlighted" onclick="{!
c.setUtilityHighlighted}" />
    </div>

    <div class="slds-m-around_medium">
        <Lightning :button label="Toggle Modal Mode" onclick="{!
c.toggleModalMode }" />
    </div>

</aura:component>
```

The controller code that invokes various methods in the **Utility Bar** API is as follows:

```
({
    getAllUtilityInfo : function(component, event, helper) {
        var utilityAPI = component.find("utilitybar");
        utilityAPI.getAllUtilityInfo().then(function(response) {
            var myUtilityInfo = response[0];
            utilityAPI.openUtility({
                utilityId: myUtilityInfo.id
            });
        })
        .catch(function(error) {
            console.log(error);
        });
    },

    getEnclosingUtilityId : function(component, event, helper) {
        var utilityAPI = component.find("utilitybar");
        utilityAPI.getEnclosingUtilityId().then(function(utilityId) {
            console.log(utilityId);
        })
        .catch(function(error) {
            console.log(error);
        });
    },

    openUtility : function(component, event, helper) {
        var utilityAPI = component.find("utilitybar");
        utilityAPI.openUtility();
    },

    setUtilityHighlighted : function(component, event, helper) {
        var utilityAPI = component.find("utilitybar");
        utilityAPI.setUtilityHighlighted({
            highlighted: true
        });
    },

    toggleModalMode : function(component, event, helper) {
        var utilityAPI = component.find("utilitybar");
        utilityAPI.toggleModalMode({
            enableModalMode: true
        });
    },


})
```

The **Utility Bar** can be added to the app by editing the Lightning Application, as shown in the following screenshot:

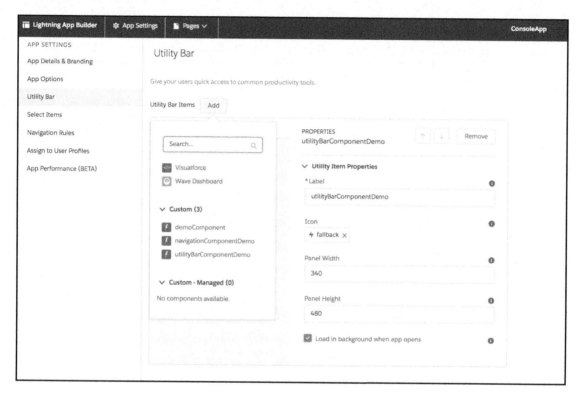

The Lightning bar component sits at the footer, shown as follows:

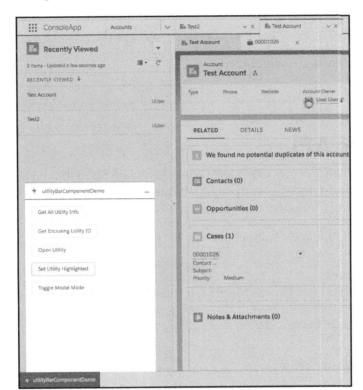

Page context in the Utility Bar API

To view the page context, use a change-event handler in the **Utility Bar** component. If a user navigates to a different page, the recordId of the view is captured. The following code snippet shows a simple demonstration:

```
<aura:component
implements="force:hasRecordId,flexipage:availableForAllPageTypes"
access="global">
    <aura:handler name="change" value="{!v.recordId}"
action="{!c.onRecordIdChange}"/>
    <div>
        <p>The current recordId is {!v.recordId}.</p>
    </div>
</aura:component>
```

The controller code for the preceding component is as follows:

```
({
    onRecordIdChange : function(component, event, helper) {
        var newRecordId = component.get("v.recordId");
        console.log(newRecordId);
    }
})
```

Workspace API

The workspace API allows you to perform console-related tasks that include opening tabs and subtabs and to adding focus to opened tabs and subtabs. To use the API, you need to include the Lightning Component Lightning :workspaceAPI in the component.

The following shows the code snippet on how to use the API:

```
<aura:component implements="flexipage:availableForAllPageTypes"
access="global">
    <Lightning :workspaceAPI aura:id="workspace"/>
    <Lightning :button label="Close Focused Tab"
onclick="{!c.closeFocusedTab}"/>
</aura:component>
```

The controller code is as follows:

```
({
    closeFocusedTab : function(component, event, helper) {
        var workspaceAPI = component.find("workspace");
        workspaceAPI.getFocusedTabInfo().then(function(response) {
            var focusedTabId = response.tabId;
            workspaceAPI.closeTab({tabId: focusedTabId});
        })
        .catch(function(error) {
            console.log(error);
        });
    }
})
```

To understand the various methods provided by the workspace API, refer to the official documentation at https://developer.Salesforce.com/docs/atlas.en-us.api_console.meta/api_console/sforce_api_console_methods_Lightning _tabs.htm.

To demonstrate how to leverage the workspace API, let's create a demo component that opens contacts linked to the account, which are currently viewed as the tabs and cases as subtabs.

Again, the demo component is a simple **Utility Bar** component and listens for the **Account view** and uses a record change event to find the `recordId`. We implement two buttons: one to open tabs and another to open subtabs. The following screenshot shows the component screen:

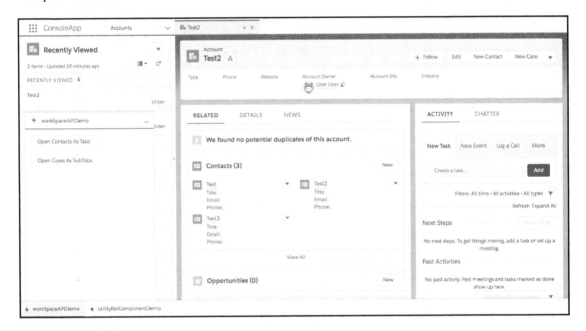

The component markup code is shown as follows (note the snippets highlighted in bold, which are used to observe the handler and the API markup):

```
<aura:component
implements="force:hasRecordId,flexipage:availableForAllPageTypes"
controller="AccountController">

    <aura:handler name="change" value="{!v.recordId}"
action="{!c.onRecordIdChange}"/>

    <aura:attribute name="currentFocusedTabId" type="String" />
    <Lightning :workspaceAPI aura:id="workspace"/>

    <div class="slds-m-around_medium">
        <Lightning :button label="Open Contacts As Tabs" onclick="{!
c.openContacts }" />
```

```
        </div>
        <div class="slds-m-around_medium">
            <Lightning :button label="Open Cases As SubTabs" onclick="{!
    c.openCases }" />
        </div>

    </aura:component>
```

The controller code is as follows (notice that we use the ES6 arrow functions and promises extensively):

```
({
    onRecordIdChange : function(component, event, helper) {
        var newRecordId = component.get("v.recordId");
        console.log(newRecordId);
        //Get the Focused TabId
        var workspaceAPI = component.find("workspace");
        workspaceAPI.getFocusedTabInfo().then(function(response) {
            var focusedTabId = response.tabId;
            component.set("v.currentFocusedTabId",focusedTabId);
        })
    },

    openContacts : function(component, event, helper) {
        helper.getAccountPromise(component, event).then(
            // resolve handler
            $A.getCallback((result) => {
                var accountObj = JSON.parse(result);
                var workspaceAPI = component.find("workspace");
                var promiseArray = [];
                accountObj.Contacts.records.forEach((element) => {
                    var workSpaceAPIPromise = workspaceAPI.openTab({
                        recordId: element.Id,
                        focus: true
                    });
                    promiseArray.push(workSpaceAPIPromise);
                });
                promiseArray.all(promiseArray);//open all the Windows using
    Promise.all
            }),
            // reject handler
            $A.getCallback((error) => {
                console.log("Promise was rejected: ", error);
            })
        )
    },

    openCases : function(component, event, helper) {
```

```
helper.getAccountPromise(component, event).then(
    // resolve handler
    $A.getCallback((result) => {
        var accountObj = JSON.parse(result);
        var workspaceAPI = component.find("workspace");
        var promiseArray = [];
        accountObj.Cases.records.forEach((element) => {
            var workSpaceAPIPromise = workspaceAPI.openSubtab({
                parentTabId:
component.get("v.currentFocusedTabId"),
                recordId: element.Id,
                focus: true
            });
            promiseArray.push(workSpaceAPIPromise);
        });
        promiseArray.all(promiseArray);//open all the Windows using
Promise.all
    }),
    // reject handler
    $A.getCallback((error) => {
        console.log("Promise was rejected: ", error);
    })
  )
},


})
```

The `helper` function holds the promise to make Apex calls to find the cases and contacts:

```
({
    getAccountPromise : function(component, event) {
        return new Promise($A.getCallback( (resolve, reject) => {

            var action = component.get("c.getAccountInfo");

            action.setParams({ recordId : component.get("v.recordId") });
            action.setCallback(this, (response) => {
                var state = response.getState();
                if (state === "SUCCESS") {
                    resolve(response.getReturnValue());
                }
                else {
                    reject(response.getError());
                }
            });

            $A.enqueueAction(action);
```

```
            }));
        },

    })
```

The Apex controller code is as follows:

```
public with sharing class AccountController {
    @AuraEnabled
    public Static String getAccountInfo(String recordId){
        String response = '{}';
        list<Account> lstaccounts = [Select Id,
                                     Name ,
                                     (Select Id FROM Contacts),
                                     (Select Id from Cases)
                                     FROM Account
                                     WHERE ID =:recordId];
        if(lstaccounts.size() >0 ){
            response = JSON.serialize(lstaccounts[0]) ;
        }
        return response;
    }
}
```

The following screenshot shows how the user interface opens tabs and subtabs upon clicking the relevant buttons:

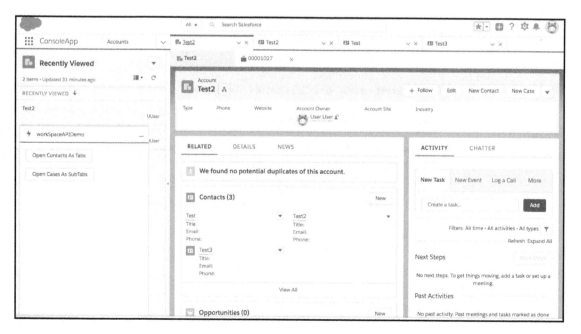

Standard Lightning tab events in the console

Lightning Experience is based on event-driven architecture. When a tab is focused, closed, or opened, there are standard handlers that Salesforce provides, which a component can handle.

The following table lists some of the events provided out of the box in the console API to detect changes to the tabs:

Event name	Component markup to handle events	Controller action on event handlers
Lightning :tabClosed	```<aura:component implements="flexipage:availableForAllPageTypes" access="global" > <aura:handler event="Lightning :tabClosed" action="{! c.onTabClosed }"/> </aura:component>```	```({ onTabClosed : function(component, event, helper) { var tabId = event.getParam('tabId'); console.log("Tab closed: " +tabId); } })```
Lightning :tabCreated	```<aura:component implements="flexipage:availableForAllPageTypes" access="global" > <Lightning :workspaceAPI aura:id="workspace" /> <aura:handler event="Lightning :tabCreated" action="{! c.onTabCreated }"/> </aura:component>```	```({ onTabCreated : function(component, event, helper) { console.log("Tab created."); var newTabId = event.getParam('tabId'); var workspaceAPI = component.find("workspace"); workspaceAPI.setTabLabel({ tabId: newTabId, label: 'New Tab' }); }, })```
Lightning :tabFocused	```<aura:component implements="flexipage:availableForAllPageTypes" access="global" > <Lightning :workspaceAPI aura:id="workspace" /> <aura:handler event="Lightning :tabFocused" action="{! c.onTabFocused }"/> </aura:component>```	```({ onTabFocused : function(component, event, helper) { console.log("Tab Focused"); var focusedTabId = event.getParam('currentTabId'); var workspaceAPI = component.find("workspace"); workspaceAPI.getTabInfo({ tabId : focusedTabId }).then(function(response) { console.log(response); }); } })```

Lightning
:tabRefreshed
	`<aura:component`
	`implements="flexipage:availableForAllPageTypes"`
	`access="global" >`
	`<Lightning :workspaceAPI aura:id="workspace" />`
	`<aura:handler event="Lightning :tabRefreshed"`
	`action="{! c.onTabRefreshed }"/>`
	`</aura:component>`
		`({`
		`onTabRefreshed :`
		`function(component, event,`
		`helper) {`
		`console.log("Tab Refreshed");`
		`var refreshedTabId =`
		`event.getParam("tabId");`
		`var workspaceAPI =`
		`component.find("workspace");`
		`workspaceAPI.getTabInfo({`
		`tabId : refreshedTabId`
		`}).then(function(response) {`
		`console.log(response);`
		`});`
		`}`
		`})`

Lightning
:tabReplaced
	`<aura:component`
	`implements="flexipage:availableForAllPageTypes"`
	`access="global" > <Lightning :workspaceAPI`
	`aura:id="workspace" /> <aura:handler`
	`event="Lightning :tabReplaced" action="{!`
	`c.onTabReplaced }"/> </aura:component>`
		`({`
		`onTabReplaced :`
		`function(component, event,`
		`helper) {`
		`console.log("Tab Replaced");`
		`var replacedTabId =`
		`event.getParam("tabId");`
		`var workspaceAPI =`
		`component.find("workspace");`
		`workspaceAPI.getTabURL({`
		`tabId : replacedTabId`
		`}).then(function(response) {`
		`console.log(response);`
		`});`
		`}`
		`})`

Lightning
:tabUpdated
	`<aura:component`
	`implements="flexipage:availableForAllPageTypes"`
	`access="global" >`
	`<Lightning :workspaceAPI aura:id="workspace" />`
	`<aura:handler event="Lightning :tabUpdated"`
	`action="{! c.onTabUpdated }"/>`
	`</aura:component>`
		`({`
		`onTabUpdated :`
		`function(component, event,`
		`helper) {`
		`console.log("Tab Updated");`
		`var updatedTabId =`
		`event.getParam("tabId");`
		`console.log(updatedTabId);`
		`},`
		`})`

Summary

This chapter covered some useful code snippets to understand the Salesforce navigation APIs, the Console API, and the workspace API. Using these navigations, you can navigate between custom components, standard components, pages, and tabs. These navigations are also faster, since they leverage caching.

In the next chapter, we will focus on how to test custom Lightning Components using the Lightning Testing Service and Jasmine.

14
Unit Testing Lightning Components

Creating unit tests for code components helps in quickly figuring out issues with the component when a piece of code is redesigned or additional logic is added to enhance the functionality. Unit tests test a single function or object in isolation. Salesforce provides Apex unit tests for all the backend business logic written in Apex. For Lightning Components, Salesforce provides the **Lightning Testing Service** (**LTS**). The LTS is a set of wrappers for Jasmine and Mocha JavaScript testing frameworks. Jasmine is a popular framework to test JavaScript applications on, and uses a wide set of features, assisting in **behavior-driven development** (**BDD**), while Mocha is an emerging framework and requires additional frameworks (such as Chai, Sinon, or Cucumber) to work with it in order to provide a complete toolset to use to write unit tests. In this chapter, we will strictly cover only LTS, using Jasmine as the testing framework. The LTS (found at `https://github.com/forcedotcom/LightningTestingService`) is open source, and hence it can be easily tailored to work with any testing framework. Once we know how this works with Jasmine, a similar approach can be applied to any testing framework that one chooses to adopt.

In this chapter, we will cover the following topics:

- Introduction to Jasmine
- LTS
- Writing Jasmine test cases for two-way binding and server responses

Introduction to Jasmine

The Jasmine testing framework encourages the use of BDD in the applications on which it is used. In this section, we will briefly look into the syntax and steps needed to write a unit test for a JavaScript. The extensive documentation can be found at Jasmine's documentation site, at `https://jasmine.github.io/`.

Jasmine syntax and terminology

Before we dive into a working example of how to use Jasmine to test the JavaScript, let's look at some of the terms that will be used in the upcoming sections, such as suite, spec, matcher, spies, setup and teardown.

Suite

A suite is a set of test cases that you want to test for a JavaScript object or function. You can think of a suite as being similar to a test class in Apex, if you want to make a comparison.

A suite uses a global `describe` function, and the function has two parameters: a string that is the title of the test suite and a function that implements the test suite.

The syntax is as follows:

```
//This is Test Suite
describe("Test Lightning Components", function() {
    //.....
});
```

Let's say we have a library that has a string of util functions, which takes a string and performs camelcasing, concatenation, and so on. The following suite definition code snippet can be used to test this JavaScript file:

```
//This is test Suite
describe("StringUtils", function() {
    //.....
});
```

Spec

A spec is a test case inside the test suite. A test suite comprises one or more test specs. A test spec comprises a `describe` function and one or more `it` functions. An `it` function is comprised of two parameters, one of which is a string and the other of which is a function that implements the test case. Treat this like an Apex test method.

A spec also comprises of `expect` statements that are used for asserting the behavior. Treat asserts are equal to `system.assert` in Apex test methods. The `expect` statements compare the actual object against the `matcher` object. There are out-of-box matchers available. You can refer to the API guide to learn more about them at `https://jasmine.github.io/api/edge/matchers.html`.

The following table describes the out-of-box matchers that are available:

Matcher	Definition
`toBe()`	Passed if the actual value is of the same type and value as that of the expected value. It compares with the `===` operator.
`toEqual()`	Works for simple literals and variables; should work for objects too.
`toMatch()`	Checks whether a value matches a string or a regular expression.
`toBeDefined()`	Ensures that a property or a value is defined.
`toBeUndefined()`	Ensures that a property or a value is undefined.
`toBeNull()`	Ensures that a property or a value is null.
`toBeTruthy()`	Ensures that a property or a value is true.
`toBeFalsy()`	Ensures that a property or a value is false.
`toContain()`	Checks whether a string or array contains a substring or an item.
`toBeLessThan()`	For mathematical comparisons of less than.
`toBeGreaterThan()`	For mathematical comparisons of greater than.

toBeCloseTo()	For precision math comparison.
toThrow()	For testing whether a function throws an exception.
toThrowError()	For testing a *specific* thrown exception.

For example, if we want to test a string util function and perform tests on its behavior for camelcasing, concatenation, and so on, the code syntax would look as follows:

```
describe("StringUtils", function() {
    var stringUtil;

    //This will be called before running each spec
    beforeEach(function() {
        stringUtil = new StringUtils();
    });

    describe("when string operations are performed", function(){
        //Spec for Concatenation operation
        it("should be able to concatenate hello and world", function() {
            expect(stringUtil.concatenate(Hello,World)).toEqual(HelloWorld);
        });

        //Spec for camelcase operation
        it("should be able to camelcase", function() {
            expect(stringUtil.camelcase('hello-
world')).toEqual('HelloWorld');
        });

    });
});
```

Setup and teardown

A setup allows us to set up test data and variables before each of the test specs are executed. This avoids having to repeat the same code and variables in each spec. This is equivalent to the @isTestsetup annotation in Apex.

A setup is defined using a `beforeEach()` function that takes a `closure` function as an argument.

```
//This will be called before running each spec
    beforeEach(function() {
        stringUtil = new StringUtils();
    });
```

A teardown allows us to clean the variables before continuing. Jasmine provides an `afterEach` function for teardowns; look at the following sample code for the syntax. Note that it also takes a `closure` function as an argument.

```
afterEach(function() {
        console.log("afterEach");
    });
```

Spies

Oftentimes, we do not want our test methods to work with the actual data on a JavaScript method. Let's say we are making a third-party web service callout using jQuery Ajax. During our test runs, we do not want to be calling the actual server; instead, we just watch whether the method executes with proper arguments and returns a fake response. Spies in Jasmine allow us to watch for the methods and replace them with a spy during the test run.

A simple example of a `spy` function is shown in the following code snippet:

```
spyOn(someObj, 'func').withArgs(1, 2, 3).and.returnValue(42);
someObj.func(1, 2, 3); // returns 42
```

In the preceding snippet, when every test calls the `func` function, a spy is set to watch for it, and then it returns a value once the function is called.

The comprehensive list of strategies that can be used with `spyOn` can be found at `https://jasmine.github.io/api/edge/SpyStrategy.html`.

In LTS, you will see that wherever we have Apex calls that make DML transactions, we spy on enqueue actions and create a fake response to test against.

Quickstart example

In this section, we will write some tests with Jasmine for a simple JavaScript file that has some string utilities. To begin with, let's download the Jasmine standalone from the release page at https://github.com/jasmine/jasmine/releases.

Once you download the jasmine-standalone, you will notice a folder structure, as shown in the following screenshot:

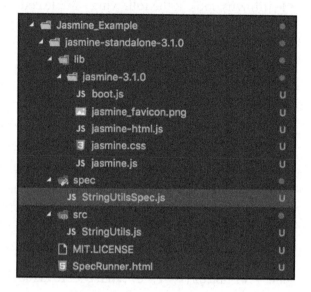

In the source directory, we keep our source code. In our example, we will use a simple StringUtils.js file that performs some operations on string variables.

The code for the StringUtils.js is as follows:

```
function StringUtils() {};

StringUtils.prototype.concatenate = function(str1,str2) {
  return str1.concat(str2);
};

StringUtils.prototype.camelcase = function(string) {
  string = string.toLowerCase().replace(/(?:(^.)|([-_\s]+.))/g,
function(match) {
      return match.charAt(match.length-1).toUpperCase();
  });
  return string.charAt(0).toLowerCase() + string.substring(1);
};
```

```
StringUtils.prototype.capitalizeFirstLetter = function(string) {
  return string.charAt(0).toUpperCase() + string.slice(1);
};
```

We will keep the test in a separate folder named `spec`. The test for the preceding JavaScript file is as follows:

```
describe("StringUtils", function() {
  var stringUtil;

  //This will be called before running each spec
  beforeEach(function() {
      stringUtil = new StringUtils();
  });

  describe("when string operations are performed", function(){
      //Spec for Concatenation operation
      it("should be able to concatenate hello and world", function() {
        expect(stringUtil.concatenate('Hello','World')).toEqual('HelloWorld');
      });

      //Spec for camelcase operation
      it("should be able to camelcase", function() {
          expect(stringUtil.camelcase('hello-
world')).toEqual('helloWorld');
      });

      //Spec for capitalizeFirstLetter
      it("should be able to capitalize First Letter", function() {
        expect(stringUtil.capitalizeFirstLetter('world')).toEqual('World');
      });
  });
});
```

The lines in bold assert the behavior.

The `SpecRunner.html` code phrase is where we add the reference to the `src` files and the test `spec` files. This is shown in the following code:

```
<!DOCTYPE html>
<html>
<head>
 <meta charset="utf-8">
 <title>Jasmine Spec Runner v3.1.0</title>
```

```
    <link rel="shortcut icon" type="image/png"
href="lib/jasmine-3.1.0/jasmine_favicon.png">
    <link rel="stylesheet" href="lib/jasmine-3.1.0/jasmine.css">

    <script src="lib/jasmine-3.1.0/jasmine.js"></script>
    <script src="lib/jasmine-3.1.0/jasmine-html.js"></script>
    <script src="lib/jasmine-3.1.0/boot.js"></script>

    <!-- include source files here... -->
    <script src="src/StringUtils.js"></script>

    <!-- include spec files here... -->
    <script src="spec/StringUtilsSpec.js"></script>

</head>

<body>
</body>
</html>
```

The highlighted lines are the ones that we have to change in the SpecRunner.html file. To run the tests, simply open SpecRunner.html in your browser. If all tests pass, you will see a green color, and any test failure is highlighted in red. Look at the following screenshot:

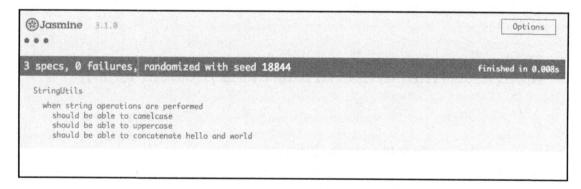

A failed test would show an error, as shown in the following screenshot:

The preceding screenshot shows the test runner screen where the test cases are failing.

LTS

LTS provides a wrapper for Jasmine and Mocha. The code for LTS is open source, so it can be easily tailored to work with other frameworks as well.

The testing service comprises a global $T object that contains methods to create components, run callbacks, fire application events, and destroy components. The code for the $T API can be found at `https://github.com/forcedotcom/`
`LightningTestingService/blob/master/Lightning-component-tests/test/default/`
`staticresources/lts_testutil.resource`.

Salesforce recommends that you write and test for the following behaviors in Lightning Components:

Test use case	Description
DOM rendering	Validates that components are added where and when they should be.
Component state	Ensures that components respond as expected.
Server-side callback response	Gets the right response from a call to another service or resource.
Validation of variables	Validates whether variables that are loaded from external sources are valid.
Conditional UI rendering	Verifies what users can see.
Event handling	Tests responses to events.

The LTS is well-integrated with the Salesforce DX. The following are some of the more useful commands related to the LTS in SFDX:

SFDX command	Description	Example command
sfdx force:Lightning:test:install	This installs the unmanaged package that contains all the code and infrastructure needed to run LTS. The wrappers are created as static resource files in Salesforce.	sfdx force:Lightning:test:install
sfdx force:Lightning:test:create	This creates a Lightning test and outputs to a testing directory.	sfdx force:Lightning:test:create -n MyLightningTest -d LightningTests
sfdx force:Lightning:test:run	This runs specified tests or all the tests, and then outputs results.	sfdx force:Lightning:test:run -a tests -r human

A simple test that uses Jasmine to test for a method call on a component is shown in the following code:

```
describe('c:egComponentMethod', function() {
    it("updates an attribute value when a method is invoked on the
component's interface", function(done) {
        $T.createComponent("c:egComponentMethod", null)
    .then(function(component) {
            component.sampleMethod();
            expect(component.get("v.status")).toBe("sampleMethod invoked");
            done();
        }).catch(function(e) {
            done.fail(e);
        });
    });
});
```

Writing tests for a YouTubeSearchApp

In this section, we will explore how to write a complete unit test suite for the YouTubeSearchApp that we created in Chapter 8, *Debugging Lightning Components* (see https://github.com/PacktPublishing/Learning-Salesforce-Lightning-Application-Development/tree/master/chapter8).

To create a scratch Org with the code samples, go through the following commands in your DX project:

```
$ git clone
https://github.com/PacktPublishing/Learning-Salesforce-Lightning-Applicatio
n-Development.git  //clone the repo

$ cd Chapter8 //cd into the chapter8 folder

$ sfdx force:auth:web:login -d -a DevHub //auth into Dev Hub

$ sfdx force:config:set defaultdevhubusername=DevHub // Set as default

$ sfdx force:org:create -s -f config/project-scratch-def.json -a testOrg //
Create a scratch Org

$ sfdx force:config:set defaultusername=testOrg //set default scratch org

$ sfdx force:source:push // push source code

$ sfdx force:org:open //open scratch Org
```

Installing LTS

To install the LTS in your scratch Org, run the following command:

```
sfdx force:Lightning:test:install
```

Once the package is installed, note that there are sample Lightning Components and tests provided in the package to help us understand how to write tests.

Now, to run the Lightning tests via the CLI, use the following command:

```
sfdx force:Lightning:test:run
```

You will see the output of the CLI, as shown in the following screenshot:

```
=== Test Summary
NAME                    VALUE
───────────────────────────────────────────────────────────────────────────
Outcome                 Passed
Tests Ran               18
Passing                 17
Failing                 0
Skipped                 1
Pass Rate               100%
Fail Rate               0%
Test Start Time         Jul 5, 2018 12:00 AM
Test Execution Time     5873 ms
Test Total Time         5873 ms
Command Time            17389 ms
Hostname                https://velocity-dream-7831-dev-ed.cs40.my.salesforce.com
Org Id                  00D540000009LcgEAE
Username                test-gn92qttmj826@example.com

Test run complete
```

You can also manually run this by opening up the Lightning app from the **Developer Console**. Run this manually by creating a Lightning app named `jasmineTests.app`. The Lightning app code for `jasmineTests.app` looks as follows:

```
<aura:application >

    <c:lts_jasmineRunner testFiles="{!join(',',
      $Resource.jasmineHelloWorldTests,
    $Resource.jasmineExampleTests,
    $Resource.jasmineLightningDataServiceTests
    )}" />

</aura:application>
```

It makes use of the `lts_jasmineRunner` component and expects an attribute that specifies that the static resource comprises of Jasmine test suites.

Creating a Lightning Component test via CLI

Let's create a test for the `YoutubeSearchApp` using the SFDX command line, as shown in the following code:

```
sfdx force:Lightning:test:create -n YoutubeSearchAppTest -d ./force-
app/main/default/staticresources
```

Upon running this command, you will notice that a JavaScript file with a `describe` function template is added in the `staticresources` folder.

We will write the test suite here and then reference them back in the `jasmineTests.app` test application.

Testing for search terms rendered via two-way binding

The first test we are going to write is for testing whether the search term entered in the text box is properly two-way bound and added on the screen.

The section of the YouTube component markup code that we test is as follows, where `{!v.searchTerm}` is an attribute:

```
<Lightning:layoutItem flexibility="auto" padding="around-large" size="6">
        <p aura:id="searchTermRendered"> You searched for
{!v.searchTerm} </p>
        </Lightning:layoutItem>
```

The test suite for testing the two-way data binding is shown in the following code:

```
describe("YoutubeSearchAppTest", function(){

    afterEach(function () {
        $T.clearRenderedTestComponents();
    });

    describe("A Suite that tests the youtube search component", function()
{
        describe('c:youtubesearch', function () {
            it('verify component rendering for search test', function
(done) {
                $T.createComponent('c:youtubesearch', {"searchTerm"
:"searchString"}, true)
                    .then(function(cmp) {
expect(cmp.find("searchTermRendered").getElement().innerHTML).toBe('searchS
tring');
                        done();
                }).catch(function (e) {
                    done.fail(e);
                });
            });
        });
    });
});
```

Note that we are creating the component using `$T.createComponent`, which has three parameters:

- The name of the component that needs to be created
- An object for the attributes
- A third parameter that is a Boolean that tells us whether to render the component or not

Note that the `$T.createComponent` returns a promise that resolves to give a function with the component that is created.

The next step before testing is to modify the `jasmineTests.app` to the following:

```
<aura:application >

    <c:lts_jasmineRunner testFiles="{!join(',',
       $Resource.youtubeSearchAppTest
    )}" />

</aura:application>
```

It's not mandatory to use the same `jasmineTests.app` as the application for the test. You can have your own, but make sure when you are running tests that you specify the app name in the test run CLI command as `sfdx force:Lightning:test:run -a tests -r human`. Here, `tests` is the Lightning app name where the test runner's components are loaded. For Jasmine, we use `lts_jasmineRunner`; for Mocha, there are similar setups in place.

To push the static resource, make sure that you run the following command:

```
sfdx force:source:push
```

To run this, you can open the `jasmineTests.app` application via the **Developer Console** or via the CLI. Upon a successful run, you should see a result similar to the following screenshot:

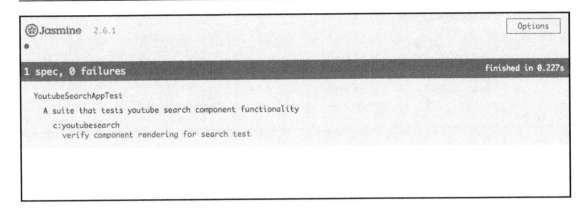

Verifying the response by mocking the server response using Jasmine spy

The next `it` function that we want to write tests the response from the server. Since we do not want to perform the actual API calls in the test method, we use mock data. We will use the `spy` function with the `callFake` strategy (this strategy is provided by the Jasmine framework) to perform testing.

Another thing to note in this example is that we have used the `Lightning:button` component, which is in the Lightning namespace, and hence it is currently not supported in the LTS service to simulate the click event. However, we can work around this by creating an `aura:method` that calls the function that is invoked on a button click.

To help us with our testing, we add the following lines to our `YouTubeSearch` component, as shown in the following code:

```
<aura:method name="search" action="{!c.handleClick}"/>
```

The test spec for this use case is shown in the following code. The complete code can be found at the Git repository at `https://github.com/PacktPublishing/Learning-Salesforce-Lightning-Application-Development/blob/master/Chapter14/force-app/main/default/staticresources/YoutubeSearchAppTest.resource`:

```
describe("YoutubeSearchAppTest", function(){

    var responseObject ;

    afterEach(function () {
        $T.clearRenderedTestComponents();
    });

    beforeEach(function (){
        //provide mock response here
```

```
            responseObject = { }
    });

    describe("A Suite that tests youtube search component functionality",
function() {
        describe('c:youtubesearch', function () {
            it('verify component rendering for search test', function
(done) {
                $T.createComponent('c:youtubesearch', {searchTerm
:"searchString"}, true)
                    .then(function(component) {
expect(component.find("searchTermRendered").getElement().innerHTML).toBe('
You searched for searchString');
                        done();
                    }).catch(function (e) {
                        done.fail(e);
                    });
            });
            //Tests for the server Response
            it('verify that server methods were called', function (done) {
                $T.createComponent('c:youtubesearch', {searchTerm
:"searchString"}, true)
                    .then(function(component) {
                        var mockResponse = {
                            getState: function () {
                                return "SUCCESS";
                            },
                            getReturnValue: function () {
                                return JSON.stringify(responseObject);
                            }
                        };
                        spyOn($A, "enqueueAction").and.callFake(function
(action) {
                            var cb = action.getCallback("SUCCESS");
                            cb.fn.apply(cb.s, [mockResponse]);
                        });
                        component.search();
expect(component.get("v.data").items.length).toBe(2);
                        done();
                    }).catch(function (e) {
                        done.fail(e);
                    });
            });
        });
    });
});
```

You can check about `responseObject = { }` at https://github.com/
PacktPublishing/Learning-Salesforce-Lightning-Application-
Development/blob/master/Chapter14/force-app/main/default/
staticresources/YoutubeSearchAppTest.resource for complete code

Observe the code in bold lines. We added the following elements to these lines:

- We added the mock response data in the `beforeEach()` so that we can use this to test against without having to call the service:

```
beforeEach(function (){
        responseObject = {} //dummy data
```

- We will leverage the `spyOn` function for the `enqueueAction` method on the `$A` object to return a `fakeresponse`, as shown in the following code:

```
$T.createComponent('c:youtubesearch', {searchTerm :"searchString"},
true)
                    .then(function(component) {
                        var mockResponse = {
                            getState: function () {
                                return "SUCCESS";
                            },
                            getReturnValue: function () {
                                return
JSON.stringify(responseObject);
                            }
                        };
                        spyOn($A,
"enqueueAction").and.callFake(function (action) {
                                var cb = action.getCallback("SUCCESS");
                                cb.fn.apply(cb.s, [mockResponse]);
                        });
                //call the search method here
```

On a successful run, you will see the following output on the CLI:

```
=== Test Summary
NAME                   VALUE
─────────────────────────────────────────────────────────────────────────
Outcome                Passed
Tests Ran              2
Passing                2
Failing                0
Skipped                0
Pass Rate              100%
Fail Rate              0%
Test Start Time        Jul 5, 2018 11:07 PM
Test Execution Time    223 ms
Test Total Time        223 ms
Command Time           10675 ms
Hostname               https://velocity-dream-7831-dev-ed.cs40.my.salesforce.com
Org Id                 00D540000009LcgEAE
Username               test-gn92qttmj826@example.com

Test run complete
```

Testing application events

The `$T` global function provides a utility method called `$T.fireApplicationEvent` to fire an event when testing components that handle the application event.

The code snippet to fire an application event from the testing service is as follows:

```
$T.fireApplicationEvent(eventName, eventParams)
```

The following is a sample code snippet that shows how to test a component that handles the application event:

```javascript
describe('c:componentsubscribingToAppEvent', function () {
    it('verify application event', function (done) {
        $T.createComponent("c:componentsubscribingToAppEvent")
            .then(function (component) {
                $T.fireApplicationEvent("c:applicationEvent", {"eventData":
"sample event Data"});
                expect(component.get("v.eventDataCaptured")).toBe("sample
event Data");
                done();
            }).catch(function (e) {
                done.fail(e);
            });
    });
});
```

The $T utility function provides other methods, and you can explore the code in the open source repository at `https://github.com/forcedotcom/LightningTestingService/blob/master/Lightning-component-tests/test/default/staticresources/lts_testutil.resource`.

Also, for more advanced use cases, such as testing for Lightning Data Services, you can refer to the sample code provided in the repository at `https://github.com/forcedotcom/LightningTestingService/blob/master/Lightning-component-tests/test/default/staticresources/jasmineLightningDataServiceTests.resource`.

> For actions that involve the DML operation in Salesforce, if you do not spy and substitute with the mock data, the test data will not be rolled back. Hence, you should always make sure that you are not running these tests in production and consider using this only in scratch Orgs or sandboxes.

Summary

This chapter showed you how to unit test the components using Jasmine. Writing unit tests allows us to find app-breaking changes whenever code is refactored or redesigned. One could also run these tests in their CI workflows.

The next chapter will help us understand how one can publish these components on Salesforce AppExchange, and how to work with these components when Salesforce Org has namespaces enabled.

15
Publishing Lightning Components on AppExchange

Salesforce AppExchange is a store where you can find prebuilt applications and components to solve specific business problems. AppExchange is similar to the Apple Store/Google Play Store (from where you can install apps on your phone). The only difference is that the apps from Salesforce AppExchange can be installed in a Salesforce sandbox, production, or developer environment (Org, where the package is installed, is termed as Subscriber Org). Customers can install the AppExchange with a single click in their Salesforce instance. AppExchange apps can be free or paid, depending on the partner agreement you have with Salesforce. The applications that are available on Salesforce AppExchange are called managed package applications. The advantages of managed package applications are that they allow developers/application owners to update the package and release new features and components.

In this chapter, we will focus on the following topics:

- Namespacing Salesforce developer instances for managed package generation
- The impact of namespacing Salesforce instances on the component bundle
- Creating scratch Orgs with namespaces
- Creating a managed package
- Documenting your components using the auradoc file
- Using the design file to allow admins to configure attributes
- Publishing components on AppExchange

Namespacing Salesforce developer instances for managed package generation

So far, we have been using either scratch Org or developer Org to build our code components and tests. However, to publish the components on AppExchange, we need to package the solution as a managed package. A managed package adds a namespace string to the fields, objects, classes, and components, and bundles all the dependencies into one unit. Manage-packaging the solution generates a URL link that can be used to install the solution in any Salesforce instance.

To package up the application as a managed package, we need a developer Org with a namespace. A developer Org can be obtained freely using the following URL: `https://developer.Salesforce.com/signup`.

To namespace an Org, navigate to the **Package Manager** from the setup using the **Setup | Apps | Package Manager** path:

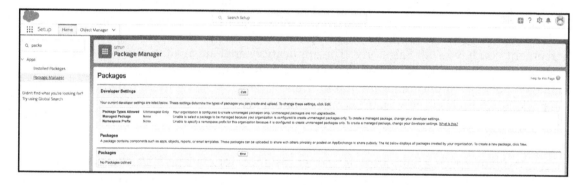

The package manager screen provides **Edit** buttons on **Developer Settings**. Choose a namespace for the application you want to package, as shown in the following screenshot:

Namespacing a developer Org is an irreversible process. Once you choose a namespace, you won't be able to edit it. To create a new namespace, you will have to create a new developer Org by signing up. More importantly, if you reference the namespace in code, you will have to change the code to use new namespaces everywhere.

Let's assume we are packaging up all the code we have for the `YouTubeSearch` application. Let's also assume that the name of the package is the `YouTubeSearch` application and the namespace we have chosen is `SearchApp`. Note that you can edit the application name any time, however, you cannot change the namespace.

The following screenshot shows how you can create a package and manage it using a checkbox. Note that a Salesforce instance can have only one managed package application:

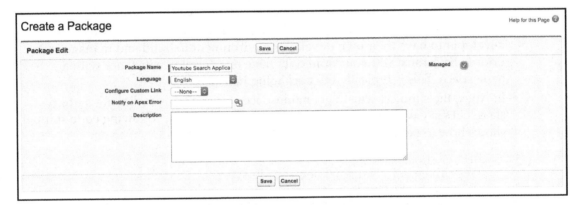

The impact of namespacing Salesforce instances on the component bundle

When you namespace a Salesforce instance for managed package creation, note that when you package, your custom objects and custom fields get namespaced. For example, let's say you have an object that is named `Project`; the object once packaged in an Org as the `SearchApp` namespace has the `SearchApp__Project` object name. The namespace is added with double underscores for all custom object and custom fields. This allows the managed package components to be unique and not conflict with the components with the same name in the Salesforce Organization where the package is installed (subscriber Org).

During the packaging process, Salesforce automatically takes care of namespacing fields and objects referenced in Apex classes in the package-generation process, so you don't have to explicitly namespace the fields in the code. This allows the developers to work in any Salesforce Org and move code to the packaging Org without having to explicitly namespace.

However, there are instances where you use strings (for example, if you write Dynamic SOQL, Dynamic DML, or JavaScript Code on a Visualforce page that doesn't have a JavaScript remoting function) instead of static bindings, in which case you will have to take care of writing code to append namespaces of the package.

There have been a couple of problems with actually hardcoding the namespaces in code:

- If ever you decide to change the namespace in the code (in my experience, I have seen this happen when a company gets acquired by another company), you will need to change it in almost every Apex class, which can be tedious.
- It becomes extremely difficult to set CI solution as that would require every developer to have their own developer environment to build and manage code. Prior to Salesforce DX, you could only have one Salesforce instance with a namespace. This is typically the packaging instance.
- In Apex, the simplest way to get namespaces for an Org is by having a utility class. Let's say we name the class as `NamespaceUtil`; the following code snippet shows how to get the namespace:

```
public class NameSpaceUtil {
  public Static String getNamespace (){
    String nameSpacePrefix =
NameSpaceUtil.class.getName().substringBefore('NameSpaceUtil').subs
tringBefore('.');
    return nameSpacePrefix;
  }
}
```

The preceding technique is widely used to get the package namespace dynamically without hardcoding the actual namespace in the Salesforce code.

For the namespaced Organizations, Salesforce recommends you use the namespace in the Lightning Component code: `https://developer.Salesforce.com/docs/atlas.en-us.Lightning.meta/Lightning/namespace_using_reference.htm`.

For organizations without namespaces, you can refer to events and components using the `c` prefix, as we have used throughout the book. However, if your Organization is namespaced, replace `c` with the actual namespace.

The following table shows how to use proper namespaces for attributes, events, and components in managed packages:

Referenced item	Example code with namespace
Component used in markup	`<namespace:myComponent/>`, **example for namespace with** `SearchApp` `<SearchApp:youtubesearch/>`
Component used in system attribute	`<aura:component extends="namespace:myComponent">` `<aura:component implements="namespace:myInterface">`
Apex controller	`<aura:component controller="namespace.controllername">`, **example for namespace with** `SerachApp` **and** `youtubeController` **is** `<aura:component controller="SearchApp.youtubeSearchController">`
Custom object or custom fields in default attribute	`<aura:attribute name="newObj"` `type="namespace__Object__c"` `default="{ 'sobjectType': 'namespace__Object__c',` `'Name': '',` `'namespace__Amount__c': 0,` `...` `}" />`
Custom fields in expression	`<Lightning:input value="{!v.obj.namespace__Amount__c}"` `label=... />`
Custom fields in JavaScript expression	`updateRow: function(component) {` `...` `for(var i = 0 ; i < obj.length ; i++){` `var newobj = obj[i];` `total += obj.namespace__Amount__c;` `}` `...` `}`
Components created dynamically in JavaScript	`var myCmp =` `$A.createComponent("namespace:myComponent",` `{},` `function(myCmp) { }` `);`
Interface comparison	`aCmp.isInstanceOf("namespace:myInterface")`
Event registration	`<aura:registerEvent type="namespace:appEvent" name=...` `/>`
Event handler	`<aura:handler event="namespace:appEvent" action=... />`
Explicit dependency	`<aura:dependency` `resource="markup://namespace:myComponent" />`

Application event in a JavaScript function	`var myEvent = $A.get("e.namespace:appEvent");`

Static resources	`<ltng:require`
	`scripts="{!$Resource.namespace__resourceName}"`
	`styles="{!$Resource.namespace__resourceName}" />`

Lightning Out script	`$Lightning.use("namespace:youtubesearchOutApp", () =>`
	`{`
	`$Lightning.createComponent("namespace:youtubesearch",`
	`{},`
	`"youtubeApp",`
	`(cmp) => {`
	`//Component COde`
	`});`
	`},LightningEndPointURI,token );`

Salesforce DX allows us to generate multiple Orgs with the same namespace. This allows for support of CI, as each developer can Org with a namespace exactly the same as that of the packaging instance. This also allows us to use the namespace prefix in the code markup.

It's still recommended not to pollute code with namespaces everywhere. For some places, this might not be possible, such as Lightning Data Services and standard Lightning base components. We can use a wrapper class to avoid tight coupling with Salesforce fields for components that require Apex.

To understand how to create the Apex class for Lightning Components and make it namespace safe, let's consider the following example, where we have a component that displays a list of accounts with a custom field. The Apex code is as follows:

```
public with sharing class AccountTest{

    @AuraEnabled
    public static list<Account> getlstacc(){
        return [Select Id , Name , NumberofLocations__c from Account order by
NumberofLocations__c limit 10];
    }

}
```

The component markup code is as follows:

```
<aura:component controller="AccountTest" access="global">
  <aura:handler name="init" action="{!c.fetchAccounts}" value="{!this}" />
    <aura:attribute name="accounts" type="Account[]" />
    <ul>
      <aura:iteration items="{!v.accounts}" var="account">
```

```
<li > <h3>{!account.name}</h3> </li>
        <li > <h3>{!account.NumberofLocations__c}</h3> </li>
    </aura:iteration>
  </ul>
</aura:component>
```

The controller code is as follows:

```
({
  fetchAccounts : function(component, event, helper) {
    var action = component.get("c.getlstacc ");
        action.setCallback(this, function(data) {
        component.set("v.accounts", data.getReturnValue());
        });
          $A.enqueueAction(action);
  }
})
```

The preceding code will not work once it is packaged as the managed package. This is because the NumberofLocations__c field requires a namespace prefix.

Changing the code to the following markup will make it work, however we ended up hardcoding the field names:

```
<aura:component controller="AccountTest" access="global">
  <aura:handler name="init" action="{!c.fetchAccounts}" value="{!this}" />
    <aura:attribute name="accounts" type="Account[]" />
    <ul>
      <aura:iteration items="{!v.accounts}" var="account">
        <li > <h3>{!account.name}</h3> </li>
              <li >
<h3>{!account.LightningTestNa__NumberofLocations__c}</h3> </li>
      </aura:iteration>
    </ul>
</aura:component>
```

Notice the preceding highlighted line has the LightningTestNa__ prefixed namespace.

The following code shows you how to completely remove the dependency on the namespace using a wrapper class. The code for the controller, component markup, and the frontend JavaScript controller is shown in the following code block. The difference is we now use an Apex wrapper class named AccountWrapper. The mapping between the wrapper class and the actual fields happens in Apex.

When the code is packaged, Salesforce takes care of namespacing Apex and we can omit the namespace references in code:

```
public with sharing class AccountTest{

    @AuraEnabled
    public static list<AccountWrapper> getlstacc(){
        list<AccountWrapper> lstWrapper = new list<AccountWrapper>();
        for(Account acc :[Select Id , Name , NumberofLocations__c from
Account order by NumberofLocations__c limit 10]){
            AccountWrapper accWrap = new AccountWrapper();
            accWrap.Name = acc.Name;
            accWrap.noOfLocations = integer.valueof(acc.NumberofLocations__c);
            lstWrapper.add(accWrap);
        }
        return lstWrapper;
    }

}
```

The Apex wrapper class is as follows:

```
public class AccountWrapper {

    @AuraEnabled
    public string name;
    @AuraEnabled
    public integer noOfLocations ;

}
```

The component code is as follows:

```
<aura:component controller="AccountTest" access="global">
    <aura:handler name="init" action="{!c.fetchAccounts}" value="{!this}" />
        <aura:attribute name="accounts" type="AccountWrapper[]" />
    <ul>
        <aura:iteration items="{!v.accounts}" var="account">
            <li > <h3>{!account.name}</h3> </li>
                <li > <h3>{!account.noOfLocations}</h3> </li>
        </aura:iteration>
    </ul>
</aura:component>
```

The JavaScript controller code is as follows:

```
({
        fetchAccounts : function(component, event, helper) {
         var action = component.get("c.getlstacc ");
             action.setCallback(this, function(data) {
             component.set("v.accounts", data.getReturnValue());
           });
         $A.enqueueAction(action);
    }
})
```

We have the freedom to use namespaces in the code, but it's still recommended to build the Apex code with a utility method that fetches namespaces dynamically, as shown in the `NameSpaceUtil` class earlier. This keeps us from polluting the code with namespaces. For Lightning Component, the component markup explicitly requires namespaces. For JavaScript bundles and events, adding namespace is handled by the Salesforce package manager on package creation. All the `auraEnabled` methods returning objects can be wrapper classes, so the component markup is not tied to the field names on the frontend.

Creating scratch Orgs with namespaces

Salesforce DX allows us to create multiple scratch Orgs with namespaces equivalent to the packaging organization. In order to do this, the first prerequisite is to link your Dev Org with namespaces to the Developer Hub Org. This process is also known as registering namespaces.

To register a namespace in your Developer Hub Org (if you do not have one, signup using `https://developer.Salesforce.com/promotions/Orgs/dx-signup`), use the **Namespace Register** tab and click on **Link Namespace**, as shown in the following screenshot:

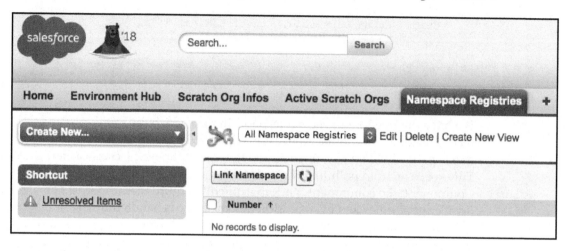

Once you click on **Link Namespace**, a login for the Salesforce instance pops up. This will be the credentials of the Org where you have namespaced and created your managed packages.

On successfully registering a namespace, you will notice a **Namespace Registry** record, as shown in the following screenshot:

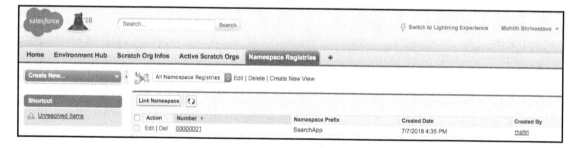

Once we register the namespace, we can create a scratch Org with the namespace by indicating the namespace in the `sfdx-project.json` file, as follows:

```
{
  "packageDirectories": [
    {
      "path": "force-app",
      "default": true
```

```
    }
  ],
  "namespace": "SearchApp",
  "sfdcLoginUrl": "https://login.Salesforce.com",
  "sourceApiVersion": "43.0"
}
```

Once you create a scratch Org using the following command, you will notice that the Org has the `SearchApp` namespace:

```
sfdx force:org:create -s -f config/project-scratch-def.json -a scratch_Org
```

You can verify this by creating a simple class in the environment and you will see that a namespace prefix has been added, as shown in the following screenshot:

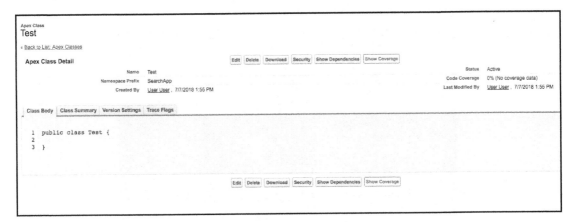

Creating a managed package

To create a managed package, the first step is to get the code and components from the scratch Org to the Developer Org where we have enabled the namespace. In order to do this, we need to convert the source code from the scratch format into the metadata API format.

To convert the source code into the metadata API format, run the following command in the Terminal in the directory where you have the Salesforce app. This command converts the source from the `force-app`, creates an API metadata equivalent, and outputs to the `mdapi_output_dir` directory. Notice that −n is followed by the name of the managed package application:

```
sfdx force:source:convert  -d mdapi_output_dir -n 'Youtube Search
Application'
```

The following screenshot shows the components in the `mdap_output_dir` directory:

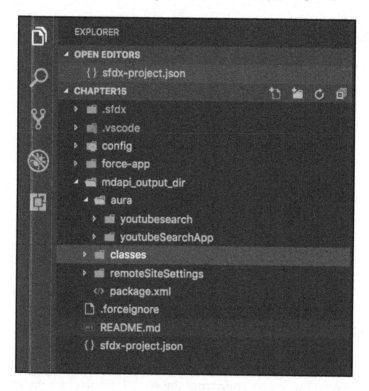

To deploy the code from `mdapi_output_dir` to the Salesforce packaging instance, we need to authenticate with the Org and then run the deploy command.

The command to authenticate with a Developer Org where we have the namespace enabled and the package installed is as follows. Log in with the Developer Org credentials:

```
sfdx force:auth:web:login -d -a DevOrg
```

Once logged in, run the following command to push the source code to the non-DX Org, which is the packaging Org:

```
sfdx force:mdapi:deploy --deploydir mdapi_output_dir -u DevOrg -w 3
```

A successful deployment will prompt on the Terminal, as follows:

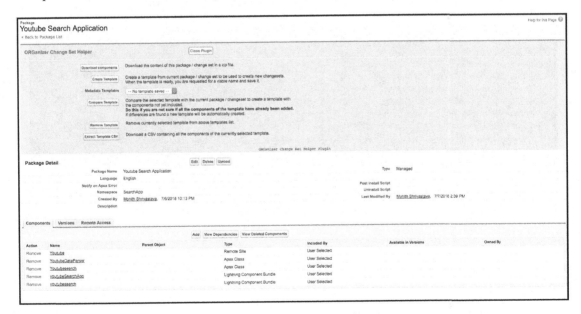

```
Deployment finished in 1000ms

=== Result
Status:  Succeeded
jobid:   0Aff20000082rdJCAQ
Completed:  2018-07-07T21:39:09.000Z
Component errors:  0
Components deployed:  5
Components total:  5
Tests errors:  0
Tests completed:  0
Tests total:  0
Check only: false
```

In the following screenshot, you can see that you also have the package with all the components after a successful deployment:

To generate a package from the Salesforce UI, simply click on **Upload** and it gives you an option to choose **BETA/Released**. A **BETA** package is non-upgradable and meant only for testing, while a release package can be upgraded and distributed on AppExchange.

You can also use the CLI to generate the package using the following command:

```
sfdx force:package1:version:create -i 033f2000000PcNg -n 'Youtube Search
Application' -u DevOrg -w 4
```

We have an ID, `-i`, which is the package ID. The package ID can be obtained from the Salesforce user interface once you create a package by observing the URL. It beings with `033`.

The command can run to create as many versions as you like. To create a release version, include `--managedreleased`, as shown in the following command:

```
sfdx force:package1:version:create -i 033f2000000PcNg -n 'Youtube Search
Application' -u DevOrg --managedreleased -w 4
```

Once a package is released, we get an installation URL that can be installed in the subscriber Org or published on AppExchange.

The following screenshot shows the successful CLI screen on page upload:

```
Mohiths-MacBook-Air:chapter15 mohith$ sfdx force:package1:version:create -i 033f
2000000PcNg -n 'Youtube Search Application' -u Devorg -w 4
Package upload is enqueued. Waiting 5 more seconds
Package upload in progress. Waiting 5 more seconds
Package upload in progress. Waiting 5 more seconds
Successfully uploaded package [04tf2000000SucXAAS]
Mohiths-MacBook-Air:chapter15 mohith$ sfdx force:package1:version:create -i 033f
2000000PcNg -n 'Youtube Search Application' -u Devorg -w 4 -m
Package upload is enqueued. Waiting 5 more seconds
Package upload in progress. Waiting 5 more seconds
Successfully uploaded package [04tf2000000T1A9AAK]
```

Once a page is created, a URL is generated that can be used by subscribers to install. The following screenshot shows the managed release package version:

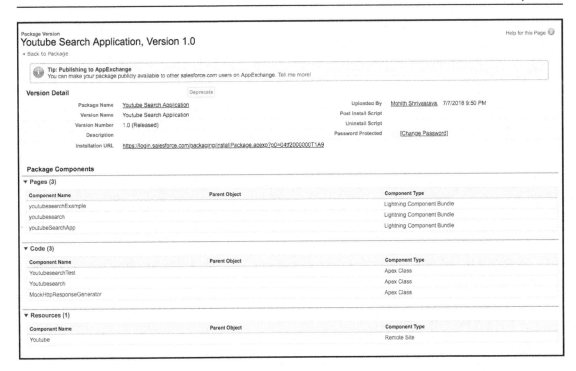

Salesforce is working toward a better packaging capability, named
Second-Generation packaging. To learn more about it, refer to the
following document: `https://developer.Salesforce.com/docs/atlas.`
`en-us.sfdx_cli_reference.meta/sfdx_cli_reference/cli_reference_`
`force_package.htm#cli_reference_force_package.`

Documenting your components using the auradoc file

The documentation can be written using the `.auradoc` file that is created every time you
create a Lightning Component. The documentation for the Lightning Component is
available at
the `https://<myDomain>.Lightning.force.com/componentReference/suite.app`
URL and any `auradocs` for custom components also appear at the same URL in your
Salesforce instance. Note that `<myDomain>` is the domain name of your Salesforce instance.

As it currently has no documentation, you will see that the component docs for `SearchApp` look as follows:

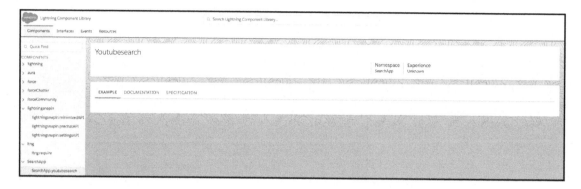

Let's prettify it by adding the proper documentation. To start, let's add a description in the `youtubesearch.auradoc` file, as follows:

```
<aura:documentation>
    <aura:description>
        <p>An <code>SearchApp:youtubesearch</code> component provides a
component with a search box to search across youtube</p>
    </aura:description>
    <aura:example name="ExampleName" ref="" label="Label">
        Example Description
    </aura:example>
</aura:documentation>
```

Using `aura:description` adds a proper description:

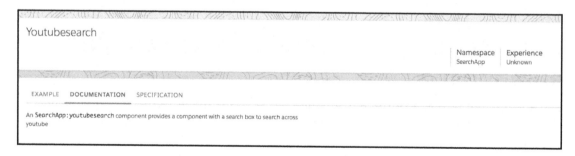

Let's add some examples and see what it this looks. To add an example, we create another component that shows how to use our component. Let's name this `youtubesearchExample`:

```
<!--The SearchApp:youtubesearchExample example component-->
<aura:component>
        <SearchApp:youtubesearch/>
</aura:component>
```

Now, we can reference this component in the `youtubesearch.auradoc` document file:

```
<aura:documentation>
    <aura:description>
        <p>An <code>SearchApp:youtubesearch</code> component provides a
component with a search box to search across youtube</p>
    </aura:description>
    <aura:example name="youtubesearchExample"
ref="SearchApp:youtubesearchExample" label="youtubesearch">
        <p>
            This example shows how to use the component in your custom code
            <code><SearchApp:youtubesearch/></code>
        </p>
    </aura:example>
</aura:documentation>
```

Once we have linked the example reference component using `aura:reference`, we can use doc previewer. Note that it also provides a working live demo and documentation:

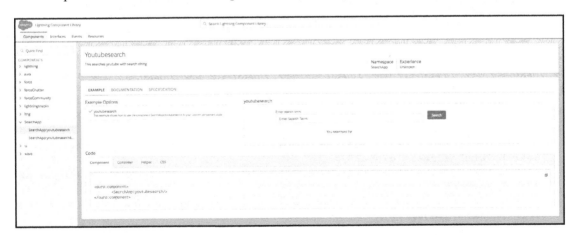

Note that for a specification section, there is a `description` attribute provided in the component, attributes, interfaces, and events. We can use the `description` attribute to describe each of these as they show up in the documentation.

If you want the components to be available outside your Salesforce instance, use a global modifier on the component. The same thing applies to events, interfaces, and attributes. Take extreme caution before you globalize an attribute or component. If you intend for it to be used by the subscriber, global is preferred. By default, the modifier is set to public.

Using the design file to allow admins to configure attributes

The Lightning Components bundle provides a design file. This can be used to add design parameters that become available for the Salesforce administrators when they drag the components using the Lightning Application Builder, Community Builder, or Flow Builder.

Salesforce provides guidelines on best practices when designing components for the Application Builder here: `https://developer.Salesforce.com/docs/atlas.en-us.Lightning.meta/Lightning/components_config_for_app_builder_template_component.htm`.

Let's imagine we want to allow admins to change labels in the YouTube component for the **Search** box placeholder, the **Search** box label, and the message that appears after the search; we can use the design file to make these configurable.

Let's expose these hardcoded values as attributes in the component markup. The following code snippet shows the changed code. Observe the lines in bold:

```
<aura:component
implements="force:appHostable,flexipage:availableForAllPageTypes"
access="global" controller="YoutubeSearch" description="This searches
youtube with search string">
    <aura:attribute name="searchTerm" type="String" />
    <!--ATTRIBUTES DECLARATION -->
    <aura:attribute name="data" type="Map"/>
    <aura:attribute name="searchBoxLabel" type="String" default="Enter
Search Term" access="global"/>
    <aura:attribute name="searchBoxPlaceHolder" type="String" default="Enter
Search Term" access="global"/>
    <aura:attribute name="resultMessage" type="String" default="You searched
for" access="global"/>

    <aura:method name="search" action="{!c.handleClick}"/>
    <div class="c-container">
        <Lightning:layout multipleRows="true" horizontalAlign="center"
verticalAlign="center">
```

```
<Lightning:layoutItem flexibility="auto" size="6">
    <div class="slds-form-element">
        <label class="slds-form-element__label" for="text-input-
id-1">{!v.searchBoxLabel}</label>
        <div class="slds-form-element__control">
            <input type="search" id="text-input-id-1" class="slds-
input" placeholder="{!v.searchBoxPlaceHolder}" aura:id="searchBox"/>
        </div>
    </div>
</Lightning:layoutItem>
<Lightning:layoutItem flexibility="auto" size="4"
padding="horizontal-small">
    <Lightning:button variant="brand" aura:id="button"
label="Search" title="" onclick="{! c.handleClick }" class="c-btn"/>
</Lightning:layoutItem>
<Lightning:layoutItem flexibility="auto" padding="around-large"
size="6">
    <p aura:id="searchTermRendered"> {!v.resultMessage}
{!v.searchTerm} </p>
</Lightning:layoutItem>
    ----

------
</div>
</aura:component>
```

Let's create a design file for the attributes highlighted in bold in the preceding code sample. A simple youtubesearch.design design file would be as follows:

```
<design:component label="Youtube Search">
    <design:attribute name="searchBoxLabel" label="Search Box Label"
description="The Label of the Search Box" default="Enter Search Term"/>
    <design:attribute name="searchBoxPlaceHolder" label="Search Box Place
Holder" description="The Placeholder of the Search Box" default="Enter
Search Term"/>
    <design:attribute name="resultMessage" label="Text Message For Results"
default="You searched for" description="Text Label for the Search Term "/>
</design:component>
```

The following screenshot shows how the design file translates to admin-friendly input to allow them to change labels:

The Lightning icon comes by default. If you are publishing components on the store, it is important to brand them. To display a custom icon, use an SVG in the `.svg` file that comes with the component bundle.

You can view the SVG code in the Git repository: `https://github.com/PacktPublishing/Learning-Salesforce-Lightning-Application-Development/blob/master/chapter15/force-app/main/default/aura/youtubesearch/youtubesearch.svg`. The following screenshot shows how the component appears in the app builder. Notice that it has its own icon:

Publishing components on AppExchange

Publishing components on AppExchange require the following steps:

1. Signup for a partner agreement with Salesforce. You can begin the process on their website: `https://partnersignup.Salesforce.com/`.

2. Once you sign the agreement, you get access to the publishing console. In the publishing console, find the **ORGANIZATIONS** tab and connect your Salesforce packaging Org with the package to the console using **Connect Organization**:

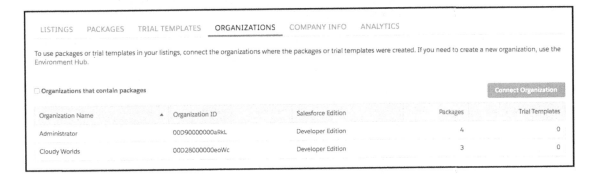

3. From the **PACKAGES** tab, you will see your listing. From here, you can create the listing and **Security Review** process:

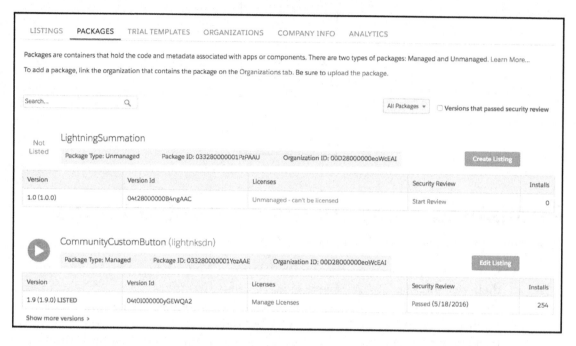

4. Create the Salesforce listing and if it is purely a Lightning Component, choose the category as Lightning Component:

5. Follow the prompts. A listing requires a security review and assets such as documentation, videos that shows demos, and other marketing assets.

6. Once your component passes the security review and adheres to guidelines from Salesforce, your app will appear on the AppExchange.

 Salesforce provides a **License Management (LMA)** application if your app is paid, where you can track leads, details about customers, Orgs that install your component, and you can manage your licenses. It's outside the scope of this book to cover all the details of the marketing assets needed for the listing. Reach out to Salesforce for any queries on their partner program and any monetization ideas you have for your app.

Summary

This chapter focused on how you can package your Lightning Components and other assets, and the steps required to publish on Salesforce AppExchange. This also brings us to the end of this book. This book covers the basics, so you can start building your Lightning Components using Salesforce DX and Lightning design systems to solve your business needs with custom Lightning Components. This book also extensively covered Salesforce DX and how it can accelerate development on the Salesforce platform. Lightning Component, along with Salesforce DX, is the future of Salesforce application development. If you are building enterprise applications, I would also recommend you build some design patterns around the framework or use open source projects, such as LAX (`https://github.com/ruslan-kurchenko/sfdc-lax`). In the coming years, it will be interesting to see how Salesforce further improves the component framework, as JavaScript and web components evolve, and the capabilities that it adds to the Salesforce DX and its packaging ability. Keep an eye on the Salesforce release notes with every release to find enhancements and improvements. Salesforce also offers Trailhead as a learning tool. I strongly recommend readers leverage `trailhead.Salesforce.com` to get hands-on experience with projects and modules for free on Trailhead.

Other Books You May Enjoy

If you enjoyed this book, you may be interested in these other books by Packt:

Learning Salesforce Einstein
Mohith Shrivastava

ISBN: 9781787126893

- Get introduced to AI and its role in CRM and cloud applications
- Understand how Einstein works for the sales, service, marketing, community, and commerce clouds
- Gain a deep understanding of how to use Einstein for the analytics cloud
- Build predictive apps on Heroku using PredictionIO, and work with Einstein Predictive Vision Services
- Incorporate Einstein in the IoT cloud
- Test the accuracy of Einstein through Salesforce reporting and Wave analytics

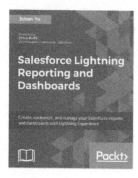

Salesforce Lightning Reporting and Dashboards
Johan Yu

ISBN: 9781788297387

- Navigate in Salesforce.com within the Lightning Experience User Interface
- Secure and share your reports and dashboards with other users
- Create, manage, and maintain reports using Report Builder
- Learn how the report type can affect the report generated
- Explore the report and dashboard folder and the sharing model
- Create reports with multiple formats and custom report types
- Explore various dashboard features in Lightning Experience
- Use Salesforce1, including accessing reports and dashboards

Leave a review - let other readers know what you think

Please share your thoughts on this book with others by leaving a review on the site that you bought it from. If you purchased the book from Amazon, please leave us an honest review on this book's Amazon page. This is vital so that other potential readers can see and use your unbiased opinion to make purchasing decisions, we can understand what our customers think about our products, and our authors can see your feedback on the title that they have worked with Packt to create. It will only take a few minutes of your time, but is valuable to other potential customers, our authors, and Packt. Thank you!

Index

$

$A top-level functions
  APIs in 112
$A.Util APIs
  exploring 112, 114

A

Aloha 9
Apex code
  data rows, limiting for lists 282
  optimizing 282
  sending responses, avoiding as wrapper objects 284
  server response time, reducing platform cache used 283
Apex controllers
  used, for wiring client-side to server 96, 98, 102
Apex debugging
  about 261
  Salesforce CLI, used to stream logs 263
  with Replay Debugger 264, 265, 266
AppExchange
  components, publishing 427
application events
  about 138
  bubbling events, handling 140
  capturing events, handling 140
  creating 139
  event attributes, obtaining from handled event 140
  firing 139
  handling 140
  registering 139
Asynchronous Module Definition (AMD) 214
attributes 89
auradoc file

used, for documenting component 421

B

behavior-driven development (BDD) 387
browser events
  about 133
  capturing 135
  event handling, in Lightning base components 137
bulk data command
  importing, in Salesforce DX 59
bulk upsert command
  limitations 60

C

carousel component
  using 201
ChartJs
  URL 203
Chrome developer console
  breakpoints, setting up 259
  Pause on caught exceptions 261
  using 258
clickjacking 108
code injection 108
component event
  about 142
  creating 142
  event attributes, obtaining from handled events 144
  events handling, alternate syntax used by child components 144
  firing 143
  handling 143
  registering 143
component get method
  using 106

component markup 70
component set method
  using 106
Component Tree tab
  $auraTemp 251
  about 250
components
  creating, $A.createComponent() used 117, 119
  destroying, destory() function used 121
Computer Telephony Interface (CTI) 20
content security policy (CSP) 108
Continuous Integration (CI) 41
cross-site scripting (XSS) 108
CRUD records
  functions 171
  record, creating 173, 175
  record, deleting 176
  record, saving 172
  SaveRecordResult, using 178
custom labels
  label parameters, populating 129
  used, in Lightning Components 128

D

data export commands
  in Salesforce DX 57, 58
data import commands
  in Salesforce DX 57, 59
data manipulation (DML) 270
datatable component
  using 197
date/DateTime
  formatting 116
  formatting, Aura Localization Service used 115
  local currency, finding 115
  local time zone, finding 115
Debug Mode
  disabling, for production 286
  enabling 245, 246
design file
  used, to allow admins to configure attributes
    424, 426
developer hub
  enabling 42, 43
  enabling, in Salesforce organization 42

DOM
  modifying, in RENDERER JavaScript file
    component 122

E

ES6 syntax
  in Lightning Component 129
events strategy
  anti-pattern 277
  for code maintenance 277
  for performance 277
  multiple items set 277
expression syntax
  using 90

F

Field Level Security (FLS) 168
find function
  used, to locate DOM 106
Flow builder
  asynchronous XHR calls, used in Lightning
    Component 322, 323, 327, 328
  custom components, adding 318, 319, 320, 321
  embedding, into Lightning Component 333, 334,
    335
  Lightning Component, used as local Flow actions
    329, 331
Flows
  about 305, 306
  debugging 318
  executing, in Lightning Experience 316, 317
  Lead Finder app, creating Flow builder used
    307, 308, 309, 310, 311, 314, 315

G

Global action 345
Global Actions, Object-Specific Actions 337

H

helper function 91, 94, 95
HighCharts
  URL 203

I

Independent Software Vendor (ISV) 42
Integrated Development Editor (IDE) 35

J

Jasmine
    about 388
    quickstart example 392
    setup 390
    spec 389
    spies 391
    suite 388
    syntax 388
    teardown 390
    terminology 388
JavaScript controller 91, 94, 95
JavaScript libraries
    in Lightning Component 204
JavaScript
    optimizing, in Lightning Component 279
JS-heavy project
    structuring, in Salesforce DX 219

L

License Management (LMA) 429
Lightning app
    creating 54
Lightning Application
    about 12
    creating 13
Lightning base components
    about 183
    access modifier 70
    aura component, definition 70
    card base component 74
    card components, example 75
    layout base component, using for horizontal
        alignment 78
    layout base component, using for vertical
        alignment 80
    LayoutItem, strrtching with flexibility attribute 81
    leveraging 281
    multiple devices, handling 83, 86
    multiple rows, creating 82

record form, creating Lightning recordForm 282
    row size, controlling 82
    used, for formatting output data 194
    using, for layout 72
    using, for layout items 72
    using, for layouts 70
    using, for nested page layout 86
Lightning commands 53
Lightning Component architecture
    about 28
    bundle 30
    web components 29
Lightning Component Bundle
    about 30
    Apex controller (.cls) 31
    controller (.js) 31
    CSS file (.css) 30
    JavaScript helper 31
    lifecycle 31
    Lightning Component Markup file (.cmp) file 30
    MVC 32
Lightning Component test
    creating, via CLI 399
    Jasmine spy, used for verifying response by
        mocking server response 401
    search terms rendered, testing via two-way
        binding 399
Lightning Component
    adding, as global and object-specific actions
        345, 347, 348
    attributes 204
    building, by setting up Salesforce developer
        organization 33
    ChartJs in 225
    client-side calls, creating to external sites using
        JavaScript 227, 231
    communicating, to Visualforce page 234
    communities, creating in Salesforce 348, 349,
        350, 351
    creating 54
    custom content layouts, creating 359, 360, 362
    custom labels, used in 128
    ES6 syntax in 129
    events 205
    hello world, creating 34

in Community Cloud 348
JavaScript libraries in 204
JavaScript libraries, integrating in 205, 206
JavaScript, optimizing in 279
Lightning container, limitations 243
Locker Service-compliant JavaScript, creating
  webpack used 213
MomentJs library, integrating in 211
navigation, adding 364, 366
profile menu, overriding 363
Promise API in 130, 131
React application rendering, Lightning container
  used 235
reactApp rendering, LCC npm module used 236,
  239, 242
Select2 JavaScript library, integrating in 207,
  210
standard search interface, overriding 363
theme layout, creating 352, 353, 354, 355, 356,
  357, 358
used, in Salesforce mobile application 338
used, overriding navigation in communities 363
used, overriding profile menu in communities
  363
used, overriding search in communities 363
Visualforce page, communicating 232
Lightning components
  creating 54
Lightning Console
  about 374
  Standard Lightning tab events 385
  Utility Bar component 375, 377, 379
  workspace API 380, 381
Lightning Data Service components
  example 179, 181, 183
Lightning Data Service
  about 167
  CRUD records, functions 171
  Salesforce record context data, loading force
  recordData used 169
Lightning data service
  using 281
Lightning Design system
  about 37
  card component, creating with SLDS 37, 39

URL 37
Lightning Experience
  about 10
  calendar, creating 24
  Component tab 16
  Global Actions 25
  Lightning App Builder 18
  Lightning Application 11
  Lightning Utility Bar 20
  list views 22
  page tabs 16
  Publisher actions 27
  tabs, creating 15
Lightning input components
  using 199
Lightning input field components
  about 184
  creating 184
  events and attributes 186
  input form, creating RecordEdit used 184
  used, for creating contact edit form 188
Lightning main frame
  versus iframe 232
Lightning Out
  about 287
  application, creating 295, 297, 298
  connected application, creating 291, 292
  considerations 303
  for unauthenticated users 299, 300, 303
  in Node.js application 291
  in Visualforce 287, 288
  JavaScript, adding to create component on
    Visualforce page 289, 290
  Lightning Component, adding for Visualforce
    JavaScript library 289
  Lightning dependency application, creating 288
  limitations 303
  Node.js application, deploying on Heroku 298
  Node.js application, setting up 293, 294
Lightning output field component
  using 189
Lightning record edit form
  events and attributes 187
Lightning Testing Service (LTS)
  about 387, 395

installing 397
Lightning Component test, creating via CLI 399
reference link 387
tests, writing for YouTubeSearchApp 396
Lightning-Quick action 345
list view component 190
Locker service 29
Locker Service-compatible bundle
  creating, with webpack 219, 224
Locker Service-compliant JavaScript
  choices.js, integrating into Lightning Components
  217
  creating, webpack used 213
Locker Service
  about 108
  DOM access containment hierarchy, in Lightning
    Components 110
  proxy object in 111
  strict mode enforcement in 108

M

Mailboxlayer
  URL 322
managed package
  creating 417, 420
managed/unmanaged package code
  converting, to DX Format 56
Metadata API commands
  about 55
  deploy command 57
  mdapi convert 55
  mdapi retrieve 55
Model, View, Controller (MVC) 32

N

navigation support
  adding, Lightning navigation used 368, 371, 373
nested aura
  $A.createComponent() 275
  avoiding 271, 274
  JavaScript, used for performance 275

P

parent and child components
  aura method, used 158, 159

aura method, used to call child method from
  parent method 156
communicating between 156
component hierarchy, passing 156
custom events, adding to component 164
optimal event architecture design pattern 160,
  163
Promise API 130

R

re-rendering the life cycle component 126
RecordEditForm components
  used, for creating contact edit form 188
rendering life cycle component 123, 125

S

sales LeaderBoard Lightning Application
  creating, events used 144, 146, 148, 150, 154
Salesforce application
  developer workflow, building 62, 63, 64, 65, 66,
  68
Salesforce community page optimizer 256, 258
Salesforce developer instances
  namespacing, for managed package 408
  namespacing, impact on component bundle 409,
  413
Salesforce developer organization
  setting up, to enable building of Lightning
    Components 33
Salesforce developer
  URL 10
Salesforce DX CLI
  installing 43, 44, 45
Salesforce DX commands
  about 45
  auth commands 45
  default Dev Hub, setting for scratch Org creation
    46
  project definition JSON, configuring 47, 48
  project, creating 46
  scratch Org definition JSON, configuring 47
  scratch Org, creating 48
Salesforce Lightning Design System (SLDS)
  about 37, 167
  URL 37

used, for creating card component 37, 39
Salesforce Lightning Inspector
  about 246, 249
  Actions tab 255
  Component Tree tab 250
  Event Log tab 254
  Performance tab 252
  Storage tab 255
  tabs 250
  Transactions tab 252
Salesforce mobile application
  Chrome browser, setting up 339
  Lightning Component, adding to 340, 341, 343, 344
  Lightning Components, used 338
Salesforce Object Query Language (SOQL) 58
SalesLeaderBoardCard component 149
scratch Org
  conflict resolution 53
  creating 48
  creating, with namespaces 415
  files, ignoring 53
  opening 49
  source code, pushing 51, 52
  source, pulling 49, 50, 51
Single-Page Application (SPA) 28
Standard Lightning tab events 385
storable actions
  about 270
  need for 271
Subversion (SVN) 41

T

Team Foundation Server (TFS) 41
Trailhead
  URL 69
tree view
  creating, tree grid components used 191

U

unbound expression
  bindings 279
Utility Bar component
  about 375, 377, 379
  page context 379, 380

V

Visual Studio extension pack
  installing, for Salesforce DX 60, 61

W

webpack
  about 214
  entry object 214
  loaders 215
  output object 215
  plugins 216
  used, for creating Locker Service-compliant JavaScript 213
workspace API 380, 381

Y

YouTubeSearchApp
  application events, testing 404
  tests, writing 396